Teaching with Authority

How to Cut through Doctrinal Confusion
& Understand What the Church Really Says

Jimmy Akin

Teaching with Authority

How to Cut through Doctrinal Confusion
& Understand What the Church Really Says

Catholic
Answers
Press

© 2018 Jimmy Akin

Published by Catholic Answers, Inc.
2020 Gillespie Way
El Cajon, California 92020
1-888-291-8000 orders
619-387-0042 fax
catholic.com

Printed in the United States of America

Cover design by ebooklaunch.com
Interior design by Russell Graphic Design

978-1-68357-094-3
978-1-68357-095-0 Kindle
978-1-68357-096-7 ePub

Dedicated to the memory of Cardinal Avery Dulles,
who went out of his way to help me, and in gratitude for the
teaching ministry of Joseph Ratzinger/Pope Benedict XVI.

Special thanks to Fr. Hugh Barbour, Mark Brumley,
and Professor Janet Smith for assistance with various aspects
of this manuscript.

Table of Contents

Introduction

There has never been a peaceful time in the history of the Church. From the ministry of Jesus straight through to today, Christians have had to deal with doctrinal conflict, heresy, and dissent.

Throughout the storm, the Holy Spirit has guided the Church and its pastors, providing a clear voice so that the Church serves as "the pillar and bulwark of the truth" (1 Tim. 3:15).

Yet few people understand their Catholic faith or know how to navigate the complex world of Church documents and teachings.

As part of my professional work, I've lived in that world for more than twenty-five years. On a daily basis, I work with the details of Church documents and teachings, and I've long wanted to write this book to share the principles that scholars use as they carefully analyze and interpret what the Church says.

We'll begin by looking at where the Church gets its teaching authority, the Magisterium of the bishops and popes. We'll cover the different kinds of doctrine and discipline that regulate Christian life, the sources of Church teaching, and the many different kinds of documents the Magisterium uses. A key issue is how to read and interpret these documents, and special attention will be devoted to the question of how to accurately assess the weight of individual statements and identify when they are infallible. Finally, we will look at how the Church's teaching develops over time, how to deal with difficulties, and how to cut through the rumors that abound today.

May God bless you as you study the teachings of the Church as the Holy Spirit continues to guide it "into all the truth" (John 16:13).

—*Jimmy Akin*
July 3, 2018
Feast of St. Thomas the Apostle

Abbreviations

CCC	*Catechism of the Catholic Church*
CDF	Congregation for the Doctrine of the Faith
CIC	*Code of Canon Law (Codex Iuris Canonici)*
D	Denzinger, *Enchiridion Symbolorum* (early editions)
DH	Denzinger-Hunermann, *Enchiridion Symbolorum* (current English edition)
DS	Denzinger-Schonmetzer, *Enchiridion Symbolorum* (common prior editions)
ITC	International Theological Commission
NT	New Testament
OT	Old Testament
PBC	Pontifical Biblical Commission
ST	*Summa Theologiae*

CHAPTER 1

Authority to Teach

How Jesus Taught

1. The Gospel of Mark tells us that, during Jesus' ministry, the people "were astonished at his teaching, for he taught them as one who had authority, and not as the scribes" (1:22).

Why would people be astonished at Jesus' authoritative manner of teaching? How was it different from the way Jewish scribes taught? We gain an insight when we look at the Sermon on the Mount, where Jesus declares:

> You have heard that it was said, "You shall not commit adultery." But I say to you that everyone who looks at a woman lustfully has already committed adultery with her in his heart (5:27–28).

The prohibition on adultery is one of the Ten Commandments (Exod. 20:14; Deut. 5:18), but in this passage Jesus indicates that it doesn't only apply to committing the outward act of adultery. We are called not only to be pure in our outward actions but in our hearts as well. To look at a woman with deliberate lust violates this commandment.

The striking thing is the way Jesus makes this application. He does so on his own authority. He takes what "you have heard" and then extends it by declaring, "but *I* say to you." He does not cite any authorities to justify his claim. He says it as if his word alone is sufficient. This dramatic statement is far from alone. In the Sermon on the Mount, he repeatedly upends common understandings of God's law on his own authority (see Matt. 5:21–22, 31–32, 33–34, 38–39, 43–44).

How Scribes Taught

2. The scribes were legal experts, and like modern lawyers, they didn't simply announce their own views as authoritative. They cited legal precedents. Today a lawyer might cite a learned jurist, he might appeal to different schools of legal thought, or he might reason from the wording of a text. The scribes and their successors did all of these things, as we see in the Mishnah—a collection of Jewish oral traditions that were compiled around A.D. 200.

Thus the Mishnah cites learned legal authorities from the past:

> Simeon the Righteous was one of the last survivors of the great assembly. He would say: "On three things does the world stand: on the Torah, and on the Temple service, and on deeds of loving kindness" (*m. Abot* 1:2).

The Mishnah contrasts the views of different schools of thought, as when it compares what the followers of the sages Shammai and Hillel said concerning the order of prayers at dinnertime:

> The House of Shammai say, "One recites the blessing over the day then one recites the blessing over the wine."
> But the House of Hillel say, "One recites the blessing over the wine and then one recites the blessing over the day" (*m. Berakhot* 8:1).

The Mishnah also reasons from the words of the biblical text, as when it discusses how much a person who has stolen must pay in restitution:

> The rule covering twofold restitution applies to something whether animate or inanimate. But the rule covering four- fold or fivefold restitution applies only to an ox or a sheep

alone, since it [Exod. 22:1] says, "If a man shall steal an ox or a sheep and kill it, or sell it, he shall pay five oxen for an ox and four sheep for a sheep" (*m. Baba Qamma* 7:1).

The traditional author of the Mishnah—the scholar Judah ha-Nasi—studiously recorded the legal traditions of which he was aware, but he and other sages did not teach in the authoritative fashion Jesus did, as if they personally had the authority to settle an issue.

What Does Teaching Have to Do with Authority?

3. We live in an age skeptical of authority. "Think for yourself" is a standard piece of advice, and slogans like "Question authority" appear on bumper stickers, buttons, and T-shirts. Following crises like the Vietnam War, Watergate, Iran-Contra, and other scandals, trust in government officials is at a historic low.

In the twentieth century, an age of radical individualism began, and even if 1960s sayings like "Do your own thing" have passed from the scene, the idea that individuals should make up their own minds about what they should do and believe has remained. The rise of modern science contributed to the anti-authoritarian attitude of our day. Scholars are not supposed to just *tell* us what to believe. Instead, they should provide evidence supporting the views they endorse.

Between science, individualism, and scandals involving authority figures, moderns are skeptical of authority, and that includes the connection between authority and teaching. People today hold that if a teaching is true, we should be able to produce reasons for it and should not simply accept it on someone's "authority."

Teaching and Evidence

4. This reasoning works in many fields. In mathematics, a teacher needs to prove what he says. Indeed, in math the standards of proof are higher than in any other field. Mathematics students must "show their work," and if a teacher is covering propositions from Euclid's *Elements of Geometry*, he needs to provide the same rigorous geometrical proofs Euclid did. Science teachers also need to provide proof, but of a different kind. Science is built on observation and experiment, and these play an important part in every science class. Even in fields like history, teachers can't simply announce their own views to students. They need to cite historical evidence, such as eyewitness accounts and archaeological remains.

Authority to Teach

5. Yet in all of these areas there is still a role for authority. Teachers are expected to be "authorities" on the subjects they specialize in, and every field has outstanding scholars and researchers who are considered high-level authorities. The authority these figures have is a function of their expertise. It's not that they don't need evidence for what they say; it's that they have such a mastery of the evidence that they can speak on the subject with authority. Consequently, those who are less familiar with the evidence owe them a certain deference.

The Importance of Teaching Authority

6. People don't always need a high level of expertise for us to accept what they say. We form beliefs based on what ordinary people tell us every day. If we're in a windowless office and a coworker tells us that it's raining outside, that the boss is in a bad mood, or that there is hot coffee in the break room, we take him at his word—unless he's a practical joker or known to be unreliable. In each case we adopt a belief based on the trustworthiness of the person, which is a form of authority.

In these situations, our coworker is acting, at least in a limited way, as a teacher. He is telling us something we previously didn't know. We do the same thing whenever we tell other people things they didn't know. Such encounters are so common that we don't usually think of them as involving *teaching authority*, but they do. In fact, *most* things we know are ones we've been taught and have accepted on the authority of others. C.S. Lewis explains:

Do not be scared by the word authority. Believing things on authority only means believing them because you have been told them by someone you think trustworthy. Ninety-nine per cent of the things you believe are believed on authority. I believe there is such a place as New York. I have not seen it myself. I could not prove by abstract reasoning that there must be such a place. I believe it because reliable people have told me so. The ordinary man believes in the solar system, atoms, evolution, and the circulation of the blood on authority—because the scientists say so. Every historical statement in the world is believed on authority. None of us has seen the Norman Conquest or the defeat of the Armada. None of us could prove them by pure logic as you prove a thing in mathematics. We believe them simply because people who did see them have left writings that tell us about them: in fact, on authority. A man who jibbed at authority in other things as some people do in religion would have to be content to know nothing all his life.[1]

That we accept teaching authority—whether of a highly credentialed expert in a technical field or an ordinary person describing his own experience—is vital. Our lives would be immensely impoverished if we tried to be systematically skeptical of every claim we encounter. In fact, to live in a human manner—or to live at all—we have to accord others a basic level of trust. We couldn't live if we constantly thought people were about to attack us or that our food was poisoned, no matter what they said. Paranoid delusions ruin people's lives, revealing how important it is we trust what others tell us—i.e., what they teach us.

Of course, what others tell us is not always correct, and sometimes our trust in what they say is misplaced. However, a basic respect for what others teach us—either formally in a classroom or informally in everyday life—is essential. A nation would be thrown into chaos if its people systematically distrusted what others told them. That society simply would not be able to function.

Governing Authority

7. Teaching authority is not the only kind that exists. Another is the authority to make and carry out decisions—what we might call *governing authority*. It also can be exercised formally or informally.

Every group needs organization, even just a group of friends planning an evening's entertainment. Though they have no formal authority, certain people are natural leaders and assume it informally. They help the group figure out what it wants to do by moving the discussion along, asking questions ("What kind of food do we want to eat?") and making suggestions ("This movie has good reviews; we could see it"). In small, informal settings, nobody needs to be appointed leader, and the group doesn't need formal rules. But this changes in groups with definite purposes. Even small social clubs have presidents, secretaries, and treasurers—as well as bylaws and rules about how the club will operate.

As the size of the group increases, so does the need for organization, from small towns to giant nation-states, and leaders take on specialized roles: legislators have the authority to make laws, judges have the authority to rule on how the laws should be applied, and executives have the authority to carry out (execute) these laws and rulings.

It's desirable that officials be skilled in their jobs, and in a democracy, elected officials try to persuade voters they have the needed skills. Even appointed officials are supposed to be well qualified for their positions. However, it's not an official's expertise that gives him authority. Even an incompetent or corrupt official has the authority his office carries. Officials can make mistakes, take bribes, show favoritism, and otherwise abuse their authority. Modern societies have procedures for removing incompetent and corrupt officials, but society would descend into chaos if nobody had governing authority. It, like teaching authority, is essential for human welfare.

Authority in Religion

8. Despite our culture's antiauthoritarian streak, we recognize the value of both teaching and governing authority. A fundamental rejection of either would have dire consequences. We thus shouldn't be scared of their role in religion. Instead, we should expect them to perform their functions in this domain as well.

The role of governing authority in religion is straightforward: a religious group needs organization as much as any other. That means it needs leaders, rules by which it operates, etc. However, the role of teaching authority in religion is unique.

Teaching authority in religion differs from other fields because of the data religion uses. In other disciplines—physics, chemistry, biology, history—experts study a particular kind of information about the natural world, which we can observe using our senses. However, religion deals with the supernatural world that lies behind and beyond nature, and we can't observe it with our senses. If we could—if we could observe and study angels the way we study lions and gazelles—then theology would be an empirical science alongside biology and the others.

For us to have information about the supernatural world, that world must make contact with ours. God or an angel has to tell us about it. Thus the prophets experienced visions, dreams, and so on, in which information about the supernatural world was *revealed* to them. We refer to this kind of information as *divine revelation*, and it is what makes theology different from other fields of study.

However, teaching authority also has similarities to other fields. Precisely because they have no natural access to the supernatural world, human religious leaders can't simply pronounce their own views as facts. This is why Jewish scribes cited precedents for their views. It is why pastors, theologians, and apologists pose arguments drawn from Scripture. Not even the prophets could simply declare things on their own authority: they were tasked with bringing people the word of the Lord. Like authorities in other area, religious ones are expected to have a basis—evidence—for what they say; it's just that the nature of their evidence is different.

But not all religious authorities are the same.

Jesus' Unique Authority

9. Jesus Christ founded a community—a Church—and during his earthly ministry he served both as its teacher and its leader, exercising both teaching and governing authority. However, he displayed a unique sense of authority that went beyond that of the scribes and even the prophets, who were limited to announcing God's will with formulas like "Thus says the Lord" (cf. Isa. 7:7, Jer. 2:2, Ezek. 2:2, Amos 1:3, Mic. 2:3, etc.). Jesus took the authority of the Lord on himself, contrasting the popular understanding of a matter ("you have heard") with his own, definitive understanding ("but I say").

He was able to settle matters this way because he was God made flesh. As John's Gospel tells us, "In the beginning was the Word, and the Word was with God, and the Word was God" (1:1). Jesus was, uniquely, the Son of God (1:14) and "the way, the truth, and the life" (14:6). Further, he had been sent as God's Messiah, allowing him to declare, "All authority in heaven and on earth has been given to me" (Matt. 28:18).

Jesus Shares Authority with the Church

10. Although Jesus' authority as the Son of God is unique to him, he chose to associate human beings with his mission and gave them a share of authority. Thus when he appoints the Twelve, we read:

> And he called to him his twelve disciples and gave them authority over unclean spirits, to cast them out, and to heal every disease and every infirmity (Matt. 10:1).

The authority he shared was not just that to work miracles. The twelve disciples were his students (that's what "disciple" means), and he prepared them to become teachers and sent them on preaching missions:

> These twelve Jesus sent out, charging them, "Go nowhere among the Gentiles, and enter no town of the Samaritans, but

go rather to the lost sheep of the house of Israel. And preach
as you go, saying, 'The kingdom of heaven is at hand'"
(Matt. 10:5–7).

Later, when sending out an even larger group, he underlined
the teaching authority he had given them, stating:

He who hears you hears me, and he who rejects you rejects me, and he who rejects me rejects him who sent me
(Luke 10:16).

Jesus also gave the Twelve the authority to govern his Church.
He first gave Peter the authority "to bind and loose" (Matt. 16:19),
and later he shared this with the other disciples (Matt. 18:18).

As the Church grew, authority to teach and govern was transmitted to others in the local churches. Thus Paul writes, "God
has appointed in the church first apostles, second prophets, third
teachers" (1 Cor. 12:28; cf. Eph. 4:11). It is because of its teaching function that the Church serves as "the pillar and bulwark of
the truth" (1 Tim. 3:15). Similarly, there are those with governing authority in the Church. The letter to the Hebrews exhorts
Christians to "obey your leaders and submit to them; for they
are keeping watch over your souls, as men who will have to give
account" (Heb. 13:17; cf. 1 Thess. 5:12). Teaching and governing
authority are therefore intrinsic to the structure of the Church.

CHAPTER 2

The Magisterium and the Bishops

The Concept of the Magisterium

11. The Church has a special term for the teaching authority it was given by Christ. This term, *magisterium,* is based on the Latin word for "teacher" (*magister*). It is used in a number of senses, two of which parallel the way the English word *authority* is used: it can refer to the power to make decisions (as in, "He has the authority to do this") or it can refer to those who have this power (as in, "He is an authority"). Similarly, magisterium can refer to the authority to teach ("The pope exercised his magisterium") and to those who have authority to teach ("The Magisterium teaches this"). A third use occurs when the word refers to a body of authoritative teachings ("This teaching is found in the magisterium of Paul VI").

12. One sometimes encounters references to the *universal magisterium.* This phrase refers to all the bishops of the world, teaching in union with the pope. It contrasts with the *personal magisterium* of an individual bishop or pope and the "particular magisterium" of a bishop, pope, or group of bishops.

13. More commonly, one encounters references to the *ordinary magisterium* and the *extraordinary magisterium.* The former includes things like a bishop giving a homily or the pope writing an encyclical letter. These forms of teaching take place on a regular basis, making them ordinary.

However, sometimes an extraordinary act of teaching occurs. This happens when a pope infallibly defines a teaching.
Ecumenical councils can also make infallible definitions, and
so both of these are referred to as acts of extraordinary magisterium. There is some ambiguity about the way this term is used.
Some authors apply it only to cases where a teaching is infallibly
defined. Others use it to refer to papal definitions and anything
an ecumenical council teaches, whether infallible or not.

Regardless of how extraordinary magisterium is understood, one
should not assume an act of extraordinary magisterium is needed
for a teaching to be infallible. As we will see in future chapters, the
Church's ordinary and universal magisterium can teach infallibly.

14. A final term we should mention is *authentic magisterium*. In
Church documents, the word *authentic* is frequently used to mean
"authoritative." Something counts as authentic magisterium if it is
an authoritative teaching or an authoritative act of teaching (§267).

The Mission to Teach

15. In the broadest sense, all Christians are called upon to proclaim the faith to others—and thus to teach. In this sense, St.
Peter says, "Always be prepared to make a defense to anyone
who calls you to account for the hope that is in you, yet do it
with gentleness and reverence" (1 Pet. 3:15). Similarly, St. Paul
tells his readers: "Let the word of Christ dwell in you richly,
teach and admonish one another in all wisdom" (Col. 3:16). This
universal teaching role is based on the fact that ordinary Christians have a share in the prophetic office of Christ. As the Second
Vatican Council stated:

> Christ conferred on the apostles and their successors the
> duty of teaching, sanctifying, and ruling in his name and
> power. But the laity likewise share in the priestly, pro-
> phetic, and royal office of Christ and therefore have their
> own share in the mission of the whole people of God in
> the Church and in the world (*Apostolicam Actuositatem,* 2).

16. Despite this, the role ordinary Christians have in teaching is limited. Thus St. James warns: "Let not many of you become teachers, my brethren, for you know that we who teach shall be judged with greater strictness" (James 3:1).

The reason some individuals have a greater teaching role is because of their spiritual gifts (Greek, *charismata*). Paul states:

> Having gifts that differ according to the grace given to us, let us use them: if prophecy, in proportion to our faith; if service, in our serving; he who teaches, in his teaching (Rom. 12:6–7).

There is thus a charismatic gift of teaching. This is true of both men and women. Thus we see Priscilla and her husband, Aquila, giving private instruction to the evangelist Apollos (Acts 18:24–28; cf. Titus 2:3–5).

17. In addition to the charismatic gift of teaching, some offices convey a teaching role. According to the Old Testament, "The lips of a priest should guard knowledge, and men should seek instruction from his mouth, for he is the messenger of the Lord of hosts" (Mal. 2:7). The New Testament similarly recognizes the teaching function of the Church offices:

> Now a bishop must be above reproach, the husband of one wife, temperate, sensible, dignified, hospitable, an apt teacher (1 Tim. 3:2).
> Let the elders who rule well be considered worthy of double honor, especially those who labor in preaching and teaching (1 Tim. 5:17).

In the first century, the titles for offices were fluid, and "bishop" (Greek, *episkopos*) and "elder" (Greek, *presbuteros*) could be used interchangeably. They were so fluid even apostles could apply them to themselves. Peter referred to himself as a "fellow elder" (1 Pet. 5:1), and Paul referred to himself as a "deacon"

(Greek, *diakonos*; Eph. 3:7). However, by the end of the first century the titles had stabilized, and St. Ignatius of Antioch could state that, without the threefold ministry of bishops, priests, and deacons, "there is no church" (*Letter to the Trallians* 3).

Since *episkopos* meant "overseer" (*epi-,* "over," *skopos,* "one who sees"), it naturally became associated with the highest of the offices, and so the Church recognizes that the authority to teach is vested in a special way in its bishops. Yet priests and deacons also have teaching roles. According to Vatican II:

> [Priests] labor in word and doctrine, believing what they have read and meditated upon in the law of God, teaching what they have believed, and putting in practice in their own lives what they have taught (*Lumen Gentium*, 28).
>
> It is the duty of the deacon, according as it shall have been assigned to him by competent authority . . . to instruct and exhort the people (ibid., 29).

Apostles, Bishops, and Theologians

18. The apostles were the original members of the Church's Magisterium. When they passed from the scene, this role passed from them to the bishops. Because the bishops are "the successors of the apostles," some have the idea bishops are simply apostles under another name, but this is not the case.

If they were, the later and less prestigious term *bishop* would never have been coined or displaced the earlier, more prestigious term *apostle*. Also, the New Testament indicates apostles had qualities no bishop meets. To be a member of the Twelve, one had to be an eyewitness to the ministry of Christ (Acts 1:21–26), and even later apostles like Paul needed to have seen Jesus (1 Cor. 9:1). Thus the Doctrinal Commission at Vatican II stated:

> The parallel between Peter and the rest of the apostles on the one hand, and between the supreme pontiff and the bishops on the other hand, does not imply the transmission of

the apostles' extraordinary power to their successors (*Lumen Gentium:* Preliminary Note of Explanation, 1).

Similarly, the U.S. bishops' Committee on Doctrine has observed:

There are some elements in the original apostolic charism—such as being eyewitnesses to the risen Lord—that episcopal consecration cannot transmit. But the college of bishops inherits the teaching office that the apostolic college once carried (*The Teaching Ministry of the Diocesan Bishop*, 3).

Some have proposed that apostles—unlike bishops—had a personal gift of infallibility and could individually define doctrines the way the pope does today. This view was expressed at the First Vatican Council by Bishop Vincent Gasser.[2] That view is a matter of theological opinion rather than a Church teaching, but it illustrates historic awareness that the two offices are different.

19. As the centuries progressed, new teaching roles developed through the work of apologists, catechists, and theologians. The latter became prominent with the rise of the university system in the Middle Ages. Colleges came to be staffed with theological experts, many of whose names are still famous today (e.g., Sts. Thomas Aquinas, Bonaventure, Anselm of Canterbury). The appearance of a large number of theological experts who were not bishops raised the question of how the two classes should relate.

The bishops had the authority to teach by virtue of their apostolic succession, but what about the theologians? Did they have some kind of teaching authority based on expertise? In some texts, Aquinas spoke of two magisteria: the bishops' *magisterium of the pastoral chair* (Latin, *magisterium cathedrae pastoralis*) and the theologians' *magisterium of the teacher's chair* (Latin, *magisterium cathedrae magistralis*).

In subsequent centuries, the term *magisterium* came to be used only in the first sense, and today "the Magisterium" refers to the bishops teaching in union with the head of the episcopal college, the pope.

Despite this, there has been an attempt to revive the other usage, and some authors speak of a *magisterium of theologians*. This effort has been led by dissidents who reject aspects of Church teaching and wish to present the magisterium of theologians as an alternative to the *ecclesiastical Magisterium*. In 1990, the Congregation for the Doctrine of the Faith commented:

> Dissent is generally defended by various arguments, two of which are more basic in character. The first lies in the order of hermeneutics. The documents of the Magisterium, it is said, reflect nothing more than a debatable theology. The second takes theological pluralism sometimes to the point of a relativism which calls the integrity of the Faith into question. Here the interventions of the Magisterium would have their origin in one theology among many theologies, while no particular theology, however, could presume to claim universal normative status. In opposition to and in competition with the authentic magisterium, there thus arises a kind of "parallel magisterium" of theologians (*Donum Veritatis*, 34).

It went on to say:

> The notion of a "parallel magisterium" of theologians in opposition to and in competition with the magisterium of the pastors is sometimes supported by reference to some texts in which St. Thomas Aquinas makes a distinction between the *magisterium cathedrae pastoralis* and *magisterium cathedrae magisterialis* (*Contra Impugnantes*, c. 2; *Quodlib. III*, q. 4, a. 1 (9); *In IV. Sent.* 19, 2, 2, q. 3 sol. 2 and 4). Actually, these texts do not give any support to this position, for St. Thomas was absolutely certain that the right to judge in matters of doctrine was the sole responsibility of the *officium praelationis* [office of the prelacy; i.e., of Church prelates] (*Donum Veritatis*, fn. 27).

This doesn't mean theologians don't have an expertise-based "authority" like experts in any field, but it is fundamentally different from the divinely given authority of bishops. The International Theological Commission observes, "The Magisterium derives its authority from sacramental ordination, which along with the task of sanctifying confers also the tasks of teaching and ruling." On the other hand, "Theologians derive their specifically theological authority from their scientific qualifications" (*The Ecclesiastical Magisterium and Theology*, thesis 6).

In fact, canon law requires that theologians teaching in academic settings obtain special recognition from their bishop:

> Those who teach theological disciplines in any institutes of higher studies whatsoever must have a mandate from the competent ecclesiastical authority (CIC 812).

In light of all this, the International Theological Commission has been prepared to speak of a magisterium of theologians only in a qualified sense:

> There is indeed in the Church a certain "magisterium" of theologians, but there is no place for parallel, opposing or alternative magisteria, or for views that would separate theology from the Church's Magisterium (*Theology Today*, 39).

Although theologians have made valuable contributions, they do not have the teaching authority of bishops. Consequently, the term *Magisterium* is used in Church documents—and in this book—to refer to the teaching role of bishops.

The Personal Magisterium of Bishops

20. Every bishop has theological training, and they are capable of teaching as private theologians. However, they also have the ability to teach authoritatively. The Second Vatican Council stated:

Bishops are preachers of the faith, who lead new disciples to Christ, and they are authentic teachers, that is, teachers endowed with the authority of Christ, who preach to the people committed to them the faith they must believe and put into practice, and by the light of the Holy Spirit illustrate that faith. They bring forth from the treasury of revelation new things and old, making it bear fruit and vigilantly warding off any errors that threaten their flock. Bishops, teaching in communion with the Roman pontiff, are to be respected by all as witnesses to divine and Catholic truth. In matters of faith and morals, the bishops speak in the name of Christ and the faithful are to accept their teaching and adhere to it with a religious assent (*Lumen Gentium*, 25).

A bishop's individual teaching authority, as well as his body of teachings, is known as his *personal magisterium*. We can unpack this concept by looking at several of its aspects.

Its Basis

21. The teaching authority bishops possess is given to them at their episcopal ordination. According to Pope John Paul II:

At his episcopal ordination, each bishop received the fundamental mission of authoritatively proclaiming the word of God. Indeed, every bishop, by virtue of sacred ordination, is an authentic teacher who preaches to the people entrusted to his care the faith to be believed and to be put into practice in the moral life. This means that bishops are endowed with the authority of Christ himself (*Pastores Gregis*, 29).

Its Audience

22. Although the college of bishops *as a whole* is capable of addressing the entire Church, a bishop acting singly can only authoritatively teach his own flock. John Paul II states:

The individual bishops, as teachers of the faith, do not address the universal community of the faithful except through the action of the entire college of bishops. In fact, only the faithful entrusted to the pastoral care of a particular bishop are required to accept his judgment given in the name of Christ in matters of faith and morals, and to adhere to it with a religious assent of soul (*Apostolos Suos*, 11).

The flock a bishop is tasked with teaching includes more than active churchgoers. The Congregation for Bishops notes:

The bishop's mission to evangelize is not restricted to his concern for the faithful, but it also reaches out to those who have abandoned Christian faith or practice, or who do not believe in Christ. He should direct the efforts of his co-workers toward this goal and should never tire of reminding everyone of the blessing and the responsibility of working with and for Christ in missionary activity (*Apostolorum Successores*, 119).

Its Subject Matter

23. The classic phrase used to describe the subjects on which the Magisterium can teach authoritatively is "matters of faith and morals" (Latin, *res fidei et morum*; cf. *Lumen Gentium*, 25). Individual bishops have the responsibility to address both. The Congregation for Bishops states:

The bishop has a *personal* obligation to preach often, proposing to the faithful, in the first instance, what they are to believe and do for the glory of God and for their eternal salvation. He proclaims the mystery of salvation accomplished in Christ, so as to demonstrate that our Lord is the one Savior and the center of the lives of the faithful and of all human history.

It is also the bishop's task to proclaim always and everywhere the *moral principles of the social order*, in this way announcing man's authentic liberation, brought about through the Incarnation of the Word (*Apostolorum Successores*, 120).

Its Exercise

24. The way a bishop exercises his personal magisterium can take many forms (homilies, pastoral letters, etc.). Regardless of the means he uses, he needs to teach faithfully and effectively:

> The word of God should be proclaimed with authority, since it proceeds not from man, but from God himself; it should be preached with conviction, never watered down to make it more palatable; and it should be presented attractively, as doctrine not only preached, but also practiced. So the bishop takes care that his preaching is firmly anchored in the doctrine of the Church and rooted in Scripture (*Apostolorum Successores*, 121).

John Paul II noted that the effectiveness of a bishop's magisterium also depends on his manner of life:

> The witness of his life becomes for a bishop a new basis for authority alongside the objective basis received in episcopal consecration. "Authority" is thus joined by "authoritativeness." Both are necessary. The former, in fact, gives rise to the objective requirement that the faithful should assent to the authentic teaching of the bishop; the latter helps them to put their trust in his message (*Pastores Gregis*, 31).

Its Authority

25. Though the bishop's teaching authority comes from God, how much authority he can individually exercise has not been fully explored. In general, the Church has discerned two concrete levels of authority its teachings can have: they can be *definitive* (infallible) or *non-definitive* (non-infallible). The Church acknowledges that non-definitive teachings have different degrees of authority, but thus far it has not developed a way of objectively classifying these.

Except for the bishop of Rome, individual bishops cannot issue definitive teachings on their own. However, when bishops teach in concert with one another, the results have greater weight, and when the whole body of bishops teaches in union, it can exercise infallibility.

Its Response

26. According to Vatican II, "in matters of faith and morals, the bishops speak in the name of Christ and the faithful are to accept their teaching and adhere to it with a religious assent" (*Lumen Gentium,* 25). It goes on to clarify that this "religious assent" involves a "religious submission of will and intellect" (Latin, *religiosum voluntatis et intellectus obsequium*).

We will explore this in more detail in future chapters, but for now it is sufficient to note that the degree of religious assent that is called for is proportional to the weight a teaching has been given. Therefore, if a teaching is found only in the magisterium of a single bishop and is not taught more broadly, it has a lower order of weight and calls for a correspondingly lower level of religious assent.

When Bishops Disagree

27. What happens when an individual bishop teaches something in his personal Magisterium that is not taught by other bishops?

In previous centuries, people did not travel much and had little contact with other dioceses. Most were not literate and were not aware of the teaching of other bishops. However, today the situation is very different due to the global rise of literacy, publishing, news media, and the internet. The faithful have much greater awareness of what bishops in other areas are teaching, and recent years have seen the media filled with stories about bishops disagreeing with one another. How are the faithful to respond?

There is an obligation to give due assent to the teaching of one's own bishop. Although this deference is real and not to be underestimated, it also is not absolute. There can be situations, particularly when there is known disagreement among the bishops, when members of the faithful may legitimately disagree (see chapter twenty).

28. Yet such situations are contrary to the will of Christ. The faithful should not be put in a position where they feel compelled to disagree with their legitimate shepherd, and the Church is sensitive to this. Thus the U.S. bishops' Committee on Doctrine states:

> Although the bishops must use the disciplines of theology and philosophy as well as personal religious insights in their teaching, they are to teach finally not theology, not philosophy, and not their personal religious insights, but the unchanging faith of the Church as it is to be understood and lived today (*The Teaching Ministry of the Diocesan Bishop,* 5).

It puts the matter succinctly when it writes:

> Each bishop has the duty to teach the Faith in his diocese, conscious that his doctrine is not simply his own (cf. John 7:16) (ibid., 8).

Because bishops are to faithfully proclaim the doctrine of the Church on settled matters, their unique, personal contributions are likely to concern new questions or those that have not yet been settled by the universal magisterium. In 1998, John Paul II addressed this matter. Although he discussed it in terms of how bishops' conferences operate, the same principles apply to individual bishops:

> In dealing with new questions and in acting so that the message of Christ enlightens and guides people's consciences in resolving new problems arising from changes in society, the bishops assembled in the episcopal conference and jointly exercising their teaching office are well aware of the limits of their pronouncements. While being official and authentic

and in communion with the Apostolic See, these pronouncements do not have the characteristics of a universal magisterium. For this reason, the bishops are to be careful to avoid interfering with the doctrinal work of the bishops of other territories, bearing in mind the wider, even worldwide, resonance which the means of social communication give to the events of a particular region (*Apostolos Suos,* 22).

The U.S. bishops' Committee on Doctrine has sought to strike a balance on this question, stating:

In our age of almost instant communication, the unity of the bishops' teaching can be greatly enhanced. Individual bishops have greater and more rapid access to their brother bishops as well as to the Holy See in the process of discernment and discussion. The unity of teaching can be thus greatly enriched by the capacities for communication in our own age. This development, however, can be harmful if it leads bishops to abdicate their own inherent teaching authority in a concession toward an excessive centralization or to defer to the statements of a regional body without personal commitment or assent. If teaching is done only at the regional or universal level, the Church may be weakened by its loss of the varied contributions of individual bishops and the churches they serve (ibid., 6).

It also said:

The college of bishops should be of immense support to the teaching of the individual bishop. A manifest continuity in Catholic teaching results when the position of one bishop is confirmed by the teaching of his brother bishops. Moral unity in teaching has been normally a sign of its authority (ibid.).

This brings us to the subject of how bishops achieve that unity. It is often done through councils, conferences, and synods.

CHAPTER 3

Bishops Teaching Together

Councils

29. A church council is a meeting called to discuss doctrinal and disciplinary matters. Although councils may involve priests, deacons, and laity, it is the bishops who ultimately preside. Councils let bishops consult and formulate their teaching in a more authoritative and united manner.

The practice of holding councils dates to the Apostolic Age. Acts 15 reports the first church council, which dealt with the question of whether Gentiles need to be circumcised. St. Paul indicates this council was prompted by the Holy Spirit (Gal. 2:2), and the council recognized that the Holy Spirit authenticated its results (Acts 15:28). It was the prototype for future councils.

There are different types of councils. The 1908 edition of the *Catholic Encyclopedia* lists seven:

1. *Ecumenical councils* are those to which the bishops, and others entitled to vote, are convoked from the whole world (*oikoumenē*) under the presidency of the pope or his legates, and the decrees of which, having received papal confirmation, bind all Christians. . . .

2. The second rank is held by the *general synods of the East or of the West*, composed of but one half of the episcopate. The Synod of Constantinople (381) was originally only an Eastern general synod, at which were present the four patriarchs of the East (viz. of Constantinople, Alexandria, Antioch, and Jerusalem), with many metropolitans and

bishops. It ranks as ecumenical because its decrees were ultimately received in the West also.

3. *Patriarchal, national, and primatial councils* represent a whole patriarchate, a whole nation, or the several provinces subject to a primate. Of such councils we have frequent examples in Latin Africa, where the metropolitan and ordinary bishops used to meet under the Primate of Carthage, in Spain, under the Primate of Toledo, and in earlier times in Syria, under the Metropolitan—later Patriarch—of Antioch.

4. *Provincial councils* bring together the suffragan bishops of the metropolitan of an ecclesiastical province and other dignitaries entitled to participate.

5. *Diocesan synods* consist of the clergy of the diocese and are presided over by the bishop or the vicar-general.

6. A peculiar kind of council used to be held at Constantinople, it consisted of bishops from any part of the world who happened to be at the time in that imperial city. Hence the name *synodoi enoemousai,* "visitors' synods."

7. Lastly there have been *mixed synods,* in which both civil and ecclesiastical dignitaries met to settle secular as well as ecclesiastical matters. They were frequent at the beginning of the Middle Ages in France, Germany, Spain, and Italy. In England even abbesses were occasionally present at such mixed councils. Sometimes, not always, the clergy and laity voted in separate chambers (s.v. "General Councils").

30. Several of these are no longer held, but canon law currently provides for:

- Diocesan synods (CIC 460–468), which may involve only a single bishop and his clergy and laity, though more than one bishop may be involved if the diocese has a coadjutor bishop or auxiliary bishops

- Particular councils (CIC 439–446), which are plenary if they includeallthechurchesinaparticularconferenceofbishops(CIC 439), or provincial if they include the churches of a particular ecclesiastical province within the conference (CIC 440)

- Ecumenical councils (CIC 337–341), which are discussed below.

The more bishops are involved, the wider the area affected by its teachings and the more authority those teachings have. Because ecumenical councils pertain to the whole world, they have universal authority and can teach infallibly.

31. Over time, terminology concerning councils has changed. The terms *council* and *synod* are sometimes used interchangeably, and ecumenical councils are sometimes referred to as universal or general councils. Confusingly, "universal council" and "general council" also have been used for any council not restricted to a single province.

Episcopal Conferences

32. Councils are occasional events in the life of the Church. They are called, they meet, and then they are over. However, bishops also collaborate in a regular, ongoing fashion. One way is through episcopal conferences. These began in the nineteenth century, and Vatican II called for bishops everywhere to form national or regional conferences (*Christus Dominus,* 37).

Conferences are required to meet at least once a year (CIC 453), and the U.S. Conference of Catholic Bishops meets twice a year, in June and November. In addition to the plenary ("full") sessions when all its members gather, there are periodic meetings of committees, and conferences maintain administrative offices to conduct routine business between plenary sessions.

33. After Vatican II, controversy developed about the teaching authority of conferences. Some, including the U.S. conference, began issuing documents whose authority was unclear. These documents were often drafted and released by a committee or group of committees and presented in the media as the teaching of the bishops, without the full conference voting on them.

Even when the conference had voted, individual bishops might disagree with the majority. Were the faithful of a particular country obliged to assent to the teaching on a mere majority? What if their own bishop was one who disagreed? And what of the bishop himself? Was he obliged to agree because most of his confreres had a different opinion? Further, episcopal conferences aren't part of the fundamental structure of the Church. They aren't divinely instituted but are created, for practical reasons, by canon law. Yet an individual bishop holds his teaching authority by divine law. How could the majority vote of a human institution overrule teaching authority held by divine right? The 1980s and 1990s saw a vigorous discussion of these questions.[3]

34. Eventually, Pope John Paul II established the following norms:

> Art. 1.—In order that the doctrinal declarations of the conference of bishops . . . may constitute authentic magisterium and be published in the name of the conference itself, they must be unanimously approved by the bishops who are members or receive the *recognitio* [i.e., approval] of the Apostolic See if approved in plenary assembly by at least two thirds of the bishops belonging to the conference and having a deliberative vote.
>
> Art. 2.—No body of the episcopal conference, outside of the plenary assembly, has the power to carry out acts of authentic magisterium. The episcopal conference cannot grant such power to its commissions or other bodies set up by it (*Apostolos Suos*).

The first norm is based on the fact that, if the bishops unanimously agree on a doctrine, it could fairly be represented as their teaching. However, the rights of individual bishops who disagree are also safeguarded. If not all agree, but if two thirds do, the Holy See can be asked to consider approving the position. If it does, the document becomes authentic magisterium and the people and bishops of the territory are expected to assent to its teaching.

The second norm guarantees that only documents that have been voted on by the whole assembly of bishops can become authentic magisterium. Documents issued between plenary sessions, by commissions or committees, or by particular officials, are not.

The Synod of Bishops

35. Another way bishops collaborate is through the Synod of Bishops, which Pope Paul VI announced in 1965. According to the *Code of Canon Law*:

> The Synod of Bishops is a group of bishops who have been chosen from different regions of the world and meet together at fixed times to foster closer unity between the Roman pontiff and bishops, to assist the Roman pontiff with their counsel in the preservation and growth of faith and morals and in the observance and strengthening of ecclesiastical discipline, and to consider questions pertaining to the activity of the Church in the world (CIC 342).

The synod is similar to national conferences in that it is a permanent body with administrative offices and staff (in this case, in Rome), and it holds periodic meetings. Unlike national conferences, its members don't all come from a single territory. It includes a representative sample of bishops, most of whom change with each meeting.

Since the first meeting in 1967, it has gathered about once every two years. Topics have included:

- Preserving and strengthening the Faith (1967)
- Evangelization in the modern world (1974)
- Catechesis in our time (1977)
- The Christian family (1980)
- The twentieth anniversary of Vatican II (1985)
- The Eucharist (2005)

- The word of God (2008)
- The family and challenges facing it (2014–2015)

Sessions also have met to discuss the pastoral situation in regions such as Africa (1994), the Americas (1997), Europe (1999), the Middle East (2010), and specific countries like the Netherlands (1980) and Lebanon (1995).

36. When the synod meets, the bishops discuss the appointed topic and prepare a document known as the *relatio synodi* (Latin, "the report of the synod"), which is given to the pope. The synod does not typically have doctrinal or legal authority but is an advisory body that provides counsel to the pope:

> It is for the Synod of Bishops to discuss the questions for consideration and express its wishes but not to resolve them or issue decrees about them unless in certain cases the Roman pontiff has endowed it with deliberative power, in which case he ratifies the decisions of the synod (CIC 343).

Afterward, the pope usually issues a document called a *postsynodal apostolic exhortation*. Such documents are primarily pastoral (indicated by the term *exhortation*), but they are documents of the pope's magisterium.

The pope may take additional actions based on suggestions by the synod. Thus the 1967 synod recommended that the 1917 *Code of Canon Law* be revised and that a commission for dialogue between theologians and the Holy See be created. Similarly, the 1985 synod recommended the writing of a universal catechism. These recommendations resulted in the 1983 *Code of Canon Law*, the International Theological Commission, and the *Catechism of the Catholic Church*. (For more on the authority of synod documents, see §158.)

The College of Bishops

37. Both the pope and the college of bishops have full and supreme power over the Church. According to Vatican II:

In virtue of his office, that is as vicar of Christ and pastor of the whole Church, the Roman pontiff has full, supreme, and universal power over the Church. And he is always free to exercise this power. The order of bishops, which succeeds to the college of apostles and gives this apostolic body continued existence, is also the subject of supreme and full power over the universal Church, provided we understand this body together with its head the Roman pontiff and never without this head (*Lumen Gentium,* 22).

The council explains:

This power can be exercised only with the consent of the Roman pontiff. For our Lord placed Simon alone as the rock and the bearer of the keys of the Church [cf. Matt. 16:18], and made him shepherd of the whole flock [cf. John 21:15ff]; it is evident, however, that the power of binding and loosing, which was given to Peter [Matt. 16:19], was granted also to the college of apostles, joined with their head [Matt. 18:18, 28:16–20] (ibid.).

38. Bishops must remain in communion with the Church to be part of the episcopal college:

One is constituted a member of the episcopal body in virtue of sacramental consecration and hierarchical communion with the head and members of the body (ibid.).

Consequently, bishops who have gone into schism (CCC 2089) cease to be members of the college of bishops. They still remain bishops in the sacramental sense, but they cannot exercise the full and supreme power over the Church, which requires the pope:

This same collegiate power can be exercised together with the pope by the bishops living in all parts of the world, provided that the head of the college calls them to collegiate action, or at least approves of or freely accepts the united action of the scattered bishops, so that it is thereby made a collegiate act (ibid.).

39. The full and supreme power over the Church includes the power to govern and the power to teach, including the power to infallibly define teachings (see chapters fifteen and sixteen). This can happen when the bishops are spread throughout the world, performing their ordinary teaching duties. In that case, a doctrine is said to be infallible by virtue of the ordinary and universal magisterium. Infallible definitions can also be made by the bishops gathered in an ecumenical council.

Ecumenical Councils

40. Ecumenical councils issue rulings that affect the whole world (Greek, *oikoumenē*), and they ideally involve bishops from the whole world. They are thus capable of exercising the Church's supreme power. According to Vatican II:

> The supreme power in the universal Church, which this college enjoys, is exercised in a solemn way in an ecumenical council. A council is never ecumenical unless it is confirmed or at least accepted as such by the successor of Peter; and it is the prerogative of the Roman pontiff to convoke these councils, to preside over them, and to confirm them (ibid.).

The first ecumenical council was held in Nicaea in A.D. 325, and it infallibly defined the divinity of Christ. The second, held in Constantinople in 381, infallibly defined the divinity of the Holy Spirit. Subsequent councils have dealt with many subjects. A total of twenty-one ecumenical councils have been held, the most recent being Vatican II (1962–1965).

Not every ecumenical council was convoked by the pope or involved bishops from the entire Christian world. The early councils were called by the emperor, though the bishops of Rome sought to participate, such as by sending legates.

Even today—when global travel is easy—not every bishop can attend. Reasons of health, local emergencies, and political persecution can prevent a bishop from doing so. In the ancient world, travel was much harder, and sometimes only a small number of bishops could attend. Several had fewer than 200 bishops, and Constantinople IV had barely more than a hundred. Also, rather than coming from all over the Christian world, the attendees of some early ecumenical councils came exclusively from the East.

41. This led the Church to reflect on what is ultimately necessary for a council to count as ecumenical. It must involve a gathering of bishops—otherwise it wouldn't be a council—and, if its results are to apply to the whole world, then the pope needs to be involved. This is why Vatican II said "a council is never ecumenical unless it is confirmed or at least accepted as such by the successor of Peter" (ibid.).

That covers historical situations. Going forward, canon law provides that only the pope can convoke an ecumenical council (CIC 338 §1), and every member of the college of bishops has the right and the duty to attend, unless legitimately prevented (CIC 339 §1). Further:

> The decrees of an ecumenical council do not have obligatory force unless they have been approved by the Roman pontiff together with the council fathers, confirmed by him, and promulgated at his order (CIC 341 §1).

List of Ecumenical Councils and Key Subjects

- 325: Nicaea I (divinity of Christ)
- 381: Constantinople I (divinity of the Holy Spirit)
- 431: Ephesus (Mary as *Theotokos*)
- 451: Chalcedon (full deity and humanity of Christ)
- 553: Constantinople II (errors of Origen)
- 680–681: Constantinople III (the divine and human wills of Christ)

- 787: Nicaea II (religious images)
- 869: Constantinople IV (the Photian schism)
- 1123: Lateran I (societal and Church reform)
- 1139: Lateran II (errors of Arnold of Brescia)
- 1179: Lateran III (errors of the Albigensians and Waldensians)
- 1215: Lateran IV (errors of Joachim of Flora)
- 1245: Lyons I (excommunication and deposition of Emperor Frederick II)
- 1274: Lyons II (procession of the Holy Spirit from the Father and the Son; union with the Eastern churches)
- 1311–1313: Vienne (the Knights Templar)
- 1414–1419: Constance (ending the Western Schism; errors of Wycliffe and Hus)
- 1432–1439: Florence (union with the Eastern churches)
- 1512–1517: Lateran V (Church reform)
- 1545–1563: Trent (errors of Protestant Reformers)
- 1869–1870: Vatican I (papal infallibility)
- 1962–1965: Vatican II (Church reform)

CHAPTER 4

The Pope and the Holy See

The Pope As Teacher

42. The pope is famous for being able to teach infallibly, but not everything he says is infallible. Most things aren't. How much authority a statement has depends on the weight the pope intends to give it.

Like every bishop, popes have training in theology, philosophy, and biblical studies. Some are even scholars in these fields, and they can write in them without invoking their teaching authority. When Pope Benedict XVI wrote his *Jesus of Nazareth* series on the life of Christ, he famously pointed out:

> It goes without saying that this book is in no way an exercise of the Magisterium, but is solely an expression of my personal search "for the face of the Lord" (cf. Ps. 27:8). Everyone is free, then, to contradict me. I would only ask my readers for that initial goodwill without which there can be no understanding (vol. 1, Foreword).

Also, as the bishop of the Diocese of Rome, the pope is capable of teaching in this capacity—simply as the bishop of his local flock. However, as the successor of Peter, the pope can teach authoritatively for the entire Church, and he is able to exercise the fullest degree of the Church's teaching authority by infallibly defining matters (see chapters fifteen and sixteen).

The Roman Curia

43. Every bishop is charged with caring for a large number of souls. That's why dioceses are divided into parishes, with priests and deacons to minister to individual Catholics. Running a diocese is a complex task, so the bishop has people who assist him. These people are known as his *curia*—a term taken from Latin roots meaning "a gathering together" (*co-*) of "men" (*viri*). The pastoral challenge facing the pope is even greater, and so he also has a curia in Rome:

> The Roman Curia is the complex of dicasteries and institutes which help the Roman pontiff in the exercise of his supreme pastoral office for the good and service of the whole Church and of the particular Churches. It thus strengthens the unity of the faith and the communion of the people of God and promotes the mission proper to the Church in the world (*Pastor Bonus,* I:1).

44. Departments of the Roman Curia are known as *dicasteries*. The Greek term *dikastērion* meant "a court of law," though today most of the dicasteries of the Roman Curia are not courts.

45. The Roman Curia has a complex structure that changes over time. In 1988, Pope John Paul II issued the apostolic constitution *Pastor Bonus* (Latin, "Good Shepherd"), which reorganized it and defined the functions of its departments. At the papal conclave of 2013, many cardinals expressed a desire for curial reform, and Pope Francis announced plans to study how the curia could be better organized to meet the needs of the Church.

There is a hierarchy among the dicasteries, which belong to categories that are ranked as follows:

1. Secretariat of State
2. Congregations
3. Tribunals
4. Pontifical councils
5. Administrative services
6. Other institutes

46. The media regularly overlooks distinctions among the dicasteries and the people who work at them. Anytime anyone connected with the Vatican says something, the press issues a headline attributing what they said directly to the pope. This is bad journalism. People who work in the Roman Curia assist the pope, but this doesn't mean they always speak for him. Hundreds of people work at the Vatican, and very few have regular, personal contact with the pope. He certainly does not give them personal instructions every time they write a letter, speak in public, or talk to a reporter.

Statements made by someone at the Vatican must be weighed in terms of who he is and what level of authority he has. Just as, with a secular organization, you can't attribute a statement made by someone who works in the mail room directly to the CEO, not every statement from a curial employee can be attributed to the pope.

47. The press also frequently mistakes every Vatican document as representing the teaching of the Church. Although such documents are meant to reflect Catholic principles, comparatively few are statements of doctrine. The Magisterium consists of the bishops of the Church, and the pope is the only bishop who can proclaim doctrines for the whole Church. Consequently, for a Vatican document to carry magisterial authority, it has to *both* be doctrinal in nature *and* be approved by the pope. If both conditions are not met, whatever other value the document may have, it is not a magisterial statement. Most documents issued by dicasteries do not fall into this category.

The Congregation for the Doctrine of the Faith

48. The dicastery that has the most to do with Church teaching is the Congregation for the Doctrine of the Faith (CDF). It is the only one that issues magisterial documents on a regular basis.

The CDF was founded in 1542 by Pope Paul III. Originally, it was called the Sacred Congregation for the Universal Inquisition, and like other inquisitions, it was tasked with protecting the Catholic faithful from heresies. Over time, its name changed. In 1908, Pope Pius X dubbed it the Sacred Congregation of the Holy Office, and for much of the twentieth century it was informally called "the Holy Office." In 1965, Paul VI renamed it the Sacred Congregation for the Doctrine of the Faith. By the mid-1980s, Vatican congregations stopped using the adjective "Sacred" in their names, resulting in its current designation.

49. *Pastor Bonus* summarizes its mission as follows:

> The proper duty of the Congregation for the Doctrine of the Faith is to promote and safeguard the doctrine on faith and morals in the whole Catholic world; so it has competence in things that touch this matter in any way (art. 48).

Note that this is not exclusively or even primarily a negative mission, focused on rooting out doctrinal error. News reports often refer to the CDF as the successor to "the Inquisition"—calling to mind torture chambers and efforts to get people to confess heresies. Not only does that kind of thing not happen today (the Church condemns torture; CCC 2297–2298), but this ignores the positive functions the CDF performs. Its fundamentally positive mission is shown by the fact that it is tasked with *promoting* Catholic doctrine, before its role in *safeguarding* doctrine is mentioned.

Pastor Bonus elaborates on this positive function:

> Fulfilling its duty of promoting doctrine, the congregation fosters studies so that the understanding of the faith may grow and a response in the light of the faith may be given to new questions arising from the progress of the sciences or human culture (art. 49).

50. When a document is issued by a dicastery of the Roman Curia, such as the CDF, this does not make it a document of the Magisterium. For that, it must carry papal approval:

The Roman pontiff fulfills his universal mission with the help of the various bodies of the Roman Curia and in particular with that of the Congregation for the Doctrine of the Faith in matters of doctrine and morals. Consequently, the documents issued by this congregation expressly approved by the pope participate in the ordinary magisterium of the successor of Peter (*Donum Veritatis,* 18; see also §361).

This principle also applies to bodies such as the Synod of Bishops. A document issued by the synod "participates in the ordinary magisterium of the successor of Peter" if it is "expressly approved by the Roman pontiff" (*Episcopalis Communio* art. 18, §1; see §158 for more on the authority of synod documents).

Other Dicasteries

51. Although the CDF is the only dicastery that regularly issues magisterial documents, other dicasteries discuss Catholic doctrine and sometimes issue documents of a doctrinal nature. For example:

- The Pontifical Academy for Life (now part of the Dicastery for the Laity, Family, and Life) published discussions of how to apply Catholic moral principles to new biomedical questions.
- The Pontifical Council for Promoting Christian Unity publishes documents discussing Catholic teaching in relation to the views of other Christians.
- The Congregation for Divine Worship and the Discipline of the Sacraments deals with Catholic teaching regarding the sacraments and aspects of popular piety.

In 2004 the Pontifical Council for Justice and Peace (now part of the Dicastery for Promoting Integral Human Development) issued the *Compendium of the Social Doctrine of the Church.* As the name indicates, it has a doctrinal nature. However, it did not carry a notification of papal approval. Consequently, it appears to be merely a summary (compendium) of existing social doctrine, rather than a new exercise of the Magisterium (§§50, 361).

52. Although most curial documents are not personally approved by the pope, the dicasteries are required to submit major decisions to him and to keep him informed of important activities. *Pastor Bonus* states:

> Decisions of major importance are to be submitted for the approval of the supreme pontiff, except decisions for which special faculties have been granted to the moderators of the dicasteries . . .
>
> It is of the utmost importance that nothing grave and extraordinary be transacted unless the supreme pontiff be previously informed by the moderators of the dicasteries (art. 18).

Documents that the pope does not personally approve are still expected to be doctrinally orthodox. To ensure this, they are only to be published after they have been reviewed and corrected by the CDF. *Pastor Bonus* requires:

> Documents being published by other dicasteries of the Roman Curia, insofar as they touch on the doctrine of faith or morals, are to be subjected to its [the CDF's] prior judgment (art. 54).

This approval by the CDF functions as an imprimatur indicating they do not contradict Church teaching, though not everything they say has magisterial authority.

Special Non-Curial Bodies

53. We also need to mention bodies that are not part of the Roman Curia but that have a special connection with it and Church doctrine. The two most important are the Pontifical Biblical Commission and the International Theological Commission.

The Pontifical Biblical Commission

54. The Pontifical Biblical Commission (PBC) originally was an organ of the Magisterium. It was founded in 1902 by Pope Leo XIII in the apostolic letter *Vigiliantiae Studiique*. At that time, it consisted of a group of cardinals, assisted by consultors, after the model of Vatican congregations. Its purpose was to engage the field of biblical scholarship and provide responses to major controversies of the day.

In 1971, Paul VI reorganized the PBC in the motu proprio *Sedula Cura*, which stated that the commission "continues in its work of promoting biblical studies and assisting the Magisterium of the Church in the interpretation of Scripture" (norm 1). However, the commission was no longer built around a group of cardinals working with consultors. Instead, it became a commission of biblical scholars who report to the CDF.

It thus ceased to have magisterial authority and became an advisory body. In his preface to the commission's 1993 document, *The Interpretation of the Bible in the Church*, Cardinal Ratzinger writes:

> The Pontifical Biblical Commission, in its new form after the Second Vatican Council, is not an organ of the magisterium, but rather a commission of scholars who, in their scientific and ecclesial responsibility as believing exegetes, take positions on important problems of scriptural interpretation and know that for this task they enjoy the confidence of the Magisterium.

The International Theological Commission

55. Unlike the Pontifical Biblical Commission, the International Theological Commission (ITC) has never been an organ of the Magisterium. It has always been an advisory body. The ITC was created in 1969 by Paul VI as a group of scholars reporting to the CDF, and its current statutes were established in 1982 by John Paul II in the motu proprio *Tredecem Anni*. According to that document:

It is the duty of the International Theological Commission to study doctrinal problems of great importance, especially those which present new points of view, and in this way to offer its help to the Magisterium of the Church, particularly to the Sacred Congregation for the Doctrine of the Faith to which it is attached (norm 1).

CHAPTER 5

Doctrines and the Realm of Belief

Introduction

56. "Is that a doctrine or a discipline?" This question is often asked in discussions of the Catholic faith. It presupposes that everything can be placed in one of these categories. Thus the Trinity is a doctrine, but the celibacy of priests is a discipline.

It's also commonly assumed that doctrines cannot change, but disciplines can. The doctrine of the Trinity is an unchangeable part of the Catholic faith. By contrast, the discipline of priestly celibacy can change.

Although the doctrine/discipline distinction can be useful, it oversimplifies matters. The two can be tightly linked, and a doctrine may require a particular discipline. It is an infallible doctrine that adultery is gravely sinful, and this requires the discipline of fidelity in marriage. Fidelity thus can be understood as a doctrine *and* a discipline. As this example illustrates, some disciplines—like marital fidelity—*cannot* change, and as we will see in later chapters, some doctrines *can* change.

Another problem is that doctrine and discipline are not exhaustive categories. Not everything is a doctrine or a discipline. Some things don't qualify as either. To see why, we need to back up and look at the broader categories to which doctrine and discipline belong: the realm of belief and the realm of action. In this chapter, we will look at the realm of belief.

Understanding Belief

57. Things people believe can be classified in various ways:

- By their relationship to reality
- By their degree of certainty
- By their subject matter
- By their relation to Church teaching

Beliefs and Reality

58. One way of classifying beliefs is by the relationship they have to reality. The two most basic classifications are true and false. Beliefs that correspond to reality are true, and those that don't are false. The belief that it is raining outside is true if and only if it really is raining outside. Otherwise, it is false.

59. The true/false distinction is useful in many situations, but not in all. Sometimes a belief is not simply true or simply false. This happens with approximations. Consider the number *pi* (π). This is an irrational number, which means it can't be expressed as the ratio of two other numbers (e.g., 1/4, 1/2, 2/3), and it can't be fully written out in decimal form. We can only write out *pi* to different degrees of approximation, such as 3.14, 3.1415, or 3.141592. These approximate *pi* with increasing precision, and to that extent they express truth. However, none is *exactly pi*. Approximation occurs in all fields, including religion. A famous example is the Bible's description of the metal basin or "sea" used for ceremonial washings in Solomon's temple. Scripture reports it was ten cubits across and "a line of thirty cubits measured its circumference" (1 Kings 7:23; 2 Chron. 4:2). This implies an approximation of *pi* as 3, which is not wrong; it's simply less precise than the approximations given above.

60. Approximations occur in religion because human speech, consciousness, and knowledge can only express the truth with a finite degree of precision. Yet God is infinite and beyond our ability to fully grasp. The *Catechism* says:

God transcends all creatures. We must therefore continually purify our language of everything in it that is limited, image-bound, or imperfect, if we are not to confuse our image of God—the inexpressible, the incomprehensible, the invisible, the ungraspable—with our human representations. Our human words always fall short of the mystery of God (CCC 42).

Nevertheless, our words do express truth:

Admittedly, in speaking about God like this, our language is using human modes of expression; nevertheless it really does attain to God himself, though unable to express him in his infinite simplicity. Likewise, we must recall that between Creator and creature no similitude can be expressed without implying an even greater dissimilitude; and that concerning God, we cannot grasp what he is, but only what he is not, and how other beings stand in relation to him (CCC 43; cf. Vatican I, *Dei Filius,* 4:4).

In addition to the degree to which beliefs correspond to reality, they can also be classified by the degree to which they are certain.

Objective and Subjective Certainty

61. Certainty can be either subjective or objective. Subjective certainty is the degree of confidence an individual person feels regarding a belief. He is subjectively certain if he has no practical doubts that it is true. This form of certainty is often called *certitude* to distinguish it from objective certainty.

Objective certainty is the degree of confidence objectively warranted by the evidence for a belief. A belief would be objectively certain if an ideal reasoner—a person making no mistakes in logic or weighing evidence—concluded the belief is certainly true.

Possibility, Probability, and Certainty

62. Beliefs can be ranked along a spectrum of certainty. A belief may be:

a) certainly true
b) probably true
c) possibly true
d) possibly untrue
e) probably untrue
f) certainly untrue

The halves of this spectrum mirror each other, so we only need concern ourselves with the possible, the probable, and the certain:

- A belief is possible if it is not certainly untrue.

- Beliefs that are possible have one or another degree of probability. Some are only barely possible (highly unlikely), others are equiprobable (as likely as not to be true), and some are highly probable. There are many ways of ranking probability, and these are only a few examples.

- The highest degree of probability is certainty. Beliefs that are certain are so well supported that doubt is excluded.

Types of Certainty

63. Scholars have distinguished different ways that a belief can be certain. One common account is as follows:

- *Metaphysical certainty* occurs when there is no possibility at all of it being incorrect. Proposed examples include the laws of logic, the laws of mathematics, and the knowledge an individual has that he exists.

- *Physical certainty* occurs when something follows from the ordinary operations of nature (barring the possibility of the extraordinary or the miraculous). Proposed examples include the laws of physics and chemistry, knowledge that one will someday die, and knowledge that the sun will rise in the morning.

- *Moral certainty* is possible when free will is involved. Proposed examples include laws developed by the social sciences, historical facts, and the certainty that one's spouse is not secretly poisoning one's food.

What is common to all these is the exclusion of doubt—the defining characteristic of certainty. Although it is *possible* one's spouse is secretly poisoning one's food, the evidence normally warrants moral certainty that this is not happening. Although it is possible a rare physical event or a miracle might prevent the sun from rising in the morning, we normally don't have evidence to warrant doubting that it will, so it is physically certain. Finally, some beliefs have no possibility of being incorrect (e.g., 1+1=2), and we can regard them as metaphysically certain.

Except in the last case, the beliefs are only highly probable. However, the human mind is configured so that it is impractical to entertain doubts about them. When a judgment is made that it is no longer worth entertaining doubts then a state of subjective certainty (certitude) has been achieved.

Certainty and Church Teaching

64. Scholars have examined the relationship between faith and reason and certainty. Not all have gotten it right. Some have exaggerated the role of faith, to the exclusion of reason. Others have done the reverse. And some have falsely minimized or maximized the possibility of certainty. Consequently, the Church has established boundaries for the discussion.

It has infallibly taught that it is possible by the natural use of reason to achieve certainty regarding the existence of God. Vatican I infallibly rejected the proposition that "the one, true God, our creator and lord, cannot be known with certainty from the things that have been made, by the natural light of human reason" (*Dei Filius,* canons 2:1; cf. CCC 36).

The *Catechism of the Catholic Church* notes the manner in which proofs for his existence work:

Created in God's image and called to know and love him, the person who seeks God discovers certain ways of coming

to know him. These are also called proofs for the existence
of God, not in the sense of proofs in the natural sciences, but
rather in the sense of "converging and convincing arguments,"
which allow us to attain certainty about the truth (CCC 31).

Vatican I also infallibly rejected the proposition "miracles can
never be known with certainty" (*Dei Filius,* canons 3:4), meaning that some miracles can be.

65. Although some things are known about God with certainty by
natural reason, not everyone is in a position to learn these proofs:

> In the historical conditions in which he finds himself,
> however, man experiences many difficulties in coming to
> know God by the light of reason alone (CCC 37).

Not everyone has the inclination or training to follow philosophical proofs about God, and we all have disordered desires that
predispose us to believe what we wish to be true rather than what
the evidence supports. Because of these difficulties, God has supplemented what can be known about him by reason with revelation:

> This is why man stands in need of being enlightened by
> God's revelation, not only about those things that exceed
> his understanding, but also about those religious and moral
> truths which of themselves are not beyond the grasp of
> human reason, so that even in the present condition of the
> human race, they can be known by all men with ease, with
> firm certainty and with no admixture of error (CCC 38).

66. To make divine revelation credible, God has given certain
signs which serve as "motives of credibility":

> So that the submission of our faith might nevertheless be
> in accordance with reason, God willed that external proofs
> of his revelation should be joined to the internal helps of

the Holy Spirit. Thus the miracles of Christ and the saints, prophecies, the Church's growth and holiness, and her fruitfulness and stability are the most certain signs of divine revelation, adapted to the intelligence of all; they are "motives of credibility" (*motiva credibilitatis*), which show that the assent of faith is by no means a blind impulse of the mind (CCC 156).

These motives of credibility bring us to the point where placing our faith in divine revelation is reasonable. They are "most certain signs of divine revelation," and scholars have generally held that the kind of certitude they provide is moral certitude.[4] They do not compel the will, but they make the choice of faith rational.

67. The points of faith themselves, however, are certain in a different way, because they are given to us by "the authority of God himself, who makes the revelation and can neither deceive nor be deceived" (*Dei Filius,* 3:2). They are therefore not just morally or physically certain but objectively certain in the most absolute sense.

Beliefs and Subject Matter

68. Another way of classifying beliefs is by subject matter. Within the realm of religion, topics of study include:

- *Christology*: The study of the Person and work of Christ
- *Pneumatology*: The study of the Person and work of the Holy Spirit
- *Protology:* The study of the "first things" (i.e., Creation)
- *Angelology*: The study of angels
- *Theological anthropology*: The theological study of man
- *Hammartiology*: The study of sin
- *Soteriology*: The study of salvation
- *Ecclesiology*: The study of the Church
- *Mariology* and *hagiology*: The studies of Mary and the saints
- *Eschatology*: The study of the "last things" (e.g., death, judgment, hell, heaven)

Belief-Related Disciplines

Identifying the Disciplines

69. In the Church there are a number of disciplines—in the sense of fields of study—related to belief. It is possible to classify them based on the goals they pursue, giving us fields like:

- *Evangelization*, whose goal is announcing the Faith
- *Apologetics*, whose goal is defending the Faith
- *Catechetics*, whose goal is basic instruction in the Faith
- *Theology*, whose goal is a deeper understanding of the Faith

70. The first field—evangelization—involves the study of how to proclaim the gospel (Greek, *euangelion*). This discipline takes first place because people must embrace the Christian gospel before they are willing to go deeper into the study of the Faith. Evangelization was a principal activity of Jesus and the apostles.

71. Once the gospel has been proclaimed, people want to know why they should believe it. They also will want objections cleared up. Apologetics offers a defense (Greek, *apologia*) of the Faith by providing the needed evidence and answers to objections. It naturally follows evangelization and began to emerge as a specialized discipline in the second century. Today in scholarly writings, apologetics is sometimes referred to as *fundamental theology* since it establishes the foundations of Christian belief, and it is often practiced in new ways.

72. After people have accepted the gospel, they need basic instruction in the Faith. This is done through catechesis (Greek, *katekhein*, "to instruct orally"). As the Church grew, catechetics became a specialized discipline, and individuals tasked with it became known as catechists.

73. As people grow in faith, they want to go deeper. This leads to theology (Greek, *theos*, "God," and *logia*, "discussion"), whose task is to discuss and understand God in a deeper way. An unofficial glossary for the *Catechism of the Catholic Church,* composed by Cardinal William Levada, defines theology as "the study of God, based on divine revelation." Everyone who seeks to understand God in a deeper way is engaging in theology, and specialists in the field are known as theologians. There have always been theologians in the Church (St. Paul being a first-century example), but as an organized field of study, theology was the last of these four disciplines to develop.

Liberty Within the Disciplines

74. Although there is overlap between Church teaching and each of the fields just discussed, there is considerable liberty within these fields. This conflicts with the stereotypical view of the Church as a dogmatic, authoritarian institution.

75. Consider evangelization: although an evangelist must announce the basics of the Christian faith (e.g., the existence of God, his love for us, our need for salvation in Christ), there is no official way of proclaiming the gospel. Instead, evangelists are called upon to use their creativity and skill to find the best ways to reach people—a complex task given the differences among people and the views they hold.

76. The Church accords similar liberty to apologists. Although it teaches that it's possible to prove God exists, the Church doesn't have an official set of arguments for God's existence. It makes general remarks on strategies for this (CCC 31–35), but it has not worked these up into detailed proofs. Not even St. Thomas Aquinas's famous "five ways" of proving God's existence (ST I:2:3) are considered official proofs. There is even less of an official stance on how to deal with arguments posed by Mormons, Jehovah's Witnesses, or other sects. Apologists thus are called on to use their skill and creativity in dealing with these.

77. The situation changes somewhat with catechesis. Since it is instruction in the basic teachings of the Faith, one would expect the Magisterium to have more to say. The Church has even produced its own catechisms, such as the *Roman Catechism* (aka the *Catechism of the Council of Trent*, promulgated by Pope Pius V in 1566) and the *Catechism of the Catholic Church* (promulgated by Pope John Paul II in 1992). National conferences of bishops have also produced catechisms, such as the *United States Catholic Catechism for Adults* (2006).

Nevertheless, catechists must still use their skill and creativity to help people understand and accept the basic teachings of the Faith. To assist them in this task, the Church gives guidance on how to implement catechesis on the practical level, as in the *General Directory for Catechesis,* published by the Vatican's Congregation for Clergy in 1997, and the *National Catechetical Directory,* published by the U.S. bishops in 2005.

Beliefs and Church Teaching

Theology and Church Teaching

78. One field that calls for special attention is theology. Like catechesis, it has a large overlap with official Church teaching. However, unlike catechesis, it goes well beyond this, for theologians are called to explore divine revelation in a deeper way.

79. At times, this causes problems. Following Vatican II, a wave of dissent spread, with many theologians rejecting magisterial teachings. These included high-profile theologians like Hans Küng, Edward Schillebeeckx, and Charles Curran, each of whom was eventually disciplined by the CDF. Catechetics was also thrown into confusion, as dissident theological ideas filtered down to parishes, leaving catechists unsure what they were to teach.

The situation was addressed in the pontificates of Popes Paul VI, John Paul II, and Benedict XVI, who released a series of documents reaffirming Church teaching. The *Catechism of the Catholic Church* also was written to address the catechetical crisis.

However, these actions—and the disciplining of dissident authors—led some theologians to object. They argued the Holy

See was infringing on their area of expertise and trying to reduce them to the status of catechists who merely repeat Church teaching rather than seek a deeper understanding of revelation.

The Holy See thus began several initiatives to clarify the task of theologians and reassure them that there was a legitimate role for their discipline. Some of these were carried out through the International Theological Commission (ITC), which Paul VI created as a way for the Holy See to consult with theologians and which is composed of theologians known for orthodoxy (see §55).

80. Several ITC studies have dealt with the relationship between the Magisterium and theologians. One document—*Theses on the Relationship Between the Ecclsiastical Magisterium and Theology* (1975)—explains the term *theologian* as follows:

> By "theologians" are meant those members of the Church who by their studies and life in the community of the Church's faith are qualified to pursue, in the scientific manner proper to theology, a deeper understanding of the word of God and also to teach that word by virtue of a canonical mission (thesis 1).

Here "canonical mission" refers to a special charge given to theologians by the Catholic universities at which they teach:

> Those who teach disciplines concerning faith or morals must receive, after making their profession of faith, a canonical mission from the chancellor or his delegate, for they do not teach on their own authority but by virtue of the mission they have received from the Church (John Paul II, *Sapientia Christiana*, art. 27:1).

In addition, "those who teach theological disciplines in any institutes of higher studies whatsoever must have a mandate from the competent ecclesiastical authority" (CIC 812), who is usually the local bishop.

To be a theologian in the formal, academic sense, one must thus have the needed canonical qualifications. However:

> All the baptized, insofar as they both really live the life of the Church and enjoy scientific competence, can carry out the task of the theologian, a task that derives its own force from the life of the Holy Spirit in the Church (thesis 7:2).

81. Concerning the enterprise of theology itself, the Congregation for the Doctrine of the Faith (CDF) explains:

> Among the vocations awakened in this way by the Spirit in the Church is that of the theologian. His role is to pursue in a particular way an ever deeper understanding of the word of God found in the inspired scriptures and handed on by the living Tradition of the Church. He does this in communion with the Magisterium which has been charged with the responsibility of preserving the deposit of faith. . . .
>
> Obedient to the impulse of truth which seeks to be communicated, theology also arises from love and love's dynamism. In the act of faith, man knows God's goodness and begins to love him. Love, however, is ever desirous of a better knowledge of the beloved (*Donum Veritatis*, 6–7).

82. As a quest to understand God in an ever deeper manner, theology goes beyond catechesis. It is an exploratory science, and theologians propose many ideas that go beyond Church teaching. In doing so, they play a valuable role, for by exploring and testing ideas, they serve the process of doctrinal development (see chapter eighteen). As time passes, the Magisterium monitors the fruits of their labor, and when a theological idea is sufficiently established, the Magisterium may elevate it to the status of a doctrine. For example, the term *transubstantiation* was originally proposed by theologians. The 1909 edition of the *Catholic Encyclopedia* notes:

The term *transubstantiation* seems to have been first used by Hildebert of Tours (about 1079). His encouraging example was soon followed by other theologians, as Stephen of Autun (d. 1139), Gaufred (1188), and Peter of Blois (d. about 1200), whereupon several ecumenical councils also adopted this significant expression, as the Fourth Council of the Lateran (1215), and the Council of Lyons (1274), in the profession of faith of the Greek Emperor Michael Palaeologus. The Council of Trent (Sess. XIII, cap. iv; can. ii) not only accepted as an inheritance of faith the truth contained in the idea, but authoritatively confirmed the "aptitude of the term" to express most strikingly the legitimately developed doctrinal concept (s.v. "Eucharist").

83. Although theologians—like everyone else—are obliged to adhere to Church teaching, they also need the proper liberty to perform their task. The CDF states:

> Freedom of research, which the academic community rightly holds most precious, means an openness to accepting the truth that emerges at the end of an investigation in which no element has intruded that is foreign to the methodology corresponding to the object under study.
>
> In theology this freedom of inquiry is the hallmark of a rational discipline whose object is given by revelation, handed on and interpreted in the Church under the authority of the Magisterium, and received by faith. These givens have the force of principles. To eliminate them would mean to cease doing theology (*Donum Veritatis*, 12).

The Magisterium thus expects theologians to adhere to Church teaching while also having the freedom to explore aspects of divine revelation on which it has not yet pronounced.

84. Sometimes people confuse ideas proposed by theologians with Church teaching. The thought of Aquinas has been so influential

historically that many have treated views he proposed as if they
were official Catholic teaching, and his thought has enjoyed special
magisterial prestige. As late as 1950, Pius XII required "that future
priests be instructed in philosophy according to the method, doctrine,
and principles of the Angelic Doctor, since as we well know from
the experience of centuries, the method of Aquinas is singularly
preeminent both for teaching students and for bringing truth to
light" (DH 3894). However, in recent years there has been a shift
in the way the Magisterium recommends Aquinas. Although "the
Church has been justified in consistently proposing Saint Thomas as
a master of thought and a model of the right way to do theology"
(John Paul II, *Fides et Ratio,* 43), it does not endorse all of his views,
and it permits and respects schools of thought besides Thomism.

Sometimes theological ideas are so common that ordinary
Catholics are surprised to learn they aren't official Church teachings. For example, many have been taught as part of their basic
catechesis about the "seal" that we receive in baptism, but, as the
Catechism of the Catholic Church notes, this image is only used "in
some theological traditions":

> The seal [as a symbol of the Holy Spirit] is a symbol close to
> that of anointing. The Father has set his seal on Christ and
> also seals us in him. Because this seal indicates the indelible
> effect of the anointing with the Holy Spirit in the sacra-
> ments of baptism, confirmation, and holy orders, the im-
> age of the seal (*sphragis*) has been used in some theological
> traditions to express the indelible "character" imprinted by
> these three unrepeatable sacraments (CCC 698).

What the Church teaches is that these three sacraments have
an indelible effect, but the image of a seal belongs to theology
rather than doctrine. This brings us to our next subject.

Doctrine and Dogma

85. "What is the difference between a doctrine and a dogma?"
Apologists are asked this question frequently, and the meaning

of the word *doctrine* is straightforward: in Latin, *doctrina* means "teaching," and a Catholic doctrine is something that the Church authoritatively teaches. Specifically, a doctrine is a matter of faith or morals taught by the Magisterium.

86. The meaning of *dogma* is less straightforward. This Greek word originally meant "opinion" or "belief." Over the centuries it has had many meanings. At times, it's been a synonym for *doctrine*. However, today it has a very specific use. Cardinal Avery Dulles explains:

> In current Catholic usage, the term "dogma" means a divinely revealed truth, proclaimed as such by the infallible teaching authority of the Church, and hence binding on all the faithful without exception, now and forever (*The Survival of Dogma*, 153).

More simply: *a dogma is a doctrine that the Magisterium has infallibly defined to be divinely revealed.* From this definition, three things are clear:

1. Dogmas are a subset of doctrines. All dogmas are doctrines, but not all doctrines are dogmas.
2. Dogmas are infallible. If a teaching has any lesser level of authority, it is not a dogma.
3. Dogmas are *also* a subset of infallible teachings. Just because the Church has infallibly taught something does not make it a dogma. For that to happen, the Church must infallibly teach that the doctrine *is divinely revealed*. This distinction is important because the Church is capable of infallibly defining some things that aren't part of divine revelation (see chapter fifteen).

Summary

87. From the foregoing, we can represent the way different beliefs relate to Church teaching as a series of concentric circles:

- The outermost circle represents *beliefs in general*—the entire range of views people might hold, regardless of the subject they concern.

- Within this, there is the realm of *theological beliefs*—beliefs about God based on divine revelation.

- Further in lies the realm of Church *doctrine*—beliefs the Magisterium teaches authoritatively.

- Near the core are *infallible doctrines*—beliefs the Magisterium teaches infallibly.

- At the center are *dogmas*—beliefs the Magisterium has infallibly taught to be divinely revealed.

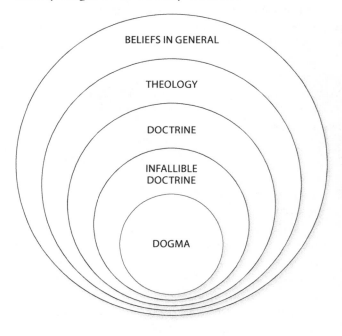

CHAPTER 6

Disciplines and the Realm of Action

88. We began the previous chapter with the question "Is that a doctrine or a discipline?" and we saw that it oversimplifies things. Not everything is a doctrine or a discipline. Doctrines are only one set within the larger category of beliefs, and the same is true of disciplines. These belong to the larger category of actions, which can be classified in various ways. Here we will look at the following:

- Actions in general
- Customs
- Disciplines
- Laws

Actions and Customs

89. An *action* is anything people do. Actions can be good, bad, or indifferent; they can be planned or spontaneous; they can be deliberate or involuntary.

90. Some actions people do on a regular basis. When a community performs an action regularly, it is known as a *custom*. These may or may not carry a sense of obligation:

- If a person or group chooses to do something differently, they may be deviating from custom, but they may not be violating any moral or legal obligation.

- On the other hand, a custom may have become so deeply ingrained in a culture that a sudden, unexpected deviation from it would cause confusion, consternation, or anxiety, and to cause others needless distress violates the moral norm to love our neighbors (Matt. 22:39).

- Customs can even obtain the force of law. The *Code of Canon Law* has a section detailing the conditions under which this happens (CIC §§23–28).

91. Over the centuries, many customs have arisen in Christian communities, such as the way they number the Ten Commandments. The *Catechism of the Catholic Church* explains:

> The division and numbering of the Commandments have varied in the course of history. The present catechism follows the division of the Commandments established by St. Augustine, which has become traditional in the Catholic Church. It is also that of the Lutheran confessions. The Greek Fathers worked out a slightly different division, which is found in the Orthodox churches and Reformed communities (2066).

Note that the *Catechism* does not say that the Commandments must be numbered the way St. Augustine proposed. It doesn't enter into the question of which numbering, if any, is superior (there is also a Jewish numbering). It simply says, "the present catechism" uses the traditional Catholic one. This is significant because there have been needless disputes among Christians on this issue, but when we recognize this is a matter of custom rather than doctrine, these can be resolved.

Consequently, we need to be sensitive to when something is a matter of custom and whether it carries an obligation. Just because something is a regular Catholic practice doesn't mean it is a matter of doctrine or that it carries a moral or legal obligation.

Disciplines

92. If a custom carries an obligation, it can be called a *discipline*. The *Oxford English Dictionary* defines "discipline" as "the system by which the practice of a church, as distinguished from its doctrine, is regulated."[5] Understood this way, disciplines involve obligations: they *regulate* the practice of a church.

93. The obligation can arise from several sources, including:

- Moral principles: The discipline of fidelity in marriage is based on the moral prohibition of adultery (Exod. 20:14; Deut. 20:18).

- Doctrinal principles: The discipline of baptizing converts is based on divine revelation (Matt. 28:19; Acts 2:38).

- Church law: Many disciplines are based on provisions found in the *Code of Canon Law* or the Church's liturgical books.

Case Study: The Discipline of Priestly Celibacy

94. Since the Protestant Reformation, the fact that most Catholic priests are unmarried (i.e., celibate) has been a lightning rod, and many Protestants have argued that the practice is "unbiblical" or contrary to the Bible. In fact, there is a strong biblical basis for it. Both Jesus and St. Paul were celibate (cf. Eph. 5:25–32, 1 Cor. 9:5), and both recommended the practice to others (Matt. 19:10–12; cf. 2 Tim. 2:3–4).

Despite its biblical basis, priestly celibacy is only a discipline. It is possible in principle for priests to be married (cf. 1 Cor. 9:5, 1 Tim. 3:2), and some Catholic priests *are* married. Eastern Catholic churches ordain married men, and the Western church sometimes ordains married men who previously were ministers in other denominations. Thus, although the Latin church's *Code of Canon Law* requires celibacy for clerics (CIC 277 §1), this law could one day be modified or abolished.

Laws

95. St. Thomas Aquinas provides the classic definition of a law as "an ordinance of reason for the common good, made by him who has care of the community, and promulgated" (ST I–II:90:4). Similarly, the *Catechism of the Catholic Church* says a "law is a rule of conduct enacted by competent authority for the sake of the common good" (1951). These definitions have the same essential elements:

- Laws are rules of conduct (i.e., "ordinances").
- They are created by a legislator ("him who has care of the community"/the "competent authority"). This is one of the differences between laws and mere customs. Laws require a legislator, whereas customs can be introduced by a community (CIC 23).
- They are published ("promulgated"/"enacted") so that the community knows about them.
- They promote the common good of the community to which they apply. Thus laws must be "ordinances of reason." A law that worked against the common good would be unreasonable and thus an unjust rule rather than a true law.

Divine and Human Laws

96. Laws can be classified by the legislator who issues them. Thus laws given by God are divine laws. Because God has shared the authority to rule with men, their laws—known as human laws—are backed by God's authority when they are just.

Since laws create a moral obligation to follow them, we can view all true laws as expressions of an overall moral law. The *Catechism* states:

> There are different expressions of the moral law, all of them interrelated: eternal law—the source, in God, of all law; natural law; revealed law, comprising the Old Law and the New Law, or Law of the Gospel; finally, civil and ecclesiastical laws (1952).

We will look briefly at each of these.

The Eternal Law

97. The most fundamental form of divine law is the eternal law, which is God's wisdom, the providential plan by which he rules the world. Aquinas explains:

> The whole community of the universe is governed by divine reason. Wherefore the very idea of the government of things in God, the ruler of the universe, has the nature of a law. And since the divine reason's conception of things is not subject to time but is eternal, according to Proverbs 8:23, therefore it is that this kind of law must be called eternal (ST I–II:91:1).

Since God is the source of everything, all law is ultimately rooted in God's wisdom, and laws are only binding to the extent that they participate in the eternal law.

Natural Law

98. The term *natural law* can be a source of confusion. In English, it often refers to laws proposed by the natural sciences, such as Newton's laws of motion. Although these are part of God's plan for the universe, they are not what theologians refer to as natural law. In this case, *natural* isn't a reference to the natural world but to *human* nature, which includes the gift of reason:

> This law is called "natural," not in reference to the nature of irrational beings, but because reason which decrees it properly belongs to human nature (CCC 1955).

Reason enables us to understand the aspects of God's plan that apply to us—to how we should direct our actions—and the Church uses *natural law* to refer to the rational creature's participation in the eternal law:

The natural law is a participation in God's wisdom and goodness by man formed in the image of his Creator. It expresses the dignity of the human person and forms the basis of his fundamental rights and duties (CCC 1978; cf. ST I–II:91:2).

99. Natural law applies to all people, in all times, and must undergird all human laws:

- Because human beings share the same nature, natural law applies to all people, in all cultures. Sin interferes with our awareness of it, but reason enables us to understand its requirements. Thus St. Paul says when Gentiles naturally perform good actions, "they show that what the law requires is written on their hearts" (Rom. 2:14–15).

- Human nature does not vary through the centuries. Consequently, although how the principles of natural law are to be applied in particular situations varies (CCC 1957), they are the same at all times.

- Since laws must promote the common good and be in accordance with reason, human laws must be in conformity with natural law.

The *Catechism* summarizes these points when it says:

The natural law is immutable, permanent throughout history. The rules that express it remain substantially valid. It is a necessary foundation for the erection of moral rules and civil law (1979).

Revealed Law

100. The gift of reason is not the only way God communicates with man. He also uses revelation, producing revealed law. Theology divides this into two bodies: the Old Law and the New Law.

101. The first is the law God gave to the people of Israel. The "Law of Moses" is found in the first five books of the Bible

(Genesis through Deuteronomy). Although these books contain many individual laws, they are summed up in the Ten Commandments (Exod. 20:1–17; Deut. 5:6–21).

"The Law of Moses expresses many truths naturally accessible to reason" (CCC 1961), such as the prohibition of murder, adultery, and theft. Because these requirements are part of natural law, they apply to all people, even those who are not Israelites. In addition, God gave the Israelites laws to regulate life as his covenant people. These included circumcision, dietary laws, holy days, and laws of sacrifice. Since these precepts go beyond natural law, they didn't apply to all people. Aquinas explains:

> The Old Law showed forth the precepts of the natural law, and added certain precepts of its own. Accordingly, as to those precepts of the natural law contained in the Old Law, all were bound to observe the Old Law; not because they belonged to the Old Law, but because they belonged to the natural law. But as to those precepts which were added by the Old Law, they were not binding save on the Jewish people alone (ST I–II:98:5).

102. The Old Law prepared the Jewish people for the coming of Christ. It thus gave way to the New Law (Gal. 3:23–25), which is referred to as "the Law of Christ" (1 Cor. 9:21, Gal. 6:2) and "the Law of the Gospel."

This law is expressed in the revelation found in the New Testament. Like the Old Law, it communicates truths that are accessible to reason and thus belong to natural law. It also establishes principles to regulate the lives of Christians as God's New Covenant people. These include provisions regarding Church government (e.g., Matt. 16:18–19), the Christian day of worship (e.g., 1 Cor. 16:2, Rev. 1:10), and the sacraments (e.g., Matt. 28:19, Luke 22:19).

Unlike the Old Law, the New Law is accompanied by the gift of the Holy Spirit, who works through charity in the hearts of Christians to enable them to fulfill the law. The role of the Holy

Spirit is so important that Aquinas can say that "the New Law is chiefly the grace itself of the Holy Ghost, which is given to those who believe in Christ" (ST I–II:106:1). Similarly, the *Catechism* states: "The New Law is the grace of the Holy Spirit received by faith in Christ, operating through charity. It finds expression above all in the Lord's Sermon on the Mount and uses the sacraments to communicate grace to us" (1983).

Civil Law

103. We now come to laws for which human beings serve as legislator. A true law must promote the common good. Consequently, such laws participate in the natural law and are morally obligatory. St. Paul says:

> Let every person be subject to the governing authorities. For there is no authority except from God, and those that exist have been instituted by God. Therefore he who resists the authorities resists what God has appointed, and those who resist will incur judgment. For rulers are not a terror to good conduct, but to bad. Would you have no fear of him who is in authority? Then do what is good, and you will receive his approval, for he is God's servant for your good. But if you do wrong, be afraid, for he does not bear the sword in vain; he is the servant of God to execute his wrath on the wrongdoer. Therefore one must be subject, not only to avoid God's wrath but also for the sake of conscience (Rom. 13:1–2).

Similarly, St. Peter says:

> Be subject for the Lord's sake to every human institution, whether it be to the emperor as supreme, or to governors as sent by him to punish those who do wrong and to praise those who do right (1 Pet. 2:13–14).

104. Although the civil law participates in natural law, it does not simply copy it. Instead, it takes natural law principles and applies them to particular situations. This is why civil law can vary in different places and times.

Natural law contains a principle that we should not create unnecessary dangers to others' lives, but this principle can be applied in different ways. Thus, in the U.S., traffic laws require cars to drive on the right side of the road, but in the U.K., they must drive on the left. Both applications of the principle are legitimate and promote the common good.

Civil laws also can vary across time. The invention of wheeled transport and especially the automobile created a need to legislate which side of the road to use. But it's possible future technologies like self-driving cars could remove the need. Human legislators can thus change laws to respond to changing conditions.

Ecclesiastical Law

105. God has given Church leaders the authority to establish laws. This power was given to Peter and his successors when Jesus declared:

> And I tell you, you are Peter, and on this rock I will build my church, and the powers of death shall not prevail against it. I will give you the keys of the kingdom of heaven, and whatever you bind on earth shall be bound in heaven, and whatever you loose on earth shall be loosed in heaven (Matt. 16:18–19).

The authority to bind and loose was later shared with the other Church leaders (Matt. 18:18), and the New Testament exhorts Christians to obey them:

> Obey your leaders and submit to them; for they are keeping watch over your souls, as men who will have to give account. Let them do this joyfully, and not sadly, for that would be of no advantage to you (Heb. 13:17; cf. 1 Thess. 5:12).

106. Like the civil law, ecclesiastical law takes principles found in divine law and applies them in concrete situations. Thus the

Code of Canon Law contains provisions taken directly from divine law and provisions of human origin:

> In the measure in which a human law gathers and formulates a command of divine origin, it participates in the superior and universal binding force of the latter. Sometimes the legislator declares the divine foundation possessed by the law which he has made (for example, c. 207 §1 indicates that the clergy exists in the Church "by divine institution"; likewise, c. 1084 §1 says that impotence in certain cases "by reason of its very nature" invalidates marriage); but there are many other canons which translate a divine precept into law even though this is not expressly indicated. In any case, their binding force is the same.
>
> On the other hand, laws which have their origin in the authority of the human legislator are called "merely ecclesiastical laws" and have the binding force that the legislator has established (and always under the condition that they do not contradict the divine law).[6]

Case Study: The Manner of Performing Penance

107. Human leaders cannot overrule God, from whom their authority comes. Consequently, Church leaders cannot modify the requirements of divine law. They can only modify what they have established. Consider the following canon from the *Code of Canon Law*:

> The divine law binds all the Christian faithful to do penance each in his or her own way. In order for all to be united among themselves by some common observance of penance, however, penitential days are prescribed on which the Christian faithful devote themselves in a special way to prayer, perform works of piety and charity, and deny themselves by fulfilling their own obligations more faithfully and especially by observing fast and abstinence, according to the norm of the following canons (CIC 1249).

This describes both the divine law requirement that Christians do penance and how this obligation is to be fulfilled through days of penance. The first requirement cannot change. Even if a future edition of the *Code* deleted this canon entirely, the obligation would remain. However, the way the obligation is fulfilled can change. Thus the *Code* provides that:

It is only for the supreme ecclesiastical authority to establish, transfer, and suppress feast days and days of penance common to the universal Church.

Diocesan bishops can decree special feast days or days of penance for their dioceses or places, but only in individual instances (CIC 1244 §§1–2).

The conference of bishops can determine more precisely the observance of fast and abstinence as well as substitute other forms of penance, especially works of charity and exercises of piety, in whole or in part, for abstinence and fast (CIC 1253).

Summary

108. From the foregoing, we can represent the way different actions can be classified as a series of concentric circles:

- The outermost circle represents *actions in general*—the entire range of things people do, whether they are occasional or habitual.

- Within this, there are *customs*—actions done habitually by a group of people, whether or not they are obligatory.

- Further in lie *disciplines*—actions members of a community are obliged to do.

- At the center are *laws*—"a rule of conduct enacted by competent authority for the sake of the common good" (CCC 1951).

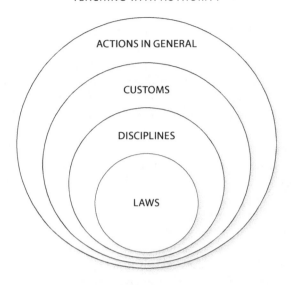

109. We can classify laws in a similar way:

- Within this realm there are two great divisions—*divine law* and *human law*—based on whether God or man is the legislator.

- The realm of divine law contains the *eternal law*—God's providential plan for all of creation.

- The eternal law includes the *natural law*—those aspects of God's plan that pertain to man and can be learned by reason.

- The natural law intersects with *revealed law*—those aspects of God's plan that are known by divine revelation.

- Revealed law includes the *Old Law* (given to Israel) and the *New Law* (given to the Church).

- Finally, human law includes the *civil law* (established by the state) and *ecclesiastical law* (established by the Church).

This way of visualizing matters does not take into account all of the distinctions we have covered. Thus for the sake of simplicity, it does not show that civil and ecclesiastical law participate in different aspects of divine law, but it provides a basic way of understanding the relationships among the categories.

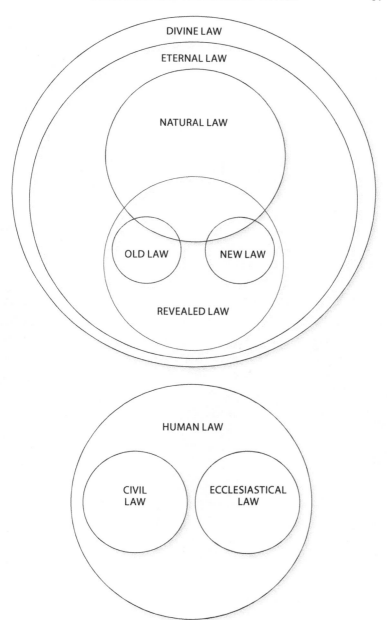

CHAPTER 7

Sources of Church Teaching

Truths of Reason

110. Some of our beliefs can be supported by natural reason, and some can only be supported by divine revelation.

The first category involves most of the beliefs we have—everything from the findings of the sciences, to knowledge of history, to the details of our own lives. Most of the time, beliefs based on natural reason don't have directly religious content. However, sometimes they do. As previously noted (§64), reason is capable of establishing certain facts about God, and there is more overlap between reason and revelation than sometimes supposed:

> All creatures bear a certain resemblance to God, most especially man, created in the image and likeness of God. The manifold perfections of creatures—their truth, their goodness, their beauty—all reflect the infinite perfection of God. Consequently, we can name God by taking his creatures' perfections as our starting point, for from the greatness and beauty of created things comes a corresponding perception of their Creator (CCC 41).

Everything about creation reveals something about God, and the Church is able to draw on natural reason for some of its teachings. It is even capable of teaching certain reason-based truths infallibly.

111. As we will see in chapter fifteen, the Church's gift of infallibility can be exercised regarding two kinds of truth: truths of revelation and additional truths needed to properly explain and defend the contents of revelation. Cardinal Avery Dulles explains:

> It is generally agreed that the Magisterium can infallibly declare the "preambles of faith," that is, naturally knowable truths implied in the credibility of the Christian message, such as the capacity of the human mind to grasp truth about invisible realities, to know the existence of God by reasoning from the created world ([DH 3004, 3026, 3538]), and to grasp the possibility of revelation ([DH 3027]) and miracles ([DH 3033–34]).[7]

These truths also include what are known as "dogmatic facts," such as "the ecumenical authority of a given council or the validity of the election of a given pope, since this information might be essential to establish the validity of a dogmatic definition. Unless the Church could identify her popes and ecumenical councils with full authority, her dogmatic teaching would be clouded by doubt."[8]

Finally, the Magisterium is able to teach certain moral truths infallibly. Even if they are not divinely revealed, they are knowable by reason, making them part of natural law. The degree to which the Church's infallibility extends to these truths has not been fully clarified, but it at least allows the Church to infallibly define the intrinsic evil of certain actions, since it is necessary to avoid such actions for salvation (see §§442–446).

Revealed Truths

112. Despite the possibility of the Church defining truths known by natural reason, these are not the principal object of its teaching mission.

> By natural reason man can know God with certainty, on the basis of his works. But there is another order of knowledge, which man cannot possibly arrive at by his own powers: the order of divine revelation. Through an utterly

free decision, God has revealed himself and given himself to man. This he does by revealing the mystery, his plan of loving goodness, formed from all eternity in Christ, for the benefit of all men. God has fully revealed this plan by sending us his beloved Son, our Lord Jesus Christ, and the Holy Spirit (CCC 50).

113. We often think of revelation as being given in the form of words, such as the words found in Scripture. However, God also reveals truths about himself by his actions, such as performing miracles, being born in human form, and being crucified for our sake.

> This plan of revelation is realized by deeds and words having an inner unity: the deeds wrought by God in the history of salvation manifest and confirm the teaching and realities signified by the words, whereas the words proclaim the deeds and clarify the mystery contained in them (*Dei Verbum,* 2).

114. By means of revelation, God allows us to know theological "mysteries"—things that cannot be deduced by reason alone. An example is the fact God is one being in three Persons:

> The Trinity is a mystery of faith in the strict sense, one of the mysteries that are hidden in God, which can never be known unless they are revealed by God. To be sure, God has left traces of his trinitarian being in his work of creation and in his revelation throughout the Old Testament. But his inmost being as Holy Trinity is a mystery that is inaccessible to reason alone or even to Israel's faith before the Incarnation of God's Son and the sending of the Holy Spirit (CCC 237).

115. Some Christians use different terms for the things that can be known about God through reason and those that must be known by revelation. Since the created world reveals things about God, at least in a general way (Rom. 1:19–20), some in the Protestant community have referred to this mode of knowledge as *general revelation*. By contrast, information given through prophets, in Scripture, and by Jesus Christ is referred to as *special revelation*.

116. A division made in Catholic circles concerns the difference between *public* and *private revelation*. When the word *revelation* is used without a further qualifier, it refers to public revelation. According to Cardinal Joseph Ratzinger:

> The term "public revelation" refers to the revealing action of God directed to humanity as a whole and which finds its literary expression in the two parts of the Bible: the Old and New Testaments ("Theological Commentary" in *The Message of Fatima*).

Note that Scripture is only the *literary* expression of public revelation. As we will see, it is also found in Sacred Tradition.

117. Since the time of the apostles, the body of public revelation—a body referred to as "the deposit of faith"—has been closed. The *Catechism of the Catholic Church* explains:

> The Christian economy, therefore, since it is the new and definitive covenant, will never pass away; and no new public revelation is to be expected before the glorious manifestation of our Lord Jesus Christ. Yet even if revelation is already complete, it has not been made completely explicit; it remains for Christian faith gradually to grasp its full significance over the course of the centuries (CCC 66).

118. In contrast to public revelation, private revelation is not directed to the entire world but to an individual or group. Pierre Adnes, professor of dogmatic theology at the Gregorian University in Rome, explains:

The adjective *private*, which is added to distinguish them from the earlier revelation (sometimes called "public" because it is addressed, through the ministry of the church, to the human beings of every time and place), does not mean that these revelations are necessarily meant only for a single individual. In fact, they often apply to an entire group, an entire milieu, or even the entire Church at a given moment of its history. It would undoubtedly be better to call these revelations "special" or "particular," as the Council of Trent does ([DH 1540, 1566]).[9]

119. Though Scripture as a whole is directed to the entire Church, it contains accounts of God giving revelations to particular people for use in their own day. Thus scholars have seen the Bible as containing private revelations that were later preserved as part of public revelation. Adnes writes:

Sacred Scripture and particular revelations are not mutually exclusive. Revelations of the second kind are not to be defined by the fact that they are outside the biblical setting but by their object, purpose, and addressee. If these elements are particular, then the revelations are particular and remain such even if guaranteed by biblical inspiration, since the latter does not alter their characteristics but only ensures their authenticity. The Acts of the Apostles is full of examples. After having proclaimed on Pentecost the age of the Spirit, who works through visions, dreams, and prophecies (2:16–21), Peter learns through a particular revelation how he should act in regard to Cornelius the centurion (10:3–8). Paul is converted as the result of a revelation he receives on the road to Damascus (9:3–9), and he will be constantly guided in his missionary activity by particular revelations (16:9; 18:9; 20:23; 27:23–24), to which are to be added those revelations of a strictly personal and mystical kind about which he tells the Corinthians (2 Cor. 12:1–6) (ibid.).

120. Public revelation is closed, whereas private revelation continues to be given:

> Throughout the ages, there have been so-called "private" revelations, some of which have been recognized by the authority of the Church. They do not belong, however, to the deposit of faith. It is not their role to improve or complete Christ's definitive revelation, but to help live more fully by it in a certain period of history. Guided by the Magisterium of the Church, the *sensus fidelium* ["the sense of the faithful"] knows how to discern and welcome in these revelations whatever constitutes an authentic call of Christ or his saints to the Church.
>
> Christian faith cannot accept "revelations" that claim to surpass or correct the revelation of which Christ is the fulfillment, as is the case in certain non-Christian religions and also in certain recent sects that base themselves on such "revelations" (CCC 67).

121. Because they cannot supplement or correct public revelation, private revelations have a different purpose and level of authority. Cardinal Ratzinger explains:

> The authority of private revelations is essentially different from that of the definitive public revelation. The latter demands faith; in it in fact God himself speaks to us through human words and the mediation of the living community of the Church. Faith in God and in his word is different from any other human faith, trust, or opinion. The certainty that it is God who is speaking gives me the assurance that I am in touch with truth itself. It gives me a certitude which is beyond verification by any human way of knowing. It is the certitude upon which I build my life and to which I entrust myself in dying.
>
> Private revelation is a help to this faith, and shows its

credibility precisely by leading me back to the definitive public revelation. In this regard, Cardinal Prospero Lambertini, the future Pope Benedict XIV, says in his classic treatise, which later became normative for beatifications and canonizations: "An assent of Catholic faith is not due to [private] revelations approved in this way; it is not even possible. These revelations seek rather an assent of human faith in keeping with the requirements of prudence, which puts them before us as probable and credible to piety" ("Theological Commentary" in *The Message of Fatima*).

122. When private revelations are approved by Church authority, the implications are modest. Cardinal Ratzinger notes:

The Flemish theologian E. Dhanis, an eminent scholar in this field, states succinctly that ecclesiastical approval of a private revelation has three elements: the message contains nothing contrary to faith or morals; it is lawful to make it public; and the faithful are authorized to accept it with prudence. Such a message can be a genuine help in understanding the gospel and living it better at a particular moment in time; therefore, it should not be disregarded. It is a help which is offered, but which one is not obliged to use (ibid., citing E. Dhanis, "*Sguardo su Fatima e bilancio di una discussione*," in *La Civiltà Cattolica* 104 [1953]: II:392–406, in particular 397).

123. Private revelations can give rise to devotions and even find a place in the liturgy:

We might add that private revelations often spring from popular piety and leave their stamp on it, giving it a new impulse and opening the way for new forms of it. Nor does this exclude that they will have an effect even on the liturgy, as we see for instance in the feasts of Corpus Christi and of the Sacred Heart of Jesus (ibid.).

Divine Mercy Sunday (the Sunday after Easter) is another devotion derived from private revelation (the apparitions of Jesus
reported by St. Faustina Kowalska). It was added to the liturgical
calendar by Pope John Paul II.

The Magisterium and the Word of God

124. The Greek word for revelation, *apokalupsis*, appears in the
New Testament, but not often. At the time, there was a more
common term: the word of God. The function of the Church's
Magisterium is to proclaim the word of God, which is why
"the church of the living God" is "the pillar and bulwark of the
truth" (1 Tim. 3:15).

It is common in the Protestant community to speak of the
word of God as if it were identical with Scripture. The Catholic
Church is then accused of "adding to the word of God" since it
does not use Scripture alone to support its teachings.

The Church acknowledges that "Sacred Scripture is the word
of God inasmuch as it is consigned to writing under the inspiration of the divine Spirit" (*Dei Verbum,* 9). However, even a cursory
reading of Scripture shows that the word of God is not limited to
Scripture. It is a complex reality that includes several things:

- In the first chapter of the Bible, we read about the power
  of God's creative word, as he speaks created realities into
  existence: "'Let there be light'; and there was light" (Gen.
  1:3). This understanding of God's creative word is found
  in the Psalms, which state: "By the word of the Lord the
  heavens were made" (Ps. 33:6).

- The Bible records the word of God being given to prophets
  who wrote no Scripture at all, such as Samuel (1 Sam. 9:27),
  Shemaiah (1 Kings 12:22), and John the Baptist (Luke 3:2).

- The New Testament describes the oral apostolic preaching of
  the Christian faith as the word of God (Acts 4:31, 6:7, 16:6).

- Most fundamentally, Scripture describes Jesus himself as
  the Word of God (John 1:1–18; Rev. 19:13).

Consequently, Scripture is simply the portion of God's word that was consigned to writing under divine inspiration.

125. The proper response to the word of God is to accept the whole of it as authoritative. Everything God speaks—everything he reveals—is authoritative, for "man shall not live by bread alone, but by every word that proceeds from the mouth of God" (Matt. 4:4; cf. Deut. 8:3). It would be wrong to close our ears to God's word when it is found outside of Scripture (2 Thess. 2:15).

Tradition

The Value of Tradition

126. Tradition is what is handed down from one generation to another. The Latin word *traditio* comes from the roots *trans-* ("across") and *dare* ("to give"). The term the Greek New Testament uses for tradition, *paradosis,* similarly means "to hand down/over."

In the Protestant community, *tradition* has a negative ring. Protestant apologists cite Jesus' condemnation of the scribes and Pharisees: "You leave the commandment of God, and hold fast the tradition of men" (Mark 7:8). But Jesus did not condemn all traditions. He condemned only those that contradict or "make void" the word of God (Mark 7:13). Furthermore, other passages show a positive attitude toward tradition. Paul states:

> I commend you because you remember me in everything and maintain the traditions even as I have delivered them to you (1 Cor. 11:2).
>
> So then, brethren, stand firm and hold to the traditions which you were taught by us, either by word of mouth or by letter (2 Thess. 2:15).
>
> Now we command you, brethren, in the name of our Lord Jesus Christ, that you keep away from any brother who is living in idleness and not in accord with the tradition that you received from us (2 Thess. 3:6).

These use the same Greek word (*paradosis*) that Jesus uses. Thus, tradition itself is not a problem. When a tradition contradicts the word of God, it is to be shunned, but when it conveys the word of God, it is to be embraced.

127. Fundamentally, the Christian faith as a whole is a tradition—or a collection of traditions handed down from Christ and the apostles. Thus Luke says he is compiling a narrative of events "just as they were delivered to us by those who from the beginning were eyewitnesses and ministers of the word" (Luke 1:2). The word he uses for "delivered" is *paradidōmi,* the verb corresponding to *paradosis.* If *tradition* were a common verb in English, this passage could be translated "just as they were traditioned to us." The same is reflected in Jude's epistle, which says:

> Beloved, being very eager to write to you of our common salvation, I found it necessary to write appealing to you to contend for the faith which was once for all delivered to the saints (Jude 3).

Again, the verb is *paradidōmi*: the faith has been once for all handed on or "traditioned" to the saints. Tradition thus is not a negative concept. It is fundamental to the Christian faith.

Tradition and Traditions

128. In addition to traditions that violate the word of God (Mark 7:8) and traditions that convey the word of God (2 Thess. 2:15), there is a middle category: traditions that are neither required by the word of God nor are contrary to it.

Jesus and the first Christians used the Aramaic, and this has been handed down to today. Aramaic is still used in worship in Chaldean and Maronite Catholic churches. Even Christians who don't speak Aramaic use Aramaic words and phrases like *Abba* ("Father") and *Maran atha* ("our Lord, come"). Yet Jesus and the apostles didn't mandate Aramaic. The New Testament is even written in Greek. The use of Aramaic as a worship language thus falls into the category of a tradition that is permitted but not required by divine law.

129. We thus could divide tradition into three categories:

- Traditions that are required
- Traditions that are permitted
- Traditions that are prohibited

130. More often, traditions are divided into just two categories: (1) Those that are required and (2) those that are not required. A way of visually signaling which of the two types is meant has developed. Traditions that are obligatory are referred to with a capital "T" ("Traditions") whereas non-obligatory ones receive a lower case "t" ("traditions"). When a mix of obligatory and non-obligatory traditions are in view, the lower case is used. We will follow these conventions in this book.

131. Under the heading "Apostolic Tradition and ecclesial traditions," the *Catechism* says:

> The Tradition here in question comes from the apostles and hands on what they received from Jesus' teaching and example and what they learned from the Holy Spirit. The first generation of Christians did not yet have a written New Testament, and the New Testament itself demonstrates the process of living Tradition.
>
> Tradition is to be distinguished from the various theological, disciplinary, liturgical, or devotional traditions, born in the local churches over time. These are the particular forms, adapted to different places and times, in which the great Tradition is expressed. In the light of Tradition, these traditions can be retained, modified or even abandoned under the guidance of the Church's Magisterium (CCC 83).

Tradition thus comes to us from the apostles. This is why the *Catechism* refers to it as "apostolic Tradition." It is also frequently called "Sacred Tradition," and it is distinguished from lowercase "ecclesial traditions." The latter have been approved "under the guidance of the Church's Magisterium," and so they are not contrary to the word of God. However, they also are not obligatory under divine law, meaning they correspond to the middle category in §129.

This passage doesn't refer to traditions contrary to the word of God. Because Christians are sinners, such traditions arise, but they are not approved by the Magisterium and so are not ecclesiastical traditions in the proper sense, even if common in Christian circles.

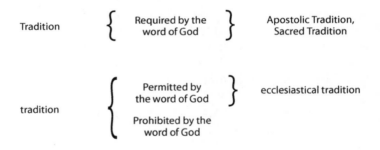

Scripture and Tradition

132. In the broad sense, apostolic Tradition includes everything authoritatively passed down to the Church by the apostles, and that would include Scripture. They were handed down, too! However, a narrower and more common usage conceives of Tradition as the word of God passed down to us in ways *other than* Scripture. Scripture and Tradition are then seen as the two modes by which divine revelation is handed on.

133. Tradition is passed on by several means, including oral preaching, the liturgy, and the writings of the Church Fathers. Since Scripture is also written, how is it different from the writings of the Church Fathers—or other ways of passing down

Tradition? The answer is that only Scripture is divinely inspired. According to Vatican II:

> There exists a close connection and communication between Sacred Tradition and Sacred Scripture. For both of them, flowing from the same divine wellspring, in a certain way merge into a unity and tend toward the same end. For Sacred Scripture is the word of God inasmuch as it is consigned to writing under the inspiration of the divine Spirit, while Sacred Tradition takes the word of God entrusted by Christ the Lord and the Holy Spirit to the apostles, and hands it on to their successors in its full purity (*Dei Verbum,* 9).

134. Because God's word has been passed on through both Scripture and Tradition, the Church does not rely exclusively on Scripture:

> Consequently, it is not from Sacred Scripture alone that the Church draws her certainty about everything which has been revealed. Therefore, both Sacred Tradition and Sacred Scripture are to be accepted and venerated with the same sense of loyalty and reverence (ibid.)

135. What does it mean for Scripture to be divinely inspired? The council explains:

> Because written under the inspiration of the Holy Spirit, [the scriptures] have God as their author and have been handed on as such to the Church herself. In composing the sacred books, God chose men and while employed by him they made use of their powers and abilities, so that with him acting in them and through them, they, as true authors, consigned to writing everything and only those things which he wanted (*Dei Verbum,* 11).

The scriptures thus do not contain material that God did not want included in them.

136. By contrast, the writings of the Church Fathers do not have this quality. They contain added material that individual Fathers chose to include, and this material is not always authoritative or even accurate. They thus present authoritative Traditions alongside non-authoritative ones.

137. There thus needs to be a sifting of apostolic Tradition from other traditions. This is the function of the Magisterium. Christ's pastors have received the task of guiding his sheep by discerning what is authentically of God and what is not. This task applies both when the word of God is written in the form of Scripture and when it is handed on in other ways.

138. The Magisterium thus received the task of identifying genuinely apostolic scriptures from among the array of "scriptures" (apocryphal gospels, etc.) circulating in the early Church. It made its decision on the basis of Tradition—on which books had been handed on to the Church as authoritative by the apostles and had been read in the churches as such. This included both the books of the Old and the New Testaments, and it included books written by apostles (Romans, 1 Peter) and their associates (Mark, Luke). If there was no tradition of a book being read in the churches, or if it disagreed with the teachings handed on from the apostles, it was regarded as inauthentic. Tradition thus proved the key to the Magisterium identifying the books of Scripture. Vatican II notes:

> Through the same Tradition the Church's full canon of the sacred books is known, and the sacred writings themselves are more profoundly understood (*Dei Verbum,* 8).

Now that the canon has been identified, the Magisterium continues to authoritatively discern the elements that represent apostolic Tradition and those that are merely traditions.

139. To summarize the relationship of Scripture, Tradition, and the Magisterium:

- Scripture passes on divine revelation in the form of inspired writings.
- Tradition communicates it in other forms.
- The Magisterium distinguishes apostolic Scripture and Tradition from other scriptures and traditions.

According to Vatican II:

> It is clear, therefore, that Sacred Tradition, Sacred Scripture and the teaching authority of the Church, in accord with God's most wise design, are so linked and joined together that one cannot stand without the others, and that all together and each in its own way under the action of the one Holy Spirit contribute effectively to the salvation of souls (ibid., 10).

140. Although the three are closely linked, there are important differences among them. Scripture alone is divinely inspired, so it has a special primacy. The formulations of divine revelation in Tradition and the teachings of the Magisterium are true, but they aren't authored by God the way Scripture is.

Another difference is that Scripture and Tradition represent sources of divine revelation. The Magisterium does not. It merely proclaims what is found in Scripture and Tradition. Thus Vatican II stated:

> [T]he task of authentically interpreting the word of God, whether written or handed on, has been entrusted exclusively to the living teaching office of the Church, whose authority is exercised in the name of Jesus Christ. This teaching office is not above the word of God, but serves it, teaching only what has been handed on, listening to it devoutly, guarding it scrupulously and explaining it faithfully in accord with a divine commission and with the help of the Holy Spirit, it draws from this one deposit of faith everything which it presents for belief as divinely revealed (ibid.).

The Magisterium therefore occupies a place below Scripture and Tradition, even when it teaches infallibly. This raises the question of how infallibility relates to inspiration and the related concept of inerrancy.

Inerrancy, Infallibility, and Inspiration

Inerrancy

141. Scripture is often said to be inerrant. This is the quality of not containing error. However, even merely human documents can be inerrant. A geometry textbook that contains no errors is inerrant. So is any statement a person makes that does not contain a falsehood. Even badly worded and partial expressions of truth are not erroneous. Consequently:

- Any true statement in an ordinary, human document is inerrant.
- True statements in Church documents are inerrant.
- Statements of apostolic Tradition are inerrant.
- Statements in Sacred Scripture are inerrant.

Infallibility

142. Infallibility is greater than inerrancy. It is the quality of not being *able* to make an error. Since "to err is human," God alone is intrinsically infallible. However, God can protect people from making errors, and when he does so, they are given a measure of infallibility. The authors of Scripture had this quality while writing under divine inspiration, as do members of the Magisterium when infallibly defining a teaching.

Although in the proper sense infallibility applies to persons, in common usage the term also covers statements made by people God protects from error. Thus Church teachings and not just Church teachers are described as infallible.

The fact that a person is protected from making an error doesn't mean what he says will be well phrased, complete, or timely. It just means it won't be false. This means infallible statements by the Magisterium could be confusing, partial, or given at an inopportune time. However, they are guaranteed to be true.

Since the authors of Scripture were protected from error, one could also say that Scripture is infallible, but this usage is not standard since their authors were divinely inspired.

Inspiration

143. Inspiration is greater than inerrancy and infallibility. The term comes from the Latin *inspirare* (*in-*, "in/on/into" + *spirare*, "to breathe"). As used in theology, it refers to the quality of being "breathed by God." The Greek equivalent is *theopneustos* (*theos*, "God" + *pneō*, "breathe out"). Thus Paul says "all Scripture is inspired by God" (2 Tim. 3:16)—or, more literally, "every Scripture is breathed by God."

Theologians have not fully explored the depths of the mystery of inspiration, but one of its consequences is that God is the ultimate author of Scripture, though he used human authors as his agents. Another consequence is that the human authors "consigned to writing everything and only those things which he wanted." From this, Vatican II drew the conclusion:

> Therefore, since everything asserted by the inspired authors or sacred writers must be held to be asserted by the Holy Spirit, it follows that the books of Scripture must be acknowledged as teaching solidly, faithfully, and without error that truth which God wanted put into sacred writings for the sake of salvation (*Dei Verbum*, 11).

The gift of inspiration thus entails the lesser gift of protection from error (infallibility), resulting in an absence of error (inerrancy). However, it goes beyond both of these in that the Holy Spirit is not simply preventing error.

Like infallibility, inspiration in the proper sense applies to persons rather than documents. The Pontifical Biblical Commission notes:

Inspiration as an activity of God, therefore, directly concerns the human authors: they are the ones who are personally inspired. But then the writings composed by them are also called inspired (*The Inspiration and Truth of Sacred Scripture*, 5).

Like infallibility, inspiration only occurs on certain occasions: the pope and the bishops are not infallible all the time, and the biblical authors were divinely inspired when they wrote Scripture. The Holy Spirit should not be regarded as the author of everything they did or said, as illustrated by the fact they sometimes were in conflict with each other (Gal. 2:11–14; cf. 1 Cor. 14:33).

Living Tradition and Doctrinal Development

144. Though the contents of the deposit of faith are unchanging, the way in which it is expressed is not. For this reason, theologians often speak of the Church as possessing a "living tradition."

One way it is living is how it is applied to changing circumstances. As the centuries progress, cultures develop and the Faith that was "once for all delivered to the saints" (Jude 3) is manifested in new ways. It gives rise to new expressions, customs, and rules. The process of "inculturation" occurs across many fields, including theology, liturgy, popular piety, and canon law.

Another way Tradition is living is described by Vatican II:

Tradition which comes from the apostles develops in the Church with the help of the Holy Spirit. For there is a growth in the understanding of the realities and the words which have been handed down. This happens through the contemplation and study made by believers, who treasure these things in their hearts (see Luke 2:19, 51) through a penetrating understanding of the spiritual realities which they experience, and through the preaching of those who have received through episcopal succession the sure gift of truth. For as the centuries succeed one another, the Church constantly moves forward toward the fullness of divine truth until the words of God reach their complete fulfillment in her (*Dei Verbum*, 8).

This "growth in the understanding of the realities and the words which have been handed down" is known as *doctrinal development* (see chapter eighteen).

Case Study: The Trinity

145. The divinity of the Father, the Son, and the Holy Spirit is taught in the New Testament, but not in a concise way or in a single place. It took time for the biblical data to be formulated as the doctrine of the Trinity. This happened as heretics of various kinds began denying aspects of the truth about God and the Church was forced to assert her faith in clearer and more precise terms.

It thus developed a special vocabulary that had not existed before. At the First Council of Nicaea (325), the bishops combatting the Arian heresy found the Arians had discovered ways of reinterpreting the language of Scripture to deny the divinity of Christ. To make it clear this was not the faith of the Church, the fathers of the council needed to use a new, postbiblical term to express the relationship of the Father and the Son. This is why the Nicene Creed states the Son is "consubstantial" (Greek, *homoousion*) with the Father.

Through the centuries, numerous terms have been coined to describe realities connected with the Faith—for example, Trinity, original sin, Bible, purgatory, transubstantiation. As this happened, truths implied in the apostolic deposit became explicitly formulated.

CHAPTER 8

The Documents of Bishops and Popes

146. Christianity has always valued the written word, beginning with Scripture. As the ages progressed, Christians produced an extensive and ever-growing body of literature. Today the Magisterium produces a blizzard of documents. Keeping up with the hundreds of documents issued each year by the pope alone is nearly impossible, and they come in a bewildering number of kinds.

Of course, bishops and popes don't just teach in documents. The original proclamation of the Faith was oral, and it continues to be taught orally today. Hypothetically, a pope or council could even infallibly define a dogma by oral means, though if this were done, it would be written down immediately and then transmitted to the Church in documentary form. In this chapter we will look at major types of Church documents.

The Documents of Bishops

An Individual Bishop's Documents

147. Bishops express their personal magisteria in a number of ways. The Congregation for Bishops lists two major ones:

The Homily. As an integral part of the liturgy, which is the source and summit of the Church's entire life, the homily is the most excellent and, in a certain sense, the sum of all forms of preaching. The bishop should seek to expound

Catholic truth in its fullness, in simple, familiar language, suited to the capacities of his hearers, focusing—unless particular pastoral reasons suggest otherwise—on the texts of the day's liturgy. He should plan his homilies so as to elucidate the whole of Catholic truth.

Pastoral letters. On special occasions in the life of the diocese, the bishop should also propose doctrine by means of pastoral letters and messages, addressed to the whole Christian community. These may appropriately be read out in Churches and oratories and also distributed in printed form among the faithful (*Apostolorum Successores,* 122a–b).

The congregation lists other ways a bishop may teach, though these means typically are not expressions of authoritative magisteria:

Other forms of preaching. The bishop should never miss an opportunity to communicate the doctrine of salvation, making full use of the possibilities offered by the mass media: newspaper articles, television and radio broadcasts, conferences, or lectures on religious topics, particularly when he is addressing those responsible for disseminating ideas in the professional worlds of education and information (ibid., 122c).

Joint Bishops' Documents
Local Joint Documents

148. Sometimes bishops issue documents jointly. This can happen when the bishops from two or more neighboring dioceses decide to issue a pastoral statement on an issue affecting their territory. These are usually released on an ad hoc basis. They are commonly pastoral, and—apart from repeating things the Church already teaches—doctrines they express represent the personal magisterium of the individual bishops involved.

National Joint Documents

149. Often joint documents are issued by the national bishops' conference. At its regularly scheduled meetings, it is common for bishops to approve documents on doctrinal and pastoral issues.

Beginning in the 1960s, the U.S. bishops have been particularly active and have issued a series of pastoral letters on topics including war, the economy, racism, and other subjects. In addition, they periodically produce new revisions of documents such as *Forming Consciences for Faithful Citizenship* (on moral principles in voting) and *Ethical and Religious Directives for Catholic Health Care Services.*

150. Committees of the conference also issue documents. The U.S. Committee on Divine Worship publishes a newsletter ten times a year to update bishops, priests, and liturgists on developments in the liturgical sphere. Other committees issue booklets or pamphlets for a broad audience, such as the Committee for Divine Worship's booklet *Pastoral Care of the Dying* or the Committee for Evangelization and Catechesis's pamphlet *Marriage and Family: The Home of the New Evangelization.*

Of special interest for our purposes are documents released by the U.S. bishops' Committee on Doctrine. These are frequently styled "statements," and they may address topics of general doctrinal interest (*The Teaching Ministry of the Diocesan Bishop: A Pastoral Reflection*), particular moral questions (*The Distinction Between Direct Abortion and Legitimate Medical Procedures*), non-Catholic practices that are having an impact in Catholic circles (*Guidelines for Evaluating Reiki As an Alternative Therapy*), or the problems in the works of a particular theologian (*Statement on Quest for the Living God by Sr. Elizabeth A. Johnson*). Many are available on the Committee on Doctrine's web page at usccb. org; others are available from USCCB Publishing.

151. Officers of a national conference may also issue documents, as when the head of the USCCB issues press releases when a news story breaks that affects the Catholic world.

152. Employees of the conference also release various publications. The USCCB operates Catholic News Service, which provides reporting on stories of interest to Catholics, including items relating to popular culture, such as movie reviews.

153. Comparatively few conference documents are official acts of the Magisterium. Movie reviews obviously are not. Although meant to reflect Catholic principles, they are only the opinion of the reviewer. When the head of the conference issues a press statement, it represents his personal sense of how the bishops, or many of them, would react to a breaking story. Documents issued by committees can be theologically valuable, but they represent only the views of their signatories. This applies even to the Committee on Doctrine.

As we saw in §34, the only way for a joint episcopal document to "constitute authentic magisterium" is if it is of a doctrinal nature and is either approved unanimously by the full body of bishops or receives the approval (*recognitio*) of the Holy See after being approved by at least two thirds of the conference.

154. In fact, sometimes documents issued by the conference can draw criticism from the bishops themselves:

- In 1997, the USCCB's Committee on Marriage and Family issued a document titled *Always Our Children: A Pastoral Message to Parents of Homosexual Children and Suggestions for Pastoral Ministers*. This document was widely criticized as downplaying Catholic teaching on homosexuality, and the Congregation for the Doctrine of the Faith requested revisions.

- In 2002, a group of scholars connected with the Committee on Ecumenical and Interreligious Affairs released *Reflections on Covenant and Mission,* which was seen as discouraging Jews from becoming followers of Christ. In response, the Committee on Doctrine issued a critical statement titled *A Note on Ambiguities Contained in "Reflections on Covenant and Mission."*

- A review of the 2005 movie *Brokeback Mountain*, which deals with a homosexual romance, was initially classified by its reviewer as L ("limited adult audience, films whose problematic content many adults would find troubling"). Following a backlash, it was reclassified as O ("morally offensive").

155. Although few documents meet the conditions necessary to count as authentic magisterium, they can still contain important doctrinal and pastoral statements. Pope Francis frequently quotes documents issued by episcopal conferences. In his encyclical *Laudato Si'*, he quotes documents by the episcopal conferences of Australia, Bolivia, Brazil, the Dominican Republic, Canada, Germany, Japan, Mexico, New Zealand, Paraguay, the Philippines, Portugal, South Africa, and the United States.

Joint International Documents

156. Sometimes conferences from different nations work together. The Council of Latin American Bishops (Spanish, *Consejo Episcopal Latinoamericano*, better known as CELAM) includes episcopal conferences from Latin America and the Caribbean. Like an individual national conference, it meets annually and has a permanent administrative staff. Periodically, CELAM holds general conferences, such as at Medillin, Colombia, in 1968, at Puebla, Mexico, in 1979, and at Aparecida, Brazil, in 2007. These conferences issue "concluding documents" of a pastoral nature that sum up the thoughts of the conference.

Apostolos Suos does not discuss documents issued by bodies like CELAM, but the same principles presumably apply to them. Even if they do not "constitute authentic magisterium," they are still influential. Thus in his apostolic exhortation *Evangelii Gaudiam*, Pope Francis quotes from CELAM's Puebla and Aparecida documents, and in *Laudato Si'* he quotes from the Aparecida document and a similar document issued by the Federation of Asian Bishops' Conferences (FABC).

The Synod of Bishops

157. The Synod of Bishops issues several major documents:

- Initially, its Secretariat in Rome prepares a document known as the *lineamenta* (Latin, "outlines"), which sketches out the topics to be covered at the synod and includes a questionnaire. It is then circulated to episcopal conferences for feedback.

- The Secretariat then incorporates this feedback and drafts the *instrumentum laboris* (Latin, "working document"), which serves as the starting point for discussion when the synod meets.

- At the synod, the bishops draft and vote on a document that is submitted to the pope. Often it takes the form of a series of *propositiones* (Latin, "proposals"); however, it can take other forms, such as a *relatio synodi* (Latin, "report of the synod").

158. Following its founding in 1965, some early meetings of the synod tried to draft documents for public consumption, but this only came to fruition at the 1971 synod, which released a document titled *Justice in the World*. Usually, the brief time the synod meets (less than a month) was not enough to prepare a document addressed to the public. However, beginning in the reign of Benedict XVI, it became common for the pope to publicly release the document it submits to him.

Because most of its documents have not been addressed to the faithful, and because bishops cannot authoritatively teach the pope, such documents are not acts of authoritative magisterium, though they refer to things the Magisterium has already taught and provide a valuable look at the mind of the world episcopate.

In September of 2018, Pope Francis issued the apostolic constitution *Episcopalis Communio*, in which he indicated that a synod's final document could participate in the pope's ordinary magisterium in the following situations:

§1. Having received the approval of the members [of the synod], the final document of the assembly is offered to the Roman pontiff, who decides whether to publish it.

If expressly approved by the Roman pontiff, the final document participates in the ordinary magisterium of the successor of Peter.

§2. If the Roman pontiff granted the deliberative power to the assembly of the synod, in accordance with can. 343 of the *Code of Canon Law,* the final document participates in the ordinary magisterium of the successor of Peter once ratified and promulgated by him.

In this case the final document is published with the signature of the Roman pontiff together with that of the members (art. 18).

Conciliar Documents

159. Councils have produced many types of documents in Church history. The earliest we have is the letter sent by the Council of Jerusalem around A.D. 49 (see Acts 15:23–29). Here we will focus on the documents of ecumenical councils.

160. Ecumenical councils produce many background documents—speeches, reports, drafts, etc. These are referred to as the "acts" of the council. Although generally only studied by scholars, they shed valuable light on the final, public documents the council issues.

161. There is no established form the public documents must take, and their nature has varied considerably over time.

The first ecumenical council—First Nicaea (325)—published two major documents; the first was a profession of faith known as the Creed of Nicaea (not the same as the Nicene Creed[10]) and the second was a series of canons (rules) dealing with matters of early canon law.

162. Subsequent councils developed new forms of documents, and by Trent (1545–1563), the most significant conciliar documents were known as "decrees," which alternately dealt with Church doctrine and Church reform. Some doctrinal decrees included a general treatise on a subject, followed by a series of canons emphasizing the key doctrinal points (e.g., the *Decree on Justification*). Other decrees consisted of a brief introduction followed by canons (e.g., the *Decree on the Sacraments*). Trent's "decrees on reformation" have a pastoral character and affected then-current canon law.

163. Vatican I (1870) issued two documents, both of which are styled "dogmatic constitutions." *Dei Filius* contains a doctrinal treatise followed by canons. *Pastor Aeternus* deals with papal authority and infallibility, and it has the canons embedded in the doctrinal treatise, with one at the end of each chapter. This council planned to produce more documents, but it was suspended due to the events of the Franco-Prussian War and the capture of Rome by the Kingdom of Italy.

164. Vatican II (1962–1965) produced three types of documents, known as constitutions, declarations, and decrees. The constitutions also fall into two kinds, styled either "dogmatic" or "pastoral." Francis Morrisey observes:

> It is still rather difficult to state precisely why one document was given a specific qualification rather than another. It could be noted, though, that the constitutions—such as the dogmatic and pastoral ones—are fundamental documents addressed to the Church universal, while the decrees, which build upon constitutional principles, are directed more specifically to a given category of the faithful or to a special form of apostolate. The declarations were policy statements giving the teaching of the Church on certain more controverted matters, and thus are more liable to be revised with time.[11]

All of the Vatican II documents take the form of treatises, and they do not contain canons.

165. Just as it is difficult to say why particular documents were issued as constitutions, declarations, or decrees, it is also difficult to say precisely what weight these carry. As the documents of an ecumenical council, they are all important. However, the council did not provide an explanation of their exact nature and weight.

The constitutions are the most authoritative documents, and the dogmatic constitutions—*Dei Verbum* (on divine revelation) and *Lumen Gentium* (on the Church)—are the most authoritative of all. The pastoral constitutions—*Sacrosanctum Concilium* (on the liturgy) and *Gaudium et Spes* (on the Church in the modern world)—have a somewhat lesser status.

The declarations and decrees have less authority than the constitutions, but it is not altogether clear which is weightier. Authors such as Morrissey seem to hold that the declarations have the lesser rank, as they generally deal with more controversial subjects. This is true: two deal with non-Christian religions and religious freedom (the third is on Christian education). By contrast, the decrees are generally on less controversial topics (means of social communication, bishops, religious life, etc.), though one deals with the sensitive issue of ecumenism. In addition, one could argue that the term "decree" has a longer history as a type of council document and thus decrees should be given more weight.

The nature of a conciliar document is one factor affecting the weight of a teaching it mentions, but ultimately every statement it makes must be assessed individually.

Papal Documents

166. The teaching ministry of the pope mirrors that of other bishops. Like them, he gives homilies, makes speeches, writes letters, and so on. However, the number and types of documents a pope issues goes far beyond those of an ordinary bishop, and—confusingly—the names and nature of these documents has changed over time and is not always consistent.

Papal Bulls and Briefs

167. Papal bulls are among the most famous documents a pope issues, and many people have heard of them, even if they have no idea what they are. This term is especially confusing because it doesn't deal with the content of the document but the physical form it takes. The *Catholic Encyclopedia* explains:

> A *bulla* was originally a circular plate or boss of metal, so called from its resemblance in form to a bubble floating upon water (Latin *bullire*, to boil). In the course of time

the term came to be applied to the leaden seals with which papal and royal documents were authenticated in the early Middle Ages, and by a further development, the name, from designating the seal, was eventually attached to the document itself. This did not happen before the thirteenth century and the name *bull* was only a popular term used almost promiscuously for all kinds of instruments which issued from the papal chancery. A much more precise acceptance has prevailed since the fifteenth century, and a bull has long stood in sharp contrast with certain other forms of papal documents. For practical purposes a bull may be conveniently defined to be "an apostolic letter with a leaden seal" (s.v. "Bulls and Briefs").

Because a bull was simply any letter issued with a *bulla*, this didn't reveal much about its content, though the use of a leaden seal adds solemnity and importance. In practice bulls were issued on doctrinal, legal, and practical matters.

168. Eventually, papal briefs—a simpler form of document—began to replace the bull:

> The introduction of briefs, which occurred at the beginning of the pontificate of Eugenius IV [1431–1447], was clearly prompted from the same desire for greater simplicity and expedition which had already been responsible for the disappearance of the greater bulls and the general adoption of [other, less cumbersome documents]. A brief (*breve*, i.e., "short") was a compendious papal letter which dispensed with some of the formalities previously insisted on. It was written on vellum, generally closed, i.e., folded, and sealed in red wax with the ring of the fisherman (ibid.).

The use of a wax seal conveyed less formality, and in the 1800s, the wax seal was replaced with a simple stamp in red ink.

169. Today, most papal letters are issued in the form of briefs, although bulls are issued in particularly solemn cases. In 1961, Pope John XXIII issued the bull *Humanae Salutis* convoking Vatican II, and in 2015, Pope Francis issued the bull *Misericordiae Vultus* to announce an extraordinary jubilee year of mercy.

Modern Papal Documents by Type

170. Setting aside the physical form they take, papal documents usually are classified by the type of content they contain and the occasions on which they are issued. They fall along a spectrum of solemnity, which very roughly is as follows:

- Apostolic Constitutions
- Encyclicals
- Motu Proprios
- Other Apostolic Letters
- Apostolic Exhortations
- Letters
- Homilies
- Speeches
- Catecheses
- *Angelus/Regina Caeli* addresses
- *Fervorinos*
- Books
- Interviews

Apostolic Constitutions

171. Apostolic constitutions are considered the most solemn papal documents. Francis Morrisey explains:

> They deal with doctrinal or disciplinary matters, but are issued only in relation to very weighty questions. They are now generally reserved for acts of the pope related to

important matters regarding the Church universal or a particular church, such as the erection of dioceses.[12]

Today most apostolic constitutions are short and deal with local matters (e.g., creating dioceses or ecclesiastical provinces). However, popes also use them to issue solemn decisions affecting the whole Church, as with:

- *Ineffabilis Deus* (1854), in which Pope Pius IX infallibly defined the Immaculate Conception of Mary.
- *Munificientissimus Deus* (1950), in which Pope Bl. Pius XII infallibly defined the Assumption of Mary.
- *Depositum Fidei* (1992), in which Pope John Paul II promulgated the *Catechism of the Catholic Church*.

They also can deal with worldwide disciplinary matters, as with:

- *Sacrae Disciplinae Legis* (1983), in which John Paul II promulgated the current *Code of Canon Law*.
- *Anglicanorum Coetibus* (2009), in which Pope Benedict XVI allowed personal ordinariates to be erected for Anglicans entering the Church.
- *Vultum Dei Quaerere* (2016), in which Pope Francis revised the laws governing women's contemplative life.

Apostolic Letters

172. As the name indicates, these take the form of letters addressed to specific audiences. There are several types:

- *Decretal letters* are particularly solemn and used to declare the canonization of saints.
- *Encyclical letters* are the most authoritative teaching documents apart from certain apostolic constitutions.
- *Apostolic letters given "sub plumbo"* (Latin, "under lead") are modern papal bulls.

- *Apostolic letters given "motu proprio"* (Latin, "by my own initiative") represent special initiatives on the part of the pope, as opposed to being documents initiated on the suggestion or advice of others.

- *Apostolic letters* are sometimes issued without further qualification and tend to be the least authoritative of this category.

Several of these categories warrant further discussion.

Encyclicals

173. Encyclicals are not as common as many think and are typically issued only every couple of years. The word *encyclical* (Greek, *en-*, "in" and *kuklos,* "circle") arose because they are not addressed to a particular person and are meant to be circulated widely. According to Pope Paul VI:

> [An encyclical is] a document in the form of a letter sent by the pope to the bishops of the entire world; "encyclical" means circular. It is a very ancient form of ecclesiastical correspondence that characteristically denotes the communion of faith and charity that exists among the various "churches," that is, among the various communities that make up the Church (Audience, August 5, 1964).[13]

The New Testament includes letters intended to be circulated among different churches (cf. James 1:1, 1 Pet. 1:1, Rev. 1:4), and many bishops in the early Church issued such letters. However, the custom fell out of use, and when it was revived, it became associated with the popes. J. Michael Miller explains:

> Benedict XIV (1740–1758) is credited with reviving the ancient tradition of a pope writing a common letter either to a specific group of bishops or to the episcopate as a whole. Not long after his election, Pope Benedict sent out the circular letter *Ubi Primum* (1740) to all members of the college of bishops. Because of this gesture, collections of

papal encyclicals now routinely begin with his pontificate. Gregory XVI (1831–1846) called these papal letters "encyclicals" and, during his papacy, this term passed into general use. For many papal documents published before the mid-nineteenth century, however, scholars fail to agree on which ones can properly be classified as encyclicals. Only for those issued after the First Vatican Council (1870) is there a consensus about the attribution of this designation to specific papal writings. . . .

Since Pius XI, the popes have distinguished between encyclical "letters" and encyclical "epistles." The latter treat a question of interest either to a restricted group or to the bishops of a specific country or region of the Church. In theory, because encyclical epistles are not addressed to the whole Church, they are considered less solemn and therefore enjoy less formal authority than encyclical letters.[14]

The distinction between encyclical letters and encyclical epistles is confusing since "epistle" (Greek, *epistolē*) means "letter" (Latin, *littera*). Consequently, the distinction is largely ignored in practice:

In fact, contemporary theologians regularly overlook the distinction, using the term "encyclical" to refer both to encyclical epistles and encyclical letters.[15]

174. Today, encyclicals are often addressed to more than just bishops. Benedict XVI addressed *Caritas in Veritate* (2009) "to the bishops, priests, and deacons, men and women religious, the lay faithful, and all people of good will." Going even further, Pope Francis said in *Laudato Si'* (2015), "I wish to address every person living on this planet" (n. 3).

175. The doctrinal weight of encyclicals varies. Pope Benedict XV's *In Praeclara Summorum* (1921) celebrated the literary contributions of medieval Italian poet Dante Alighieri. It was thus of less doctrinal weight than John Paul II's *Evangelium Vitae* (1995), which contained solemn papal reaffirmations of Church teaching on the killing of innocents, abortion, and euthanasia.

Sometimes people ask if encyclicals are infallible. Although they can reaffirm teachings that are already infallible, popes do not use encyclicals to issue new infallible teachings. The documents used for that are apostolic constitutions. J. Michael Miller comments:

> While no canonical or theological reason would prevent the successor of Peter from making an *ex cathedra* pronouncement in an encyclical, no pope has solemnly defined a dogma of faith in this way. In other words, the contents of an encyclical are presumed to belong to the ordinary magisterium unless the opposite is clearly manifested.[16]

Motu Proprios

176. The name *motu proprio* indicates that a letter originated with the pope himself, though this may not always be meant literally. Motu proprios deal with disciplinary matters. Francis Morrisey explains:

> Of all the papal legislative texts, the motu proprio is probably the most common source of canonical legislation after the *Code* itself. . . . Originally used to settle the affairs of the Curia or to administer the Papal States, today they deal with matters that are significant but would not merit a constitution; they are legislative in nature. While encyclicals and other papal letters are addressed to certain categories of persons, a *motu proprio* is directed to the Church at large.[17]

Examples of motu proprios include:

- *Ecclesia Dei* (1988), in which John Paul II declared the excommunication of the bishops of the Society of St. Pius X and established provisions for members of that movement who wished to remain in communion with the Church.

- *Summorum Pontificum* (2007), in which Benedict XVI clarified and liberalized the use of the traditional Latin Mass.
- *Mitis Iudex Dominus Iesus* (2015), in which Pope Francis revised the *Code of Canon Law*'s provisions regarding annulments.

Other Apostolic Letters

177. Some apostolic letters don't fall into the categories above. They are sometimes called "apostolic epistles." Francis Morrisey explains:

> In distinction from encyclical letters, apostolic epistles are sent to a particular category of persons, such as a group of bishops. These documents . . . contain social and pastoral teachings, but are not legislative texts.[18]

Examples include:

- *Ordinatio Sacerdotalis* (1994), in which John Paul II solemnly confirmed that priestly ordination is reserved to men alone.
- *Lux Sui Populi* (2012), in which Benedict XVI proclaimed St. Hildegard of Bingen a Doctor of the Church.
- *Vidimus Stellam Eius* (2015), in which Pope Francis proclaimed St. Gregory of Narek a Doctor of the Church.

Apostolic Exhortations

178. As the name suggests, these are documents in which the pope exhorts (urges, advises, counsels). They are pastoral rather than doctrinal in the formal sense, though they routinely restate Church doctrine. As teaching documents, they rank lower than encyclicals, though it would be inaccurate to represent them as non-magisterial documents. They also aren't legislative and don't create or modify laws. However, they can indicate how popes believe moral and canon law should be applied.

After it became clear that the Synod of Bishops often couldn't effectively prepare public documents in its own name (see §158), popes began releasing apostolic exhortations following its meetings. These are known as "postsynodal apostolic exhortations."

Examples of apostolic exhortations include:

- *Familiaris Consortio* (1981), a postsynodal exhortation in which John Paul II discussed the role of the Christian family in the modern world.

- *Verbum Domini* (2011), a postsynodal exhortation in which Benedict XVI discussed the word of God.

- *Amoris Laetitiae* (2016), a postsynodal exhortation in which Pope Francis discussed love in the family.

Letters

179. Popes often write letters that don't have the modifier "apostolic." They are just "letters" or "epistles" (Latin, *epistulae*) and are correspondingly less weighty. These documents are not usually known by a Latin incipit (that is, the first few words of the document in Latin). Instead, they are referred to by the person or group addressed and by date. Examples include:

- Benedict XVI's *Letter to the Participants of the Plenary Session of the Congregation for the Causes of Saints* (April 24, 2006), in which he clarified the way the term "martyr" should be used.

- Benedict XVI's *Letter to the Bishops of the Catholic Church Concerning the Remission of the Excommunication of the Four Bishops Consecrated by Archbishop Lefebvre* (March 10, 2009), in which he explained why he lifted the penalty of excommunication from the Society of St. Pius X bishops.

- Pope Francis's *Letter to the Italian Journalist Dr. Eugenio Scalfari* (September 11, 2013), in which he responded to a letter published in the newspaper *La Repubblica*.

Chirographs

180. Sometimes popes write letters in their own hand, in which case the resulting document is known as a chirograph (Greek, *kheir,* "hand" and *graphē,* "writing"). These are usually short and composed when the pope does not wish to prepare a more formal document. This can mean either that the matter is of lesser weight or that it is so urgent the pope wants to address it immediately. Examples include:

- John Paul II's *Chirograph for the Centenary of the Motu Proprio "Tra le Sollecitudini" on Sacred Music* (November 22, 2003)
- Pope Francis's *Chirograph by Which a Council of Cardinals Is Established* (September 28, 2013)
- Pope Francis's *Chirograph for the Institution of a Pontifical Commission for the Protection of Minors* (March 22, 2014)

Audiences

181. Every Wednesday, the pope holds a formal meeting or "audience" (Latin, *audientia,* "hearing") with people gathered in St. Peter's Square. Although lower than encyclicals in doctrinal authority, they are an unusually rich resource since they are used to give cycles of catechetical instruction, such as John Paul II's "Theology of the Body" series (periodically given from 1979 to 1984).

John Paul II did many cycles of catechesis on various subjects, essentially working his way through the contents of the Creed and providing a parallel to the *Catechism of the Catholic Church.* He also did series on subjects such as priests, the Psalms, and the canticles of the Liturgy of the Hours. The last series was continued by Benedict XVI, who went on to discuss Christ and the Church, the twelve apostles and St. Paul, the Fathers and Doctors of the Church, prayer, and faith. The last was continued by Pope Francis, who has also conducted series on the sacraments, the gifts of the Holy Spirit, the Church, the family, and others.

The series do not run continuously. Popes will interrupt them with audiences for liturgical days and seasons, and whenever the pope returns from a major apostolic journey he usually devotes his next audience to reflecting on the trip.

Audiences are especially valuable from a doctrinal perspective because of their weekly frequency and the broad range of topics they cover. High-level documents like encyclicals only appear every couple of years, but in the same period popes give about a hundred audiences. They thus cover numerous topics that never make it into encyclicals.

Homilies

182. Popes, like other members of the clergy, give homilies. They are the most ancient regular form of papal teaching. Today transcripts of the pope's homilies are published in the journal *Acts Apostolicae Sedis* (see §231) and on the Vatican website (www.vatican.va). Sometimes they are televised, streamed, or broadcast live on radio.

Popes do not use homilies as major teaching occasions, and they tend to be brief reflections on the biblical readings or liturgical themes. Speeches styled "homilies" are given at major public liturgies. They are different from the *fervorinos* given at daily Masses (see §186).

Speeches

183. Popes give many speeches, both in Rome and during travels. In Rome, the pope addresses:

- Dicasteries of the Roman Curia and bodies affiliated with the Holy See
- Bishops from particular territories who are making their *ad limina* visits
- Dignitaries such as ambassadors and heads of state
- Religious and lay groups from different parts of the world

When the pope travels, among the first speeches he gives is an address to representatives of the local government. He also addresses the local Catholic bishops, representatives of other churches and faiths, and groups gathered for major events, such as World Youth Day.

Speeches usually are not major teaching occasions and tend to be primarily pastoral or diplomatic. However, the speeches popes give to Roman dicasteries can be very informative about the way the pope wishes them to carry out their work, and they contain references to projects the departments are pursuing that are not yet publicly announced. The speeches popes give to bishops making *ad limina* visits are informative about the problems he sees in their territories and how he wants them to respond.

Messages

184. Popes issue a large number of "messages" every year. These are published in a different section than the speeches in *Acts Apostolica Sedis* (see §231) and on the Vatican website. The most famous is the *Urbi et Orbi* (Latin, "to the city and the world") message, which occurs every Easter and Christmas. In it, the pope reflects on these holidays and discusses various world situations. Currently, in addition to an annual message for Lent, there are annual messages for:

- World Communications Day
- World Food Day
- World Mission Day
- World Day for Consecrated Life
- World Day for Migrants and Refugees
- World Day of Peace
- World Day of the Sick
- World Day of Prayer for Vocations
- World Day of the Poor
- World Youth Day (including the annual local celebrations)

For the most part, messages are pastoral and reiterate familiar themes. However, messages can occasionally be more significant. On October 22, 1996, John Paul II gave a message to the Pontifical Academy of Sciences that made world headlines because he indicated a more positive attitude toward certain versions of evolution than he and other popes had previously taken.

Angelus/Regina Caeli Addresses

185. Every Sunday at noon the pope gives a brief address from the window of the papal apartment in which he reflects on the Sunday readings or the liturgical day. At its conclusion, he says a brief prayer with the crowd, which will be the *Angelus* ("The Angel of the Lord declared unto Mary . . .") or, during Easter, the *Regina Caeli* ("Queen of Heaven, rejoice, alleluia . . ."). These addresses are thus referred to by the prayer he recites. They are among the least authoritative papal addresses, though they contain valuable spiritual insights.

Fervorinos

186. Canon law requires homilies be given on Sundays and holy days of obligation (CIC 767 §1). On other days, they are only recommended (§2). Daily homilies tend to be short and informal. Known as *fervorinos* (from an Italian word meaning "a little fire") they are meant to be brief motivational or inspirational talks.

In the reign of Pope Francis, the Holy See began to publish accounts of his *fervorinos*, which appear on the Vatican website (www.vatican.va) under the English title "Daily Meditations." Unlike his formal homilies, they are improvised and—at Pope Francis's request—only summaries rather than transcripts are made available. Apparently, he feels the *fervorinos* provide a benefit, but he did not want to spend time every day reviewing, correcting, and approving such short, informal statements. Consequently, they do not participate in the papal magisterium the way formally prepared homilies do, and they are not published in *Acta Apostolicae Sedis* (see §231). Accounts of them can be useful for understanding the pope's thought, but without full transcripts, the details are not to be pressed.

Other Official Papal Statements

187. The categories above represent the major types of papal statement, but there are others, including:

- Greetings popes send from the papal plane to world leaders whose territories they are flying through

- Telegrams to express prayer and condolences in the wake of tragedies
- Papal tweets sent from @Pontifex on Twitter—a practice begun by Benedict XVI to engage internet culture

Although every papal statement presupposes doctrinal principles, such statements do not participate significantly in the pope's magisterium.

Non-Official Papal Statements

188. Popes also make non-official statements. Some have published books during their pontificate, such as John Paul II's interview book, *Crossing the Threshold of Hope,* and Benedict XVI's three-volume series, *Jesus of Nazareth.* Modern popes also frequently give interviews with the press. In principle, nothing stops a pope from exercising his magisterium in such statements. However, typically he does not. In the case of *Jesus of Nazareth,* Benedict XVI made it explicit that he was not exercising his magisterium (see §42).

189. Some authors have expressed puzzlement at the idea that a pope could discuss doctrinal matters without these statements becoming part of his magisterium.[19] However, this idea has long been recognized. It is presupposed by the fact that popes and councils can determine what level of doctrinal authority to invest in their statements. If, by exercising the fullest extent of their authority, they can set the level of authority to "infallible," they can also set it to "zero," enabling them to *propose* theological ideas for the consideration of the faithful without *imposing* them as matters of doctrine.

This was made explicit in the briefing (Latin, *relatio*) given by Bishop Vincent Gasser to the fathers of Vatican I as they prepared to define papal infallibility. He indicated that the pope is infallible:

> when the supreme pontiff speaks *ex cathedra*, not, first of all, when he decrees something as a private teacher, nor only as

the bishop and ordinary of a particular See and province, but when he teaches as exercising his office as supreme pastor and teacher of all Christians.[20]

Gasser thus indicates that a pope can speak "as a private teacher," or theologian, rather than as pope.

The same is indicated by Vatican II, which taught that when he teaches infallibly, "the Roman pontiff is not pronouncing judgment as a private person, but as the supreme teacher of the universal Church" (*Lumen Gentium,* 25). It is up to the pope to determine the capacity in which he is speaking, as when Pope Benedict determined to write his *Jesus of Nazareth* series as a private author.

190. In 1990, the CDF noted that theologians need to "assess accurately the authoritativeness of the interventions, which becomes clear from the nature of the documents, the insistence with which a teaching is repeated, and the very way in which it is expressed" (*Donum Veritatis,* 24).

Regarding the manner in which something is phrased, if a pope says it "is in no way an exercise of the magisterium," as Benedict XVI did, then it obviously is not.

Regarding the nature of a document like a papal book or interview, the pope has his own means of publishing official documents, via the Vatican publishing house (*Libreria Editrice Vaticana*). Consequently, it's significant if he chooses someone else to issue it. A rule of thumb is that if a secular book publisher, newspaper, magazine, or other media outlet is the originating publisher of a papal statement then it should be regarded as an unofficial one unless the pope indicates the contrary.

191. This doesn't mean that non-magisterial papal statements have no value. They have an intrinsic value based on the arguments the pope uses, and they have a practical value in understanding the mind of a pope.

Something similar is true of writings made before a man became pope. They may or may not have been part of his magisterium as a bishop, and his later election to the papacy does not confer papal authority on them retroactively. However, they provide valuable insights on his thought. Thus the extensive body of theological literature Joseph Ratzinger penned provides insights for understanding the magisterium of Benedict XVI.

CHAPTER 9

Curial and Other Documents

Curial Documents

192. The Roman Curia issues a huge number of documents. With more than a billion Catholics in the world, the need to relate to the nation-states in which they reside, and the need to evangelize the cultures of the world, a plethora of documents is only to be expected. Here we will look at the major types of curial documents dealing with Church teaching. Most of these are issued by the Congregation for the Doctrine of the Faith (CDF). Note that curial documents must carry express papal approval to be acts of the Magisterium—a rule that applies even to the CDF (see §50).

Responses/Dubia

193. The shortest documents to engage Church teaching are known, variously, as replies, responses, *dubia,* or *responsa ad dubia.* All of these refer to the same thing. In Latin, *dubium* means "a doubt," but it can colloquially refer to a question. A *responsum ad dubium* is therefore a response to a question. Various dicasteries have used this Q & A format to answer inquiries sent by bishops. *Dubia* are strikingly brief, the question is carefully worded, and the reply is often just a single word: *affirmative* or *negative.*

194. Here is the complete text of one such *dubium*:

RESPONSE TO A "DUBIUM"
on the validity of baptism conferred by "The Church of Jesus Christ of Latter-day Saints," called "Mormons"

Question: Whether the baptism conferred by the community "The Church of Jesus Christ of Latter-day Saints," called "Mormons" in the vernacular, is valid.

Response: Negative.

The supreme pontiff John Paul II, in the audience granted to the undersigned cardinal prefect, approved the present response, decided in the Sessione Ordinaria *of this congregation, and ordered it published.*

From the Offices of the Congregation for the Doctrine of the Faith, 5 June 2001.
+ Joseph Cardinal RATZINGER
Prefect
+ Tarcisio BERTONE, S.D.B.
Archbishop emeritus of Vercelli
Secretary

This *dubium* considers only a single question, but others include a series of questions. As you can see, in this case the question is a single sentence, and the response is a single word. Everything else consists of formalities letting you know that the pope approved the response (making it a magisterial statement), and when and by whom it was issued.

One-word answers provide decisive responses, but they leave one wanting an explanation of the reasoning behind the response. In some cases, the text of a *dubium* will contain a few words of explanation, but longer explanations are typically found in an accompanying document.

Accompanying Documents

195. Upon the release of major documents, the Holy See holds press conferences in which official representatives comment on them. The texts of these presentations—or other signed or unsigned commentaries—are then made available.

When the CDF released the *dubium* on Mormon baptism, it knew people would want some kind of explanation of why

Mormon baptisms are invalid (especially since the Holy See previously had treated them as valid). It therefore released two accompanying documents—one by Fr. Luis Ladaria, S.J., and another by Fr. Urbano Navarrete, S.J., both of whom were involved in preparing the *dubium*. Their commentaries were published in the Vatican newspaper *L'Osservatore Romano*.

Accompanying documents are helpful in understanding the reasoning and significance of documents, but they do not carry papal approval and are not magisterial. Their authors, if known, are giving their own understanding of matters. Unsigned accompanying documents can be regarded as reflecting the thought of the authors in a general way, but they also are not on the same level as the official text.

Notes

196. In recent years the CDF has issued "notes," which are a step up from *dubia* in terms of length, typically being a few pages long. Like most Church documents, they use ordinary prose instead of a Q & A format. As the somewhat informal name "note" suggests, they are documents of a lesser order. Examples include:

- *Note on the Expression "Sister Churches"* (2000), in which the CDF explains the proper use of a conceptually tricky phrase.

- *Note on the Force of the Doctrinal Decrees Concerning the Thought and Work of Fr. Antonio Rosmini Serbati* (2004), in which the CDF discussed the fundamental orthodoxy of a nineteenth-century philosopher and theologian whose works were once prohibited.

- *Note on the Banalization of Sexuality, Regarding Certain Interpretations of "Light of the World"* (2010), in which the CDF responded to a controversy concerning remarks Pope Benedict XVI had made in the interview book *Light of the World*.

197. In some cases, the CDF qualifies a document as a "doctrinal note," giving it greater weight. Examples include:

- *Doctrinal Note on Some Questions Regarding the Participation of Catholics in Political Life* (2002), in which the CDF discusses the moral obligations of Catholic politicians and citizens.

- *Doctrinal Note on Some Aspects of Evangelization* (2007), in which the CDF discusses the importance of evangelization and its implications.

Notifications

198. Though "notification" and "note" share the same root, notifications play a different function: usually they are warnings, most frequently about a book or books that contain problematic theological ideas. Examples include:

- *Notification on the Book "Church: Charism and Power, Essays on Militant Ecclesiology" by Fr. Leonardo Boff, O.F.M.* (1985)

- *Notification Concerning the Text "Mary and Human Liberation" by Fr. Tissa Balasuriya* (1997)

- *Notification Concerning the Writings of Fr. Anthony De Mello, S.J.* (1998)

In recent years, CDF notifications have become less common, as the congregation has been shifting the burden of dealing with problematic theologians to national bishops' conferences. Consequently, the U.S. bishops' Committee on Doctrine has begun issuing similar statements on books by American theologians.

199. Notifications sometimes concern individuals, their ideas, and problematic activities they have undertaken, including ecclesiastical crimes such as schism or performing illicit ordinations. Examples include:

- *Notification Regarding the Canonical Penalties Incurred by His Excellency Mons. Pierre Martin Ngo-Dinh-Thuc and Other Completely Illicit Ordinations* (1983)

- *Notification Regarding Rev. George de Nantes* (1983)

- *Notification Regarding Sr. Jeannine Gramick, S.S.N.D., and Fr. Robert Nugent, S.D.S.* (1999)

200. Notifications are sometimes issued to warn the faithful about problematic reports of apparitions:

- *Notification Regarding the Alleged Apparitions and Revelations of "Our Lady of All Nations" in Amsterdam* (1974)
- *Notification on the Writings and Activities of Mrs. Vassula Ryden* (1995)

201. In two cases notifications were issued concerning the validity of baptisms in non-Catholic communities. It is not clear why these were not issued as *dubia*, especially since they were written as a question followed by a one-word response ("Negative" in both cases):

- *Notification Regarding the Validity of the Baptism Conferred by the "Christian Community" of Rudolph Steiner* (1991)
- *Notification on the Validity of the Baptism Conferred in "The New Church"* (1993)

202. Though most notifications are warning against specific individuals and things, there are a few that serve other functions:

- *Notification Regarding the Abolition of the Index of Books* (1966), in which the CDF notes that the Index of Prohibited Books has been abolished, though one still has a moral duty to guard one's faith.
- *Notification Regarding the Devotion to Divine Mercy in the Form Proposed by Sr. Faustina Kowalska* (1978), in which the CDF announces that a previous notification regarding the Divine Mercy devotion is no longer in force.

Decrees

203. A step up from notifications are decrees, which establish or concretely apply a law. Francis Morrisey explains:

The *Code* provides for two types of decrees: general and individual. A general decree is issued for a community capable of receiving a law (c. 29), while an individual decree is an administrative act in which a decision is given or a provision is made in a particular case in accord with the norms of law (c. 48).[21]

Canon 29 provides that general decrees "are laws properly speaking."

204. Since the Second Vatican Council, the CDF has published one general decree. It was issued in 2007 following a number of attempted ordinations of women to the priesthood (see *General Decree Regarding the Delict of Attempted Sacred Ordination of a Woman*). A similar decree (without the qualifier "general") was issued in 1988, when the congregation provided automatic excommunication for anyone who records a confession or discloses it through the means of social communication. Other CDF decrees include:

- *Decree on the Ecclesiastical Burial of Manifest Sinners* (1973)
- *Decree Regarding the Censorship of Pastors of the Church on Books* (1975)
- *Decree Regarding Public Celebration of Mass in the Catholic Church for Other Christians Who Have Died* (1976)
- *Decree Concerning Certain Unlawful Priestly and Episcopal Ordinations* (1976)
- *Decree Regarding Cases in Which Impotence Renders Marriage Null* (1977)

These decrees were published before the 1983 *Code of Canon Law* and have been superseded in various ways.

205. Although CDF decrees frequently deal with unfortunate situations and can impose penalties, some have happier subjects. In 1992, a decree offered a path to regularize relations with an organization known as *Opus Angelorum*, and several decrees issued between 2011 and 2012 erected personal ordinariates for Anglicans who wish to be in full communion with the Catholic Church.

Declarations

206. Related to decrees are declarations. Morrisey explains:

> Another form of pronouncement used quite frequently in recent years is the declaration, which is an interpretation of existing law or facts, or a reply to a contested point of law or doctrine.[22]

Since Vatican II, the CDF has issued many declarations. Some of them focus on specifically doctrinal matters. These include:

- *Mysterium Ecclesiae: Declaration in Defense of Catholic Doctrine on the Church Against Certain Errors of the Present Day* (1973)
- *Inter Insigniores: Declaration on the Question of Admission of Women to the Ministerial Priesthood* (1976)
- *Dominus Iesus: Declaration on the Unicity and Salvific Universality of Jesus Christ and the Church* (2000)

207. Some declarations cover the same kind of material found in notifications and decrees—such as warnings about doctrinal errors advocated by theologians—and it is not clear why the congregation chose to issue them as declarations. These include:

- *Declaration Regarding Certain Aspects of the Theological Doctrine of Prof. Hans Kung* (1979)
- *Declaration Regarding the Dialogues with Rev. Fr. Edward Schillebeeckx on Certain Aspects of his Doctrinal Christology* (1979)
- *Declaration on the Book by Fr. Jacques Pohier, "When I Say God"* (1979)

Similarly, some declarations deal with problematic pastoral situations:

- *Declaration Concerning the Status of Catholics Becoming Freemasons* (1981)
- *Declaration on Masonic Associations* (1983)
- *Declaration on the "Clandestine Church" in the Czech Republic* (2000)

Letters

208. The CDF occasionally issues public documents in the form of letters. In some cases, these are important items of individual correspondence, such as a 1980 letter to the Belgian theologian Edward Schillebeeckx, concerning problematic statements in his writings. Another is a 1982 letter to Bishop Alan Clark about the progress of his dialogue with representatives of the Anglican communion.

209. However, usually the CDF doesn't publicly release correspondence directed to individuals. But it does publish letters issued to a broader audience, such as the heads of episcopal conferences. These are known as circular letters (*litterae circulares*) because they are meant to be widely circulated. Despite having a similar function to papal encyclicals, they are called "circular letters" to prevent confusion.

Such documents deal with disciplinary matters, though they involve doctrinal principles. Examples include:

- *Circular Letter Regarding the Indissolubility of Marriage* (1973)
- *Circular Letter to All Presidents of the Episcopal Conferences Concerning the Use of Low-Gluten Altar Breads and Mustum as Matter for the Celebration of the Eucharist* (2003)
- *Circular Letter to Assist Episcopal Conferences in Developing Guidelines for Dealing with Cases of Sexual Abuse of Minors Perpetrated by Clerics* (2011)

210. Interestingly, the CDF sometimes issues letters to a broad audience but omits the qualifier "circular." When a Latin version of these documents exists, they are often called *epistulae* rather than *litterae*, though both terms translate in English as "letters." Examples include:

- *Letter to Ordinaries Regarding Norms on Exorcism* (1985)
- *Letter to the Bishops of the Catholic Church on the Pastoral Care of Homosexual Persons* (1987)
- *Letter to the Bishops of the Catholic Church on Some Aspects of Christian Meditation* (1991)

Instructions

211. Among the more authoritative documents issued by the CDF are instructions. According to the *Code of Canon Law*, instructions "clarify the prescripts of laws and elaborate on and determine the methods to be observed in fulfilling them" (CIC 34). Instructions of this type issued by the CDF include:

- *Instruction on Mixed Marriages* (1966)
- *Instruction on the Necessity to Establish Doctrinal Commissions in Episcopal Conferences* (1967)
- *Instruction Regarding the Burial of the Deceased and the Conservation of the Ashes in the Case of Cremation* (2016)

These can contain extensive discussions of doctrine, but they also prescribe how the laws on these subjects are to be applied. In some cases, instructions establish new legal norms.

212. On the other hand, some CDF instructions are devoted to doctrinal rather than legal matters. These include:

- *Instruction on Certain Aspects of the "Theology of Liberation"* (1984)
- *Donum Veritatis: Instruction on the Ecclesial Vocation of the Theologian* (1990)
- *Dignitas Personae: Instruction on Certain Bioethical Questions* (2008)

These represent an extension of the category of "instruction" as defined in the *Code of Canon Law*, which may be one reason why Francis Morrisey observes:

> It is this form of document, along with the declaration, that has given rise to the greatest difficulty in interpretation in the post-conciliar era. Since the texts are not strictly speaking legislative—at least according to their nature—their application certainly allows for more leeway than would a decree.[23]

The CDF's decision to publish some purely doctrinal documents as instructions may be a desire to signal their authority. The canonical use of the term, as well as the greater formality of the word "instruction" compared to "note" or "letter," lends additional gravitas.

Other CDF Documents

213. Some CDF documents do not fall into the above categories. Examples include:

- *Christian Faith and Demonology* (1975), a document styled a "study" by an anonymous expert the CDF commissioned to prepare it
- *Regulations for Doctrinal Examination* (1997), a set of procedural norms the CDF employs when evaluating reports of doctrinal error
- *Documents Regarding "The Message of Fatima"* (2000), a collection of several documents dealing with the Fatima apparitions and their famous "third secret"
- *Doctrinal Assessment of the Leadership Conference of Women Religious* (2012), an evaluation of problematic ideas and activities in a leadership group for women religious

Directories

214. The final kind of curial document we will consider is the directory. Thus far the CDF has not issued any directories, but other dicasteries have, and they often touch on matters of doctrine. Morrisey explains:

> Another relatively new type of act is the directory, wherein guidelines are given for the application of accepted principles. . . . The interest of a directory is to provide the basic principles of pastoral theology, taken from the Magisterium of the Church, by which pastoral action in the ministry can be more fittingly directed and governed. This outlook explains why the theoretical aspect is given primary emphasis in a directory without, however, neglecting the practical aspects. Consequently, directories are addressed more particularly to bishops to give them assistance in practical matters.[24]

Examples of directories touching on doctrinal matters include:

- *Directory for the Application of the Principles and Norms on Ecumenism* (Pontifical Council for Promoting Christian Unity, 1993)
- *General Directory for Catechesis* (Congregation for the Clergy, 1997)
- *Directory on Popular Piety and the Liturgy* (Congregation for Divine Worship and the Discipline of the Sacraments, 2001)
- *Apostolores Succesores: Directory for the Pastoral Ministry of Bishops* (Congregation for Bishops, 2004)

Commission Documents

215. From time to time, the Holy See has created commissions to study particular subjects. These meet either on a temporary or an ongoing basis. Under canon law, these commissions are not organs of the Magisterium, but their documents are only published if they receive Church approval. Two current commissions of special significance are the Pontifical Biblical Commission and the International Theological Commission.

The Pontifical Biblical Commission

216. The Pontifical Biblical Commission (PBC) began its life in 1902 as an organ of the Magisterium. However, in 1971 it was reorganized by Pope Paul VI as an advisory body run under the auspices of the CDF (see §54). Its documents fall into two groups, based on these periods.

Early PBC Documents

217. The PBC's best-known early documents were issued between 1905 and 1933 and were written in the *dubia* format. They principally concerned questions about particular books of the Bible (e.g., did Moses write the Pentateuch, how many authors contributed to Isaiah, in what order were the synoptic Gospels written), and they largely reaffirmed views that had been widely accepted in recent centuries and were being challenged by modern biblical scholarship. At the time, these responses had magisterial authority, at least when they touched on matters of doctrine. This was confirmed by Pope Pius X in the 1907 motu proprio *Praestantia Scripturae*.

218. Over time, this changed. In 1948, the PBC issued a letter to Cardinal Emmanuel Suhard of Paris concerning certain early responses. This letter was written at the direction of Pope Bl. Pius XII and carried his approval. It concluded that, in light of subsequent magisterial teaching (including Pius XII's 1943 encyclical *Divino Afflante Spiritu*), key findings of the early PBC *dubia* "are in no way a hindrance to further truly scientific examination of these problems in accordance with the results [of biblical scholarship] acquired in these last forty years."

In 1990, Cardinal Joseph Ratzinger gave a press conference for the release of *Donum Veritatis* in which he discussed the early PBC decisions, stating:

> As a warning cry against hasty and superficial adaptations they remain fully justified; a person of the stature of Johann Baptist Metz has said, for example, that the anti-Modernist decisions of the Church rendered a great service in keeping

her from sinking into the liberal-bourgeois world. But the details of the determinations of their contents were later superseded once they had carried out their pastoral duty at a particular moment.[25]

In a 2003 speech to the PBC, he again stressed the theme of the early decisions as valid warnings for their time but which since have been superseded:

> It is true that, with the above-mentioned decisions, the Magisterium overly enlarged the area of certainties that the faith can guarantee; it is also true that with this, the credibility of the Magisterium was diminished and the space necessary for research and exegetical questions was excessively restricted. . . .
> At first it seemed indispensable for the authenticity of Scripture, and therefore for the faith founded upon it, that the Pentateuch be indisputably attributed to Moses or that the authors of the individual Gospels be truly those named by tradition.[26]

He concluded:

> Meanwhile, not only those decisions of the Biblical Commission which had entered too much into the sphere of merely historical questions were corrected; we have also learned something new about the methods and limits of historical knowledge.

The matter was put succinctly by Cardinal Ratzinger's successor as prefect of the CDF, Cardinal William Levada, when in a 2005 speech he remarked that the early decisions of the PBC are "now viewed as transitory judgments."[27]

Recent PBC Documents

219. Since its reorganization as an advisory body, the PBC's documents have not carried magisterial authority. However, there are safeguards in place to ensure they are in line with Catholic teaching:

a) The man in charge of the commission is the head of the CDF and thus the chief official entrusted with guarding the Church's doctrine. According to the PBC's statutes:

> The cardinal prefect of the Sacred Congregation for the Doctrine of the Faith serves as the president of the Biblical Commission, and he may be assisted by a vice-president selected from the members of the commission (*Sedula Cura*, norm 2).

b) Members of the commission are appointed by the pope, on the recommendation of the head of the CDF, and are chosen based on their adherence to the Magisterium:

> The Biblical Commission is composed of scholars of the biblical sciences from various schools and nations, who are distinguished for their learning, prudence, and Catholic regard for the Magisterium of the Church.
> Members of the Biblical Commission are appointed by the supreme pontiff, on the proposal by the cardinal president and after consultation with the episcopal conferences (norms 3 and 4).

c) The writings of the PBC are submitted to the pope before being given to the CDF:

> The conclusions reached by the Biblical Commission . . . shall be submitted to the supreme pontiff before being turned over for the use of the Sacred Congregation for the Doctrine of the Faith (norm 10).

d) The pope must approve PBC documents before they are published:

It is the duty of the Biblical Commission to conduct studies of proposed questions as well as to prepare instructions and decrees, which the Sacred Congregation for the Doctrine of the Faith has the right to publish, with special mention of the Biblical Commission and with the recorded approval of the supreme pontiff, unless the supreme pontiff in special cases shall have determined otherwise (norm 11).

Since they are not magisterial documents, this does not mean that Catholics are obliged to agree with everything they discuss (e.g., various theories of biblical scholarship), but the approval of the pope functions as an imprimatur (Latin, "let it be published"), indicating the fundamental orthodoxy of published PBC documents.

The International Theological Commission

220. Unlike the PBC, the International Theological Commission (ITC) has never been an organ of the Magisterium. It was founded as an advisory body run under the auspices of the CDF (see §55). Because of this, one is under no obligation to agree with its conclusions, except where they repeat Church teaching. However, there are safeguards to ensure its documents' fundamental orthodoxy:

a) The man in charge of it is the head of the CDF:

> The President of the International Theological Commission is the cardinal prefect of the Sacred Congregation for the Doctrine of the Faith, who, however, in case of necessity and for individual sessions may delegate another moderator (norm 2).

b) Members are appointed by the pope, based on the recommendation of the head of the CDF, and selected based on their doctrinal orthodoxy:

The International Theological Commission is made up of scholars of the theological sciences of different schools and nations; they should be eminent for their science, prudence, and fidelity toward the Magisterium of the Church.

The members of the International Theological Commission are appointed by the supreme pontiff, to whose judgment the cardinal prefect of this Sacred Congregation for the Doctrine of the Faith will make proposals, after having listened to the episcopal conferences (norms 3 and 4).

c) When the ITC has completed a study, it is submitted to the pope and the CDF:

The conclusions which the International Theological Commission reaches, whether in the plenary session or in the special subcommissions, as also, if it be judged opportune, the views of individual members, should be submitted to the supreme pontiff and should be given to the Sacred Congregation for the Doctrine of the Faith (norm 11).

d) Its documents are only published on the condition that the Holy See does not have "any difficulty" with them:

Documents which have been approved by the majority of the members of the International Theological Commission may also be published on condition that there is not any difficulty on the part of the Apostolic See (norm 12).

Since the statutes of the ITC don't specify that the pope himself is to authorize publication (as with the PBC), this is typically done by the head of the CDF, and so it is his authorization that functions as an imprimatur certifying the doctrinal orthodoxy of a published ITC document.

221. The ITC is not a forum for dissident theologians, and it is meant to represent a common, orthodox approach to theology. Thus in 1985, its then-head, Cardinal Joseph Ratzinger, wrote:

> It is hardly surprising that one constantly hears the criticism that the Commission is not active enough and has nothing to offer the wider life of the Church. However, anybody who has expectations that the commission might represent a kind of permanent "his majesty's opposition" to the Church's Magisterium, offering a running commentary of speculative objections against Rome for the benefit of the multitude, is going to be disappointed by a revelation of the serenity and objectivity of the commission's labors. On the other hand, anybody who is looking for world-shaking scholarly discoveries has misunderstood the whole point and nature of a commission. Thirty very different voices have to be brought to speak in harmony: the scholarly pursuits of individuals are not the object of the exercise. The special contribution of the commission is to gain a hearing for the common voice of theology amid all the diversities that exist. For notwithstanding the legitimate pluralism of theological cultures in the Church, the unity of theology must remain and empower theologians to offer some common account of their subject.[28]

Other Commission Documents

222. In addition to the PBC and ITC, other pontifical commissions have been appointed. A noteworthy example was the Pontifical Commission on Population, the Family, and Birth-Rate, which was established by John XXIII in 1963 and dealt with the question of birth control. In 1966, it issued its findings to Paul VI, but they were not approved for publication. Instead, they were leaked to the press and published in French and English editions—the latter appearing in the American newspaper *The National Catholic Reporter* (April 19, 1967).

Because the Holy See did not approve them for publication, these documents could not be relied upon to accurately reflect

Catholic principles, and they did not. The majority of commission members supported a change in the Church's position on contraception. The fact the documents did not reflect Catholic principles was confirmed in 1968 by Paul VI's encyclical *Humanae Vitae*, which reaffirmed the Church's teaching on the subject.

Special Documents

Codes of Canon Law

223. Certain documents that do not fall into the above categories also need to be considered. Among them are the codes of canon law.

Prior to the twentieth century, canon law was found in an extensive collection of documents composed over the centuries. It was a complex and confusing field needing greater organization, and in 1917, Pope Benedict XV released the first *Code of Canon Law* (Latin, *Codex Iuris Canonici* or CIC), which organized and condensed the core of canon law into a single volume.

This *Code* served as the basis of canon law for much of the twentieth century, but in 1983 Pope John Paul II issued a new edition, which replaced the original. In 1990, he released a parallel volume—the *Code of Canons for the Eastern Churches* (Latin, *Codex Canonum Ecclesiarum Orientalium* or CCEO)—which became the basis of canon law for Eastern Catholic churches.

Subsequently, popes have updated canon law by revising specific canons rather than releasing new full editions. This first occurred when John Paul II released the motu proprio *Ad Tuendam Fidem* (1998), which modified a small number of canons. Benedict XVI modified a few more in *Omnium in Mentem* (2009), and Pope Francis extensively revised the canons pertaining to the annulment process with *Mitis Iudex Dominus Iesus* (2015). Consequently, one must ensure one is reading the current edition of the affected canons.

By nature, codes are legal documents rather than teaching documents. However, they are based on doctrinal principles, and some canons involve straightforward expressions of doctrine (see §106). Consequently, the *Catechism of the Catholic Church*—a teaching document—sometimes quotes from the *Code* to document a point of doctrine.

Because the codes contain a mixture of doctrinal and legal principles, one must carefully distinguish the two to determine the degree to which their provisions can be modified (see §107).

Churchwide Catechisms

224. In two notable cases the Holy See has released Churchwide catechisms. The first was mandated by the fathers of Trent as a way to reinforce Catholic teaching against Protestant ideas. Consequently, in 1566, Pope Pius V released the *Roman Catechism* (aka the *Catechism of the Council of Trent*). It was addressed to local pastors and intended to inform their preaching and teaching.

The *Roman Catechism* became highly influential, and it is quoted numerous times in the *Catechism of the Catholic Church*, though as a creature of its time it does not reflect the subsequent 450 years of doctrinal development or the changes in Church law and practice.

225. Following Vatican II (1962–1965), a period of intense doctrinal confusion occurred, with many Catholics unsure what the Church taught. At the 1985 meeting of the Synod of Bishops, the idea of a new Churchwide catechism was proposed, and in 1992 John Paul II released the first edition of the *Catechism of the Catholic Church*. This edition was in French—the language most widely known in the working group that composed it—and it was subsequently translated into numerous languages, with an English edition appearing in 1994.

In 1997, John Paul II released a Latin edition of the text, which henceforth was the official version from which future translations would be made. This edition also included several minor modifications, so it is necessary when quoting from the affected passages to ensure they reflect the 1997 revision. In 2018, Pope Francis also authorized a revision of the passage in the *Catechism* dealing with capital punishment.[29]

226. Many had questions about the *Catechism*'s level of author-ity. Does the fact that something is mentioned in it mean that the teaching is infallible or nearly infallible? The answer is no. Cardinal Joseph Ratzinger, who headed the commission that prepared the work, explained that it did not affect the previous status of teachings:

> This brings us to the question already mentioned before, regarding the authority of the *Catechism*. In order to find the answer, let us first consider a bit more closely its juridi-cal character. We could express it in this way: analogously to the new *Code of Canon Law*, the *Catechism* is de facto a collegial work; canonically, it falls under the special juris-diction of the pope, inasmuch as it was authorized for the whole Christian world by the Holy Father in virtue of the supreme teaching authority invested in him. . . .
>
> This does not mean that the *Catechism* is a sort of super-dogma, as its opponents would like to insinuate in order to cast suspicion on it as a danger to the liberty of theology. What significance the *Catechism* really holds for the common exercise of teaching in the Church may be learned by read-ing the apostolic constitution *Fidei Depositum*, with which the pope promulgated it on October 11, 1992—exactly thirty years after the opening of the Second Vatican Council: "I ac-knowledge it [the *Catechism*] as a valid and legitimate tool in the service of ecclesiastical communion, as a sure norm for instruction in the faith." The individual doctrines which the *Catechism* presents receive no other weight than that which they already possess. The weight of the *Catechism* itself lies in the whole. Since it transmits what the Church teaches, who-ever rejects it as a whole separates himself beyond question from the faith and teaching of the Church.[30]

Consequently, the fact a teaching is included in the *Catechism* doesn't make it infallible. In Cardinal Ratzinger's words, its teachings "receive no other weight than that which they already possess." Therefore, one must look to prior and subsequent documents to determine what this is.

227. The *Catechism* had a significant impact worldwide, with many local catechisms being revised or newly composed based on its contents. It also led to two additional catechisms of a global nature.

The first, the *Compendium of the Catechism of the Catholic Church,* was released by Benedict XVI in 2005. It is written in a question-and-answer format and distills the key teachings of the larger *Catechism.*

The second, the *Youth Catechism of the Catholic Church* or *Youcat,* was issued in 2011 and has been distributed at events like World Youth Day. Unlike the *Catechism* and the *Compendium, Youcat* is not a publication of the Holy See. It was reviewed and approved by the CDF, and it carries a forward by Benedict XVI, but it is actually a local publication written under the direction of Cardinal Christoph Schonborn of Vienna.

228. A final, related document that appeared following the success of the *Catechism* is the *Compendium of the Social Doctrine of the Church* (2004). It was released by the Pontifical Council for Justice and Peace (now part of the Dicastery for Promoting Integral Human Development). As its name suggests, it seeks to summarize the social teachings of the Church. It does not carry papal approval and so it does not participate in the pope's magisterium, though it does repeat teaching of prior popes. Also, since it deals with matters of doctrine, it would have been reviewed by the CDF, ensuring its fundamental orthodoxy (see §§50–52).

Publications Linked to the Holy See

229. The Holy See has many communications initiatives to get its message out, including a press office, a publishing house, and news services for print, radio, television, and the internet. In 2015, Pope Francis decreed that these efforts would be folded into a new Secretariat for Communications.

230. Among the efforts the Secretariat oversees is the Holy See's publishing house, *Libreria Editrice Vaticana* (Italian, "Vatican Publishing Library") or LEV, which was founded in 1926. It publishes magisterial documents such as papal encyclicals and the Latin edition of the *Catechism of the Catholic Church*. However, LEV also publishes non-magisterial works including writings of scholars in biblical studies and canon law. These works do not carry magisterial authority, but they generally may be presumed to reflect Catholic teaching, especially when they carry an imprimatur.

231. Among LEV's most important publications is *Acta Apostolicae Sedis* (Latin, "Acts of the Apostolic See"), a monthly journal that prints documents issued by the pope and the dicasteries of the Roman Curia. It is considered the official record of such documents, and its authoritative status is illustrated by the fact that universal laws typically take effect three months after their appearance in *Acta Apostolicae Sedis* (CIC 8 §1).

232. The Secretariat for Communications also oversees the Vatican newspaper, *L'Osservatore Romano* (Italian, "The Roman Observer"), which began publication in 1861. It is frequently considered a semiofficial publication of the Holy See, and it prints both magisterial and non-magisterial pieces. Non-magisterial pieces appearing in *L'Osservatore Romano* are considered fundamentally orthodox, though the mere fact of publication does not carry as much weight as it used to. Beginning in the reign of Benedict XVI (2005–2013), the paper implemented an editorial policy intended to make it more engaging, and it began to print opinion pieces engaging pop culture phenomena such as Michael Jackson and *The Simpsons*.

233. Another semiofficial publication is the magazine *La Civiltà Cattolica* (Italian, "The Catholic Civilization"). It is issued by the Jesuit order rather than the Secretariat for Communications. Its semiofficial status is due to the fact that, prior to publication, it is reviewed and approved by the Holy See's Secretariat of State. It therefore serves as an indicator of the Secretariat's thought.

Denzinger's Enchiridion Symbolorum

234. A final notable work is *Enchiridion Symbolorum, Definitionum, et Declarationum de Rebus Fidei et Morum* (Latin, "Handbook of Creeds, Definitions, and Declarations on Matters of Faith and Morals"), which is commonly called "Denzinger" after its original editor—the German scholar Heinrich Denzinger—who published the first edition in 1854.

Denzinger is a collection of extracts from magisterial documents throughout the centuries. There are other, similar works, but Denzinger is by far the most influential, and it has gone through more than forty editions. Some are known by compound names reflecting later editors (e.g., "Denzinger-Schonmetzer" or "Denzinger-Hunermann").

235. The work is so influential that, although it isn't a Church publication, magisterial documents regularly cite it using abbreviations like D 1008, DS 3628, or DH 5109, reflecting numbered paragraphs in different editions of the work.

236. Denzinger documents the development of Church teaching over time, and so the excerpts it gives are in chronological rather than topical order. The work's historical nature has important implications for evaluating the weight of individual statements it contains:

- One cannot take a random statement and conclude it is infallible. Comparatively few statements are infallible, and one must determine the doctrinal weight they had *at the time* they were issued.

- One cannot assume a random statement is *currently* Church teaching. Denzinger contains non-infallible statements that have since been superseded, e.g., the early replies of the Pontifical Biblical Commission (see §218). One must take subsequent doctrinal development into account.

- Statements in Denzinger reflect the vocabulary of the time, and the use of terms can change. Thus Peter Hunermann notes, "The terms *sacramentum* and *dogma*, for example, undergo important shifts in meaning."[31]

Despite these cautions, Denzinger is an extraordinarily valuable collection of magisterial texts.

CHAPTER 10

Reading Church Documents

The Need to Read the Documents

237. For a person who wants to understand Church teaching, reading Church documents is a must. Innumerable misunderstandings arise precisely because people don't consult the documents, because they give them a hasty, inattentive reading, or because they lack the background needed to understand them.

Every day, people discuss what they've heard Church leaders say. These reports then get passed on in second- and third-hand forms—a process that produces a huge body of gossip and rumors, many completely inaccurate (see chapter twenty-one). Today, the mass media flashes inaccurate stories about Church leaders around the globe at lightning speed, misleading millions of people and making it all the more necessary that we consult the original documents to see what was said.

Case Study: Mistaken Press Accounts

238. Here is the beginning of a story published by the Associated Press about an interview Pope Francis gave during a return flight from Colombia:

> Pope Blasts Climate Change Doubters:
> Cites Moral Duty to Act
> By Nicole Winfield
> Associated Press
> ABOARD THE PAPAL PLANE (AP)—Pope Francis has sharply criticized climate change doubters, saying history will

judge those who failed to take the necessary decisions to curb heat-trapping emissions blamed for the warming of the Earth.[32]

On occasion, Pope Francis uses harsh language, and this account leads one to believe he did so here, "blasting" those who doubt man-made climate change and stating that history will "judge"—i.e., condemn—them. But when one checks a transcript of the interview, it turns out he took a far more irenic tone. When asked whether politicians have a moral responsibility for climate change and why some deny man causes it, he said:

Pope Francis: Thanks. For the last part, to not forget, whoever denies this should go to the scientists and ask them. They speak very clearly. The scientists are precise. The other day, when the news of that Russian boat came out, I believe, that went from Norway to Japan or Taipei by way of the North Pole without an icebreaker and the photographs showed pieces of ice. To the North Pole, you could go. It's very, very clear. When that news came from a university, I don't remember from where, another came out that said, "We only have three years to turn back, otherwise the consequences will be terrible." I don't know if three years is true or not, but if we don't turn back we're going down, that's true. Climate change, you see the effects and scientists say clearly which is the path to follow. And all of us have a responsibility, all . . . everyone . . . a little one, a big one, a moral responsibility, and to accept from the opinion or make decisions, and we have to take it seriously. I think it's something that's not to joke around with. It's very serious. And you ask me: what is the moral responsibility. Everyone has his. Politicians have their own. Everyone has their own according to the response he gives.

   I would say: everyone has their own moral responsibility, first. Second, if one is a bit doubtful that this is not so true, let them ask the scientists. They are very clear.

They are not opinions on the air, they are very clear. And then let them decide, and history will judge their decisions. Thanks.[33]

Pope Francis did not "blast" critics of man-made global warming. He indicated his own belief in the phenomenon and remarked that everyone has a moral responsibility, but he spoke respectfully of those who doubt humans cause it, referred them to scientists, and said that history will judge "their decisions"— i.e., determine whether they were correct—not judge or condemn "them."

239. An even more egregious example involves not just a misrepresentation of the pope's tone but his meaning. A 2015 story by Catholic news agency ZENIT carried the headline, "Pope to U.S. Christian Unity Event: Jesus Knows All Christians Are One, Doesn't Care What Type."[34] It stated:

> Francis pointed out that Jesus knows that Christians are disciples of Christ, and that they are one and brothers.
>   "He doesn't care if they are Evangelicals, or Orthodox, Lutherans, Catholics or Apostolic . . . he doesn't care!" Francis said. "They are Christians."

When one checks the transcript of the original message, it turns out Francis didn't say *Jesus* does not care what kind of Christian you are. He said *the devil* doesn't care:

> Division is the work of the father of lies, the father of discord, who does everything possible to keep us divided. . . . It is he who is persecuting us. It is he who is persecuting Christians today, he who is anointing us with (the blood of) martyrdom. He knows that Christians are disciples of Christ: that they are one, that they are brothers! He doesn't care if they are Evangelicals, or Orthodox, Lutherans, Catholics or Apostolic . . . he doesn't care! They are

Christians (Video Message on the Occasion of the Day of Christian Unity, May 23, 2015).

240. Shortly before his resignation in 2013, Pope Benedict XVI spoke with the clergy of Rome and commented on how the media distorted what happened at Vatican II. He recalled how journalists created a false image of the council, which he termed a "council of the media," and how it had disastrous consequences:

> We know that this council of the media was accessible to everyone. Therefore, this was the dominant one, the more effective one, and it created so many disasters, so many problems, so much suffering: seminaries closed, convents closed, banal liturgy . . . and the real council had difficulty establishing itself and taking shape; the virtual council was stronger than the real council. But the real force of the council was present and, slowly but surely, established itself more and more and became the true force which is also the true reform, the true renewal of the Church (Meeting with Parish Priests and the Clergy of Rome, February 14, 2013).

241. These examples illustrate how secondhand accounts can distort and misrepresent the facts, and they underscore the need to consult the original documents. This must be our constant practice, particularly when we encounter a claim about the Church that seems strange or shocking.

Key Concepts: Authorial Intent, Exegesis, Eisegesis, and Hermeneutics

242. When scholars study texts, they discuss important concepts like authorial intent, exegesis, eisegesis, and hermeneutics.

Authorial intent refers to what an author meant to communicate. Determining this is the goal of interpreting a document. If we are reading a Church document our task is to establish what the author—a bishop, a pope, or a council—wanted to communicate.

243. To achieve this goal, we employ *exegesis*, a Greek word that means explanation or interpretation (from the roots *hegeisthai*, "guide," and *ek*, "out"). The goal of exegesis is to guide the meaning out of a text so we understand it.

244. What we want to avoid is *eisegesis* or reading an unintended meaning *into* a text (Greek, *eis*, "into"). This is a real danger. People frequently read false meanings into the words of others, often unintentionally, and history shows this can easily happen with statements made by Church leaders.

245. The process by which one arrives at an interpretation is *hermeneutics* (Greek, *hermēneutēs*, "interpreter"), and an individual principle you use when interpreting is a *hermeneutic*. In recent years Benedict XVI spoke of how Vatican II should be interpreted using a "hermeneutic of renewal in continuity" rather than a "hermeneutic of discontinuity" (see §§288, 295).

The Process of Interpretation

The Authoritative Version of a Text

246. Church documents appear in many editions and translations, but the official version is known as the *editio typica* or "typical edition." Its function is to serve as the ultimate reference point for questions about a document. Regardless of what other editions and translations may say, the wording of the *editio typica* is the official, authoritative wording, and it is used to make translations into other languages.

The *editio typica* is often found in *Acta Apostolicae Sedis*, and it is often in Latin, though not always. Pope Pius XI's encyclical *Mit Brennender Sorge* (1937) was famously written in German to express the pope's horror at what was happening in Nazi Germany.

Frequently, a document will be written in a modern language and then translated into Latin to produce the *editio typica*, as with the *Catechism of the Catholic Church* (see §225).

247. The *editio typica* may differ from earlier editions. If a pope gives a speech and has a slip of the tongue, the version in *Acta Apostolicae Sedis* will correct this. Similarly, when the *Catechism* was released in Latin, a number of adjustments were made in the text. Originally, paragraph 2358 stated that people who suffer from same-sex attraction "do not choose their homosexual condition; for most of them it is a trial," but there was a concern this could be misunderstood, and it was revised to read, "This inclination, which is objectively disordered, constitutes for most of them a trial."

The typical edition can be revised with time, as with the *Roman missal* released by Pope Paul VI:

- In 1970, the first typical edition of the Missal was published.
- In 1971, an "amended typical edition" was produced.
- In 1975, a "second typical edition" that made more substantial changes came out.
- In 2002, Pope John Paul II issued the "third typical edition," which became the basis for the current rite used at Mass.
- In 2008, Benedict XVI released an "amended third typical edition," which corrected typos and made minor updates.

248. The *editio typica* can be difficult to access since it is normally used only by scholars. Books and journals printing it tend to have low print runs, and they are consequently expensive. Fortunately, the internet is changing this. *Acta Apostolicae Sedis* is now published in pdf form on the Vatican web page (vatican. va), and the site contains the original language versions of many documents in Latin.

Types of Translation

249. We are fortunate to live in an age when translations of Church documents are widely available. However, there are issues the interpreter needs to be aware of. One is translation style. Languages do not map onto each other in a word-for-word fashion, and translators have to make choices when doing their work. For example, if you translate Matthew's version of the Lord's Prayer from the original Greek in a strictly word-for-word fashion, it would read something like this:

> Father our, that in the heavens,
> let-be-sanctified the name your,
> let-come the kingdom your,
> let-happen the will your, as in heaven also on earth.
> The bread our, the daily, give us today,
> and remit us the debts our, as also we remit-to the debtors our,
> and not lead us into temptation, but deliver us from the evil
> (Matt. 6:9–13).

This is not good English, and reading this kind of translation for page after page would be frustrating and confusing. Consequently, to produce readable texts, translators have to accommodate what the original language says to the way the target language works.

250. Generally, they do this in one of two ways, producing different styles of translations. The first of these seeks to preserve as much of the form and wording of the original as possible. These "formal equivalence" translations are sometimes called "literal" translations, but that is misleading, for no translation is fully literal.

The second style places less emphasis on details of the original wording and seeks to communicate its meaning in a way that feels natural. These "dynamic equivalence" translations are sometimes called "free" translations or even "paraphrases."

All translations fall on a spectrum between formal and dynamic equivalence. Both styles have their advantages and disadvantages. Formal translations can be confusing and hard to read, but they capture more aspects of the original wording. Dynamic translations are easier to read, but they lose more aspects of the original and are more vulnerable to translator bias.

251. We see different translation styles in the Bible itself. In first-century Palestine, it was common in Aramaic to speak about sin as going into debt, and since Matthew's Gospel was written primarily for Jewish Christians, it uses a formal equivalence translation in Greek: "forgive us our *debts*" (Matt. 6:12). Luke's Gospel was written for a predominantly Gentile audience, so it uses a dynamic translation: "forgive us our *sins*" (Luke 11:4).

252. Today Church documents are translated by many different people, and they don't all use the same translation strategy. Consequently, you have to be sensitive to what kind of translation you are reading. If it is a dynamic translation, you should be particularly alert to the fact that the translator is making a lot of choices about how to put statements into smooth-flowing English, and with each choice, there is the possibility of losing or misrepresenting something from the original.

Ambiguity in the Original

253. Words and phrases can mean more than one thing. "The kitty is on the table" means one thing in a veterinarian's office and another in a poker game. When a translator encounters ambiguity in a text, he may get lucky and find a way to preserve it in translation, but often he must make a choice that collapses the ambiguity.

If we translate the final line of the Lord's Prayer word for word, Jesus says we should ask God to "deliver us from the evil." Because of how Greek works, "the evil" is ambiguous. It can refer either to evil in general or it can refer to something specific: the evil *one* (i.e., the devil). Standard English doesn't have a way of preserving that ambiguity, so translators collapse the ambiguity in favor of one meaning or another. Some choose "deliver us from evil" (Revised Standard Version), and others choose "keep us safe from the Evil One" (Good News Translation).

254. Sometimes a translator encounters a word or phrase that is so difficult that he is baffled, yet he must find *some* way to translate it.

Misleading or Mistaken Translations

259. Translators are fallible human beings, and they sometimes make mistakes. These have to be identified and handled on a case-by-case basis, and correcting them requires consulting the original language. However, you need to be aware that they do happen, even when the translator is skilled and has the best of intentions.

260. Sometimes errors are very small and simply amount to typos. Since Church documents need to be translated quickly, mistakes in spelling and punctuation often appear in the Vatican news service and on the Vatican website.

Sometimes this happens in carefully prepared translations. A few years ago I discovered a typo in the English version of the *Catechism of the Catholic Church*. Paragraph 345 describes the Sabbath as "the end of the work of the six days." In Latin there are quotation marks around "six days," which is significant because they signal the reader that the days are understood symbolically rather than literally, as in other paragraphs (cf. 337, 339, 342).

261. Sometimes a translation will be flatly erroneous. Tim Staples discovered an example in paragraph 460 of the *Catechism*. He writes:

> Where the English translation says, quoting St. Athanasius of Alexandria in the fourth century, "For the son of God became man so that we might become God," the official Latin text actually reads, *"Ipse siquidem homo factus est, ut nos dii efficeremur."* Literal translation: "For the Son of God became man so that we might be made gods." The Latin term *dii*, translated "God" in the English translation of the *Catechism*, is actually nominative plural and is *not* capitalized. Unfortunately, the English translation of the official Latin text gets it wrong. "God" should be "gods."[38]

This is significant because to be made God could mean becoming part of the Godhead, alongside the Father, the Son, and the Holy Spirit. That understanding would be heretical (and metaphysically impossible, since God is immutable and can't change). However, to become "gods" only means to share in God's communicable attributes, such as holiness, and thus "become partakers of the divine nature" (2 Pet. 1:4).

Deceptive Translations

262. Unfortunately, translators sometimes produce misleading or inaccurate translations in the service of an agenda. These aren't the norm, and one shouldn't jump to the conclusion that a translator is acting in bad faith, but they do happen.

An example occurs in many English translations of liturgical texts from the 1980s and 1990s. Following Vatican II, the Holy See allowed greater use of laity to distribute Communion when the number of available priests and deacons was insufficient. In canon law, "the ordinary minister of Holy Communion is a bishop, presbyter, or deacon" (CIC 910 §1), and anyone else is termed an "extraordinary minister of Holy Communion" (cf. CIC 910 §2).

However, an ideology grew in some liturgical circles wishing to blur the distinction between clergy and laity by having as many lay people as possible performing ministerial roles. To facilitate that, some translators began deliberately and systematically mistranslating "extraordinary minister of Holy Communion" (Latin, *minister extraordinarius sacrae communionis*) with terms that masked the extraordinary character of this role—e.g., "special minister." Of course, Latin has a word that means special (*specialis*), but it isn't used in the relevant passages.

These mistranslations grew so widespread that the Holy See demanded they be stopped. In 2004, the Congregation for Divine Worship stated:

> This function is to be understood strictly according to the name by which it is known, that is to say, that of extraordinary minister of Holy Communion, and not "special minister of Holy Communion" nor "extraordinary minister of

the Eucharist" nor "special minister of the Eucharist," by which names the meaning of this function is unnecessarily and improperly broadened (*Redemptionis Sacramentum,* 156).

Technical Meanings of Terms

263. The starting point for understanding Church texts is making sure one understands the words they use. This is not as simple as it might appear. Theology, canon law, liturgy, and biblical studies all use "terms of art"—that is, terms with technical meanings known to professionals working in the field.

Examples include *heresy, apostasy,* and *schism.* In popular speech, *heresy* is often used loosely to mean something like "false religious belief" or "really bad false religious belief," *apostasy* is used to mean the same thing as *heresy,* and *schism* is used for some kind of religious division. However, in Church documents these terms have technical meanings:

Heresy is the obstinate denial or obstinate doubt after the reception of baptism of some truth which is to be believed by divine and catholic faith; apostasy is the total repudiation of the Christian faith; schism is the refusal of submission to the supreme pontiff or of communion with the members of the Church subject to him (CIC 751, CCC 2089).

Each element in these definitions is important.

264. For *heresy* to occur:

1. A truth "which is to be believed by divine and catholic faith" must be involved. This is another way of saying a dogma (i.e., something the Church has infallibly defined to be divinely revealed; see §§271, 343). If anything less than a dogma is involved—even if it's an infallible teaching—then heresy does not exist.
2. A person must deny or doubt this truth, meaning either reject it outright or at least refuse to make a judgment about

it. (Having emotional "doubts" or lacking emotional confidence is not enough; doubt in this case means suspending
one's judgment as an act of the will.)
3. The person must be baptized. Thus Muslims, Jews, and
   other non-baptized people are not heretics.
4. The person must be obstinate. A baptized person who is
   innocently unaware that they are rejecting a dogma is not
   committing heresy.

The last requirement—which has been part of the Church's
understanding for a long time (cf. *Code of Canon Law* [1917]
1325 §2)—has an important implication. Although Protestants
have been baptized and do doubt or deny Catholic dogmas, they
typically do not do so out of bad faith (Latin, *mala fide*) and thus
don't meet the requirement of obstinacy.

Vatican II remarked: "The children who are born into
these communities and who grow up believing in Christ cannot be accused of the sin involved in the separation, and the
Catholic Church embraces upon them as brothers, with respect and affection" (*Unitatis Redintegratio,* 3). The Secretariat
for Promoting Christian Unity then indicated people raised
Protestant didn't need to make a formal abjuration of heresy
upon becoming Catholic (*Ecumenical Directory* [1967], 19–20).
Thus today Church documents refer to Protestants as "separated brethren" rather than heretics because they're not presumed to be in bad faith.

However, sometimes a distinction is drawn between "formal
heresy" and "material heresy." The former refers to the kind of
heresy defined above, in which a baptized person obstinately
refuses to embrace a dogma. "Material heresy" exists when
the person is not obstinate. Though rare, this usage is found in
Church documents (cf. Pontifical Council for Legislative Texts,
Actus Formalis Defectionis ab Ecclesia Catholica, 2006). On this
understanding, Protestants could be termed "material heretics,"
though, as a way of promoting Christian reconciliation, this
phrase is not used in contemporary Church documents.

265. The term *apostasy* must be used carefully. It refers to rejecting the Christian faith outright. If a person maintains any kind
of claim to being a Christian, he is not an apostate. He must be
willing to say, "I am not a Christian anymore."

266. Finally, *schism* has a technical meaning. It involves one of
two things: (1) refusing to submit to the pope or (2) refusing to
be in communion with those subject to him.

Whether one of these conditions exists is sometimes disputed.
The bishops of the Society of St. Pius X maintain they have
always submitted to the pope, but in 1988, John Paul II ruled
that by being consecrated as bishops *against* his instructions they
had committed a schismatic act since "*disobedience* to the Roman
pontiff in a very grave matter and of supreme importance for
the unity of the church . . . implies in practice the rejection of
the Roman primacy" (*Ecclesia Dei, 4*). He thus determined that
professing to submit was not enough if one refused to submit in
practice on a grave matter. (Note: Subsequent actions by Popes
Benedict XVI and Francis may indicate that the Society is no
longer in a state of formal schism.)

Unexpected Meanings

267. Sometimes the Church uses terms in ways quite different
from the common understanding. An example is *authentic*. In
ordinary speech, this means "genuine," as opposed to fake or
fraudulent, but in Church documents it often means something
else. The U.S. bishops' Committee on Doctrine explains:

> "Authentic" in the phrase "authentic magisterium" is
> a transliteration from the Latin and means "authorita-
> tive" (*The Teaching Ministry of the Diocesan Bishop*, note 1).

The same usage can appear in other phrases, such as
"authentic document" and "authentic teaching," which then
respectively mean "authoritative document" and "authoritative
teaching."

268. A term with a similarly unexpected meaning is *dissent*. In 1990 the Congregation for the Doctrine of the Faith defined dissent as "public opposition to the Magisterium of the Church" (*Donum Veritatis,* 32), and two years later, the U.S. bishops' Committee on Doctrine noted:

> [*Donum Veritatis*] restricts the meaning of the word *dissent* to "public opposition to the Magisterium of the Church, which must be distinguished from the situation of personal difficulties" (DV 32). This should be noted because in American usage the term *dissent* is used more broadly to include even the private expression of rejection of reformable magisterial teaching (*The Teaching Ministry of the Diocesan Bishop,* 18).

A person who privately rejects a Church teaching that is "reformable" (not infallible) is not a dissenter in the way Rome uses this term. He only becomes a dissenter if he publicly opposes the teaching (see chapter twenty). The development of the internet creates new questions regarding what constitutes private or public opposition. Some discussions (e.g., among a small group of people by email or a small group of "friends" on social media) would clearly be private, but other discussions (e.g., messages addressed to the public at large) would not.

Changes in Meaning Over Time

269. Language changes over time, so you have to ensure that you understand the way terms were used at the time a Church document was written. Here we will examine three terms—*heresy, dogma,* and *sacrament*—that have changed meaning over the centuries and illustrate the need to know the history of words when reading Church documents.

"Heresy"

270. This term did not always have the meaning it does today. Originally, the Greek term from which it is taken, *hairesis,* meant "opinion" or "choice," and it was used neutrally to refer to any distinctive group (Acts 26:5), such as Sadducees, Pharisees, and Christians (Acts 5:17, 15:5, 24:5). However, it also could indicate factionalism (Acts 24:14; 1 Cor. 11:19; Gal. 5:20; 2 Pet. 2:1) and thus signify what we would call a sect or schism.

Sects are known for having distinctive beliefs, and this meaning came to the fore. The early Church Fathers thus began to use *heresy* to refer to deviations in doctrine within the Christian community, at which point the term ceased to apply to non-Christian groups.

By the Middle Ages, it had come to refer to a specific kind of doctrinal deviation: the denial of a dogma. St. Thomas Aquinas defined heresy as "a species of unbelief, belonging to those who profess the Christian faith, but corrupt its dogmas" (ST II–II:11:1). This is close to the modern definition discussed in §264. However, it introduces a parallel term, *dogma*, which we will consider next.

In view of these uses, one must be careful when interpreting the word *heresy* in older Church documents, for they do not use it in its modern, technical sense (see §498).

"Dogma"

271. In the first century, the Greek term *dogma* meant "edict," "ordinance," or "decree." It is used in the New Testament for the decree of Caesar Augustus at the time of Jesus' birth (Luke 2:1) and decrees of later caesars (Acts 17:7). It's also used for the legal requirements of the Mosaic Law (Eph. 2:15, Col. 2:14) and the decisions reached at the Council of Jerusalem (Acts 16:4).

Outside the New Testament, *dogma* also meant "opinion," "belief," or "that which seems right," based on its root *dokein* ("to seem"). The Church Fathers began using *dogma* to refer to the teachings of Christ, but they also used it for other teachings, including "the false doctrines of philosophers or heretics, or Catholic doctrine."[39] It was thus a general term for "teaching" or "doctrine." Gradually, it came to mean a specific class of Christian doctrines:

Dogma in the sense in which the term is used nowadays in the Church and in theology (a usage which only became definite and universal in the eighteenth century) is a proposition which is the object of *fides divina et catholica* ["divine and catholic faith"], in other words, one which the Church explicitly propounds as revealed by God, in such a way that its denial is condemned by the Church as heresy and anathematized.[40]

Key to understanding this usage is the phrase "divine and catholic faith" The *New Commentary on the Code of Canon Law* comments:

The faith is called "divine" because it responds to God's self-revelation, and "catholic" because it is proposed by the Church as divinely revealed.[41]

A dogma is thus a truth that the Church has infallibly proclaimed to be divinely revealed. The fact that this usage only became widespread in the eighteenth century means that for much of Church history it was used in a looser sense, and this must be taken into account when reading older documents. In many, *dogma* will mean the same thing as doctrine (see §496).

This explains an otherwise puzzling fact: the field of dogmatic theology or "dogmatics" doesn't just involve study of dogmas but of all Church teaching. Cardinal Gerhard Muller states:

Though the name of this discipline (roughly since the eighteenth century) has been taken from the individual dogmas, dogmatics is not restricted to the dogmas in the formal sense: to certain doctrinal principles accepted in Catholic belief on divine authority due to a council or papal definition (e.g., the belief in Christ in the Nicene Creed or the dogma of the corporeal assumption of Mary in God's glory).

Dogma means here the whole of Christian belief in terms of the creed and practice of the Church.[42]

"Sacrament"

272. The Greek word for sacrament is *mustērion*. It originally meant "mystery," "secret," or "secret rite," and it is used in the New Testament to refer to "the secrets of the kingdom of God" (Matt. 13:11) and to the "mysteries of God" in general (1 Cor. 4:1), etc. The use of *mustērion* to refer to a secret or sacred rite is not found in the New Testament but begins to appear in the Church Fathers, who translated *mustērion* with the Latin word *sacramentum*.

In itself *sacramentum* had the sense of something sacred. In secular Latin it commonly denoted a deposit, and very frequently it stood for an oath, particularly the military pledge of allegiance. In the latter sense the early Church used it sometimes for the creed and associated it with baptism. The word also found a wider ecclesiastical use for signs of sacred things, whether in the more general sense of any earthly sign with a heavenly meaning or in the more specific sense of divinely given covenant signs, i.e., circumcision and the Passover in the Old Testament and baptism and the Lord's Supper in the New Testament.[43]

Because of the term's range of meanings, numerous Christian rites were called sacraments. Thus St. Augustine speaks of "the sacrament of the Lord's Prayer" (*Sermon* 228:3) and to "the sacrament of salt" administered to catechumens (*On the Catechizing of the Uninstructed* 26[50], *On the Merits and Forgiveness of Sins* 2:25[42]).

From the end of the tenth century to the time of Peter Lombard (d. 1164), we find a long list of *sacramenta* in vogue. Peter Damian (*Serm.* 69) says there are "twelve *sacramenta* in the Church." Hugo of St. Victor ("*De Sacr.*" ix. 7) counts (α) two necessary *sacramenta*—viz. Baptism and the Eucharist; (β) *sacramenta* useful for sanctification—*e.g.* sprinkling with holy water, blessed ashes, &c., &c.; (γ) those which prepare us for other sacred rites—*e.g.* ordination, &c. St. Bernard (*Serm.* "*In Coena Domini*") tells his hearers there

are many *sacramenta*, but he will only speak then of three—
viz. Baptism, Eucharist, and the washing of feet.[44]

However, a new era began when Peter Lombard introduced
his definition of the term:

> In the twelfth century Peter Lombard (d. 1164), known as the
> Master of the *Sentences*, author of the manual of systematized
> theology, gave an accurate definition of a sacrament of the
> New Law: a sacrament is in such a manner an outward sign of
> inward grace that it bears its image (i.e., signifies or represents
> it) and is its cause . . . (*IV Sent.*, d.I, n.2). This definition was
> adopted and perfected by the medieval Scholastics.[45]

This led to the definition found in the *Catechism of the Catholic
Church*:

> The sacraments are efficacious signs of grace, instituted by
> Christ and entrusted to the Church, by which divine life is
> dispensed to us (1131).

Using his definition, Lombard identified the seven sacraments
we refer to by that name today. Rites instituted by Church authority were then classified not as sacraments but as sacramentals:

> Sacramentals are sacred signs instituted by the Church.
> They prepare men to receive the fruit of the sacraments
> and sanctify different circumstances of life (CCC 1677).

Even today, the term *sacrament* is used in other senses, as when
the Church is referred to analogically as "the universal sacrament of salvation" (CCC 774–776, 780).

Personal Uses

273. Everyone speaks and writes in his own, individual way—
what linguists call his *idiolect* (from Greek *idios*, "one's own,

personal" and *dialect*). The Magisterium generally uses language in a carefully crafted and cautious way, in keeping with established usage, so it will be understood by bishops, priests, and theologians the world over.

However, each bishop and pope has his own idiolect. John Paul II could compose very dense prose that was difficult to understand (see, e.g., *Veritatis Splendor*). By contrast, Benedict XVI is recognized as a much clearer writer (see, e.g., *Jesus of Nazareth*).

Popes are so influential that their idiolects can make a broad impact on theological discourse, as when John Paul II began to speak of "the theology of the body" or when Benedict XVI introduced "hermeneutic of discontinuity" and "hermeneutic of reform."

Pope Francis also uses terms in unique ways. He frequently speaks of reaching those on "the peripheries" of society and of churchmen needing to have "the smell of the sheep." He also has a special meaning when he refers to "the corrupt." Rocco Palmo comments:

"The corrupt" are a frequent and uniquely loaded target in Francis's arsenal of criticism—a category of people who are essentially beyond redemption, having lost their sense of sin and thus an awareness of their need for God's mercy. Among other examples, in a 2013 homily, the pope put it bluntly, citing St. John: "The corrupt are the Antichrist."[46]

Pope Francis's idiolect is so distinctive that in 2018 the CDF issued a letter (*Placuit Deo*) to explain the way he uses the terms *Pelagianism* and *Gnosticism*, in preparation for the release of his apostolic exhortation *Gaudete et Exsultate*, which heavily used both terms.

It is therefore important to pay attention not only to the way terms are used in general but to the specific ways they are used by individuals.

Learning the Meanings

274. We've looked at the unexpected ways words can be used in Church documents, but how are you supposed to learn all those meanings? There is no single answer. If you're lucky, the document you're reading will contain a definition. Thus the *Code of Canon Law* gives precise legal definitions for terms like "minor" and "infant":

§1. A person who has completed the eighteenth year of age has reached majority; below this age, a person is a minor.

§2. A minor before the completion of the seventh year is called an infant and is considered not responsible for oneself *(non sui compos)*. With the completion of the seventh year, however, a minor is presumed to have the use of reason (can. 97).

Sometimes you have to read carefully to notice a definition. When *Donum Veritatis* defines dissent, it does so in a backward way that introduces the term only at the end of what it was being used to describe. It also offered the definition in the middle of a sentence rather than devoting a whole sentence to it, stating:

In particular, he [Pope Paul VI] addresses here that public opposition to the Magisterium of the Church also called "dissent," which must be distinguished from the situation of personal difficulties treated above.

It would be very easy to miss the definition, but the trailing phrase "also called 'dissent'" gives you the needed clue.

275. Much of the time documents don't define terms, in which case you must consult other resources. It's preferable to consult official documents, and the *Code of Canon Law* and the *Catechism of the Catholic Church* are particularly useful as both contain many definitions. At times the *Catechism* offers an embarrassment of riches, piling up multiple ways of defining a single concept. In other cases, definitions can be found by consulting major documents on the topic or looking in the pope's weekly catecheses.

276. When it isn't possible to find a definition in an official document, you should consult scholarly non-magisterial ones. There are numerous dictionaries, lexicons, and encyclopedias dealing with theology, biblical studies, liturgy, and canon law. Commentaries can also be very useful. Thus commentaries on the *Code of Canon Law* can clarify the meaning of terms not defined in the *Code* itself. Histories and scholarly papers are also potential resources. Finally, if you can't find a written resource that gives you a definition, you can contact an expert in the field.

In dealing with any of these non-official sources, be aware you'll be getting a non-official definition. It may be based on expertise, but it may not fully correspond to the way the term is used in the document you're examining.

CHAPTER 11

Key Principles of Interpretation

Exploring the Possibilities

277. There is much more to correctly interpreting a document than understanding the terms and knowing the rules of grammar. Because of the natural ambiguity of language, additional rules of exegesis need to be employed.

The first step is becoming aware of the ambiguity a text has. You can't eliminate possible meanings until you know what the possibilities are. Don't stop with the first meaning that occurs to you. It may not be correct. The careful way magisterial documents are written demands careful reading. If one simply goes with one's first impression, it is easy to miss something important.

Ask yourself all of the things a statement *could* mean. If there are many, make a list. Then go back through them and determine how likely or unlikely each is, based on other things you know, such as what is said in surrounding passages. Based on this, you are likely to find that a text *must mean* at least certain things, that it *could mean* other things, and that it *could not mean* further things.

278. It may not be possible to eliminate all ambiguity. The text may not contain enough information, and it may be deliberately open to more than one meaning. This happens because the Faith is rich and multilayered. The human mind can't grasp everything God has revealed. The authors of Scripture therefore

made deliberately ambiguous statements, such as using symbols
that have more than one fulfillment (cf. Rev. 17:3, 9–10). The
Magisterium also uses ambiguity to keep from oversimplifying
divine revelation, to keep options open for further doctrinal
development, and to protect legitimate diversity of opinion in
the Church.

279. This happens in the writings of popes and at every council.
When one meets, it brings together bishops with many points
of view. As they draft documents, the council fathers must find
ways to express the central points they want to make but that
don't close off legitimate viewpoints.

At Trent (1545–1563), ways needed to be found for the council
to reject erroneous Protestant ideas about justification without
closing off views held by Thomists, Scotists, etc. This led to the
council's *Decree on Justification* using partly ambiguous language
to preserve liberty of opinion among the Catholic schools. Hubert Jedin observes:

> [The *Decree on Justification*] is more than a compromise be-
> tween the great theological schools: it is clear and precise
> when treating of the essence of justification, ambiguous
> and obscure from sheer caution when dealing with partic-
> ular details, that is, the divergent opinions of the schools.[47]

The final version of the decree thus rejected Protestant errors
while allowing the legitimate Catholic schools to continue to
hold their own points of view. The takeaway for us is that, although we should eliminate meanings a text could *not* intend, we
should not minimize actual ambiguity or pretend it doesn't exist.

The Historical Context

280. Church documents are written to accomplish particular
goals at particular moments in history. Therefore, their historical context must be taken into account. For example, St. Paul
wrote his letters to address pastoral situations in local churches,

and biblical scholars try to reconstruct these situations to shed light on the meaning of his letters.

281. It is often possible to identify the central concern that led to a magisterial intervention. The first Church council (Acts 15) was called to deal with whether Gentile Christians need to be circumcised.

The first ecumenical council—Nicaea I (325)—was called in response to Arianism, which denied the divinity of Christ. Thus the Creed of Nicaea defines the divinity of Christ. However, it only makes a brief mention of the Holy Spirit and doesn't define his divinity since that wasn't the controversy under discussion.

It was under discussion at the second ecumenical council—Constantinople I (381)—which responded to the Pneumatomachians (Greek, "those who fight against the Spirit"). They denied the Holy Spirit's divinity, so the resulting Niceno-Constantinopolitan Creed (known today as the "Nicene Creed") did define the Holy Spirit's divinity.

282. Knowing the purpose for which a magisterial document was produced tells you about the authors' intent. The general rule is that what the Magisterium says should be read in light of its central purpose, and it shouldn't be regarded as settling questions apart from that purpose, unless the contrary is clear.

Since Trent's purpose was to respond to the Protestant Reformers, we shouldn't try to use its documents to settle doctrinal discussions among legitimate schools of Catholic thought (§279). Similarly, the purpose of the *Catechism of the Catholic Church* was to restate the Faith in response to confusion after Vatican II, not to further doctrinal development. Thus, the individual points mentioned in it only have the same weight they did before it was issued (§226).

Of course, the Magisterium can address matters besides those involved in its central purpose. In addition to issuing its creed, I Nicaea issued a series of canons on disciplinary matters. But the words the council used made it obvious they were going beyond the purpose of dealing with Arianism. The general rule thus remains: magisterial documents should be understood as addressing their central purpose unless the words make it clear they are addressing something else.

The Literary Context

283. One of the most familiar exhortations in biblical studies is to read Scripture passages in context. If you read them without regard for context, they could mean all kinds of things, and this creates an opportunity for you to read your own views into Scripture so that you're doing eisegesis rather than exegesis. The same is true when reading Church documents. A single statement in isolation can be read multiple ways. What context does is close off some of those possibilities so you can understand what is meant.

284. Suppose a person with no prior background in Catholic thought opened the *Catechism* at random and read this single sentence:

> Throughout the ages, there have been so-called "private" revelations, some of which have been recognized by the authority of the Church (CCC 67).

If he then closed the book and thought about what the sentence means, he might conclude the Church believes God continues to give revelations, some of which it has authoritatively recognized as being just as binding as Scripture. He might even think the Church believes God continues to disclose new mysteries. However, this is not what this sentence means, as the context makes clear. In the previous paragraph, we read:

> There will be no further revelation
> The Christian economy, therefore, since it is the new and definitive Covenant, will never pass away; and no new public revelation is to be expected before the glorious manifestation of our Lord Jesus Christ. Yet even if revelation is already complete, it has not been made completely

explicit; it remains for Christian faith gradually to grasp its full significance over the course of the centuries (CCC 66).

Continuing further in paragraph 67, we read:

They [the "private" revelations] do not belong, however, to the deposit of faith. It is not their role to improve or complete Christ's definitive revelation, but to help live more fully by it in a certain period of history. Guided by the Magisterium of the Church, the *sensus fidelium* knows how to discern and welcome in these revelations whatever constitutes an authentic call of Christ or his saints to the Church.

Christian faith cannot accept "revelations" that claim to surpass or correct the revelation of which Christ is the fulfillment, as is the case in certain non-Christian religions and also in certain recent sects which base themselves on such "revelations."

This shows how important context is: a single statement in isolation can be understood in ways that are essentially the opposite of what is being said.

285. When people speak and write, the reason they provide context is to prevent misunderstanding. If we stated our conclusions as bare, unconnected propositions, they would often be misunderstood. Thus we build up to our key sentences, unpack them, and repeat them in different words to help people understand our meaning.

286. Context can be conceived of as a series of concentric zones:

1. At the center is the *immediate context* of a statement—what is said immediately before and after it.
2. Next is the *proximate context*—what is said elsewhere in the same section or chapter.
3. Beyond that is the *documentary context*—everything said in the same document.

4. Finally, there is the *remote context*—things said in other relevant documents, especially those on the same subject or by the same author.

The first is the most important, because it's most likely to contain information bearing on the interpretation of a statement. The other contexts are progressively less likely to contain important information, but there are exceptions.

287. A helpful question to ask is, "Why is this statement made in *this* section rather than another one?" This sometimes reveals something important about the author's intention.

For example, in the *Catechism*, contraception is dealt with in the section titled "The fecundity of marriage" (CCC 2366–2372), and it only mentions contraception between a husband and a wife (CCC 2370). The subject is not dealt with in the section "Offenses against chastity," which deals with sexual sins more broadly—e.g., masturbation, pornography, prostitution, and rape (CCC 2351–2356). This reflects the fact that *Humanae Vitae* only discusses contraception within marriage (see §261), the Church having already made it clear that all forms of sex apart from marriage are impermissible.

The Hermeneutic of Continuity

288. Pope Benedict XVI several times discussed the ways the documents of Vatican II have been interpreted. He referred to one approach as a "hermeneutic of discontinuity," stating:

> The hermeneutic of discontinuity risks ending in a split between the pre-conciliar Church and the post-conciliar Church. It asserts that the texts of the council as such do not yet express the true spirit of the council. It claims that they are the result of compromises in which, to reach unanimity, it was found necessary to keep and reconfirm many old things that are now pointless. However, the true spirit of the council is not to be found in these compromises but

instead in the impulses toward the new that are contained in the texts.

These innovations alone were supposed to represent the true spirit of the council, and starting from and in conformity with them, it would be possible to move ahead. Precisely because the texts would only imperfectly reflect the true spirit of the council and its newness, it would be necessary to go courageously beyond the texts and make room for the newness in which the council's deepest intention would be expressed, even if it were still vague.

In a word: it would be necessary not to follow the texts of the council but its spirit. In this way, obviously, a vast margin was left open for the question on how this spirit should subsequently be defined and room was consequently made for every whim (*Address to the Roman Curia*, December 22, 2005).

289. The opposite of a hermeneutic of discontinuity would be one of continuity. This would understand the council not as decisively breaking with what came before but as preserving what had been handed down from the previous generations of Christians. Thus passages in Vatican II that repeated traditional Church teaching could not be set aside as things that were included merely to get a momentary majority of votes and later be discarded. Instead, they must be regarded as part of the council's authoritative teaching.

290. The hermeneutic of continuity has implications beyond the interpretation of Vatican II. At the beginning of the Christian age, Jesus gave his apostles a message and commissioned them to preach it. It is also the job of the apostles' successors—the bishops, and thus the Magisterium—to continue to proclaim this body of revelation, the deposit of faith, until Jesus returns. There is thus to be a fundamental continuity in the teaching of the Church, and this implies a hermeneutic of continuity when we read its documents.

291. One consequence of this is a presumption that the Church's teaching in one age can be harmonized with its teaching in another age. The assumption should be that the documents do not fundamentally contradict each other, just as the books of the Bible do not. When there is an apparent contradiction, it is an invitation to read more deeply and see how the two might be harmonized. That means an initial presumption that earlier documents do not contradict later ones and vice versa.

The Hermeneutic of Reform

292. Jesus told the disciples that the Holy Spirit would "guide you into all the truth" (John 16:13). This is the dynamic that drives doctrinal development (see chapters eighteen and nineteen). Through doctrinal development, the Holy Spirit helps the Church:

- Understand and articulate its faith in a more precise way (e.g., the precise language that was crafted to express the doctrine of the Trinity)
- Make things explicit that were formerly implicit in the deposit of faith (e.g., the realization that since Christ is fully God and fully man he must have two wills, one divine and one human)
- Differentiate between what is genuinely part of the deposit of faith from what are merely customary ways of thinking and acting (e.g., the realization that being circumcised and keeping the Law of Moses is not necessary to be a Christian)

The reality of doctrinal development leads to what may be termed a "hermeneutic of reform"—that is, a recognition that, despite continuity in Church teaching, the way it is expressed develops over time in a process of continual reform.

293. In practice, this means being sensitive to changes in how the Church articulates its teaching. It isn't enough to note the points of continuity with what has been said before. One also must note the differences and accept their legitimacy. The hermeneutic of reform thus complements the hermeneutic of continuity. Without it, the latter could be applied in so wooden a way that it would keep us from recognizing doctrinal development when it takes place.

294. After Vatican II (1962–1965) the hermeneutic of continuity was applied by some traditionalists in a way that didn't recognize its legitimate developments of doctrine and practice. When discussing the doctrinal objections of the traditionalist Society of St. Pius X, Benedict XVI remarked, "The Church's teaching authority cannot be frozen in the year 1962—this must be quite clear to the Society" (*Letter Concerning the Remission of the Excommunication of the Four Bishops Consecrated by Archbishop Lefebvre,* March 10, 2009).

295. Of the two hermeneutics, the more fundamental is the principle of continuity. The deposit of faith was given to the Church at its inception, and it is the Church's task to continue to proclaim its contents until Christ returns. Doctrinal development does not provide the Church with new revelation to supplement the deposit of faith, it merely allows the Church to understand the contents of the deposit in a deeper way.

Although the hermeneutic of continuity is more fundamental, the principle of reform cannot be ignored. It is based on the teaching of Christ himself and demonstrated throughout Church history. Both are essential, and Benedict XVI once referred to the two together as a "hermeneutic of renewal in continuity" (*Address to the Roman Rota,* January 27, 2007).

The Hermeneutic of Charity

296. Fallen human nature guarantees not everyone will be pleased with everything that happens in the Church. The New Testament records difficulties the early Christians had with each other, including doctrinal conflicts (Acts 11, 15) and the problem of factions (1 Cor. 1:10–3:23).

Dissatisfaction happens in every age of the Church. After Vatican II, progressives who wanted the council to go further felt unhappy with things during the pontificates of Popes Paul VI, John Paul II, and Benedict XVI. Simultaneously, traditionalists who thought the council went too far didn't like events in the reigns of these same popes, as well as Pope Francis. Disappointments can lead to cynicism, and both some progressives and some traditionalists began adopting a fundamentally uncharitable attitude toward magisterial documents, reading them in the least favorable way and seeking to maximize differences with the Magisterium. Such attitudes are part of our fallen nature, and everyone can fall into these traps.

297. The solution is a "hermeneutic of charity." Love is the fundamental Christian ethic (Matt. 22:37–40, cf. 5:43–48). Many passages in the New Testament exhort believers to be of one mind and to live in harmony (e.g., Rom. 12:16, 15:5–6; 1 Cor. 1:10; 2 Cor. 13:11; Phil. 4:2; 1 Peter 3:8–9), and charity (love) is the greatest of the theological virtues. As St. Paul says:

> If I have prophetic powers, and understand all mysteries and all knowledge, and if I have all faith, so as to remove mountains, but have not love, I am nothing. . . . Love is patient and kind; love is not jealous or boastful; it is not arrogant or rude. Love does not insist on its own way; it is not irritable or resentful; it does not rejoice at wrong, but rejoices in the right. Love bears all things, believes all things, hopes all things, endures all things (1 Cor. 13:2, 4–7).

As Christians, we must heed the New Testament's call to charity:

> So if there is any encouragement in Christ, any incentive of love, any participation in the Spirit, any affection and sympathy, complete my joy by being of the same mind, having the same love, being in full accord and of one mind. Do nothing

from selfishness or conceit, but in humility count others better than yourselves. Let each of you look not only to his own
interests, but also to the interests of others (Phil. 2:1–4).

298. When reading Church documents we must approach them
with an attitude of charity and humility. We must not automatically assume we are correct and anything in them we don't like
must be false. The bishops teaching in union with the pope are
guided by the Holy Spirit in a way that we are not.

We must not adopt a cynical or jaded attitude and must give
Church documents a favorable interpretation—the benefit of the
doubt—whenever possible. We should see the good in them (Phil.
4:8), even if it is not expressed the way we would have said it.
We should presume the goodwill of the authors and "in humility
count others better" than ourselves (Phil. 2:3). Finally, we must
recognize that—given the global nature of the Church—not every document is framed to deal with our personal concerns. It
may be addressing the situation of others, in a far-removed part of
the world. By recognizing this, we will look not just to our interests but "also to the interests of others" (Phil. 2:4).

The Hermeneutic of Precision

299. Reading someone's work charitably means reading it with
precision—paying attention to what they say and don't say. We
aren't reading charitably if we do a sloppy, inattentive job and
end up attributing things to an author he didn't say. We've all
spoken with someone who acts like he can't be bothered to pay
attention, and it's no surprise when he tries to speed things along
by stating, "So what you're saying is *this*"—revealing in the process that he completely misunderstood us. "That's not what I'm
saying *at all*," we reply.

300. Reading magisterial documents with precision means carefully noting both what they say and what they *don't* say. We must
be especially cautious when drawing inferences from them. By
definition, inferences go beyond what a person said, and the

further away we get from the actual words a person used, the higher the chances of making a mistake.

Inferences are particularly risky in doctrine and theology because many concepts in divine revelation are at the edge of our ability to understand—e.g., the Trinity, the Incarnation, the Eucharist, and the afterlife. Drawing incautious inferences from revelation is a perennial source of error and heresy. It contains many truths that need to be kept in harmony, producing the famous Catholic "both/and"—Christ is both God and man, God is both one and three, etc. Heresies often occur when someone seizes on a truth and draws incautious inferences from it. In the early Church, the Docetists inferred that since Jesus is God, he can't be man, whereas the Ebionites did the reverse. Today Oneness Pentecostals infer that since there is one God, he can't be three Persons, and Mormons infer that since there are three divine Persons, there is more than one God.

301. Another reason we must be careful with inferences is that the Magisterium usually phrases its teachings very carefully so it doesn't prematurely close off legitimate discussion. On countless subjects there are different opinions, some of which fall into broad schools of thought (e.g., Thomism, Augustinianism, *ressourcement* theology). Ordinarily, the Magisterium avoids hindering discussion among these schools. Thus Trent declined to decide between the views of Thomists, Scotists, and others on justification (§279).

One reason for this hesitancy is that theological discussion helps drive doctrinal development. It clarifies questions and eventually informs the decisions of the Magisterium. Thus the Magisterium generally leaves theological questions open and only intervenes authoritatively when there is a significant need to do so, as in the case of a pressing theological or social need.

A key question to ask yourself is thus, "What opinions were considered legitimate at the time this document was written?" If an opinion was considered legitimate, we should assume it remained so unless the words of the document clearly indicate otherwise. The latter does happen, as when Pope Pius IX defined the Immaculate Conception in 1854. He thereby indicated that some of the Dominicans of the Thomist school, who in prior centuries had opposed the teaching, were incorrect.

302. As a check on drawing incautious inferences, we also need to ask, "What are the authors *not* saying?" This is important because we are subject to a cognitive flaw known as *confirmation bias*—the tendency to read evidence in a way that favors views we already hold. All of us like seeing our views confirmed, and studies show we have a tendency to acknowledge evidence that supports them and ignore or downplay evidence that doesn't.

303. Confirmation bias affects our religious views as much as any others, and it can skew the way we read religious documents— whether biblical, Patristic, or magisterial. People often consult such documents precisely to find confirmation—a phenomenon known as prooftexting. In principle, prooftexting is fine. Texts that do support a view can be used to prove it. However, confirmation bias leads many people to think a text supports their view when it doesn't. It's too easy for us to find a passage that says *something like* what we want and just assume that it does. This gives prooftexting a bad name, and many sources now *define* prooftexting as the misuse of passages to support a view.

304. This happens both when the thing we want confirmed is something we like and when it's something we dislike. Just as we want to see authorities we respect saying things we agree with, we also want to see people we don't respect saying things we disagree with. That confirms our bias and justifies our negative attitude toward them.

Thus anti-Catholics search Catholic writings for statements that "prove" how misinformed, heretical, or evil the Church is. The same thing occurs when Catholics read the writings of those they disagree with, even if they are fellow Catholics. Following Vatican II, individuals in the progressive and traditionalist communities have read magisterial texts in unsympathetic ways to justify their criticisms.

305. This is why the hermeneutic of charity is so important and why it leads to the hermeneutic of precision. The Golden Rule demands we read others' statements the way we want ours read: sympathetically and carefully. Consequently, magisterial documents are to be given a strict reading, not the one we would prefer.

306. This principle is so important it's found expression in canon law with respect to infallible teachings. According to the *Code*:

> No doctrine is understood as defined infallibly unless this is manifestly evident (CIC 749 §3).

Note the way this is phrased: it says no *doctrine* is to be understood as infallible unless this is clearly the case. It doesn't say merely that no *text* is to be understood as infallible. Even if you have a text that meets the requirements for infallibility (and such texts are rare), you can't say that a particular doctrine is found in that text, and thus infallible, unless it's "manifestly evident" that it is. Infallible texts must be given a strict reading. We can't stretch them to make things infallible that we want to be infallible.

The same applies in principle to every text and teaching, whether it is infallible or not. They all must be read using a hermeneutic of precision.

307. When figuring out the intention of a text's authors, we even need to ask, "What are they *avoiding* saying?"

For example, when Pope Pius XII infallibly defined the Assumption of Mary, he deliberately avoided saying that she died. It was the common opinion among theologians that she did, and he even referred to her death or "dormition" in the same document, but in making the definition he merely said that Mary "having completed the course of her earthly life, was assumed body and soul into heavenly glory" (*Munificentissimus Deus,* 44).

John Paul II noted that Pope Pius "made no pronouncement on the question of Mary's death" and that "some theologians have in fact maintained that the Blessed Virgin did not die and was immediately raised from earthly life to heavenly glory. However, this opinion was unknown until the seventeenth century, whereas a common tradition actually exists which sees Mary's death as her entry into heavenly glory" (*General Audience*, June 25, 1997).

This provides a concrete example of a pope (i.e., Pius XII) deliberately avoiding saying something, even though he himself accepts it, as a way of preserving the theological liberty of others.

Case Study: Humanae Vitae and Contraception Within Marriage

308. Paul VI's encyclical *Humanae Vitae* (1968) provides an example of why it is necessary to read magisterial documents with precision. According to a common translation, after it condemns abortion and sterilization, the text says:

> Similarly excluded is any action which either before, at the moment of, or after sexual intercourse, is specifically intended to prevent procreation—whether as an end or as a means (*Humanae Vitae* 14).[48]

The problematic phrase is "sexual intercourse," which corresponds to *coniugale commercium* in Latin. But *coniugale* does not mean "sexual." There is a different adjective for that—*sexualis*—and it is used in many Church documents, so it isn't omitted here for reasons of delicacy.

Coniugale actually means "marital" (cf. *coniugatus*, "married"; *coniugare*, "to unite in marriage"; *coniunx*, "spouse"). The two-volume *Oxford Latin Dictionary* doesn't even list "sexual" as a meaning of *coniugalis*, giving its definition as:

> coniugālis ~is, ~e *adj.* [coniunx + -ālis]
> 1 Belonging or proper to marriage, marital; (of gods) presiding over marriage.

2a Belonging to a husband or wife.
b consisting of wives.[49]

Similarly, Leo F. Stelten's *Dictionary of Ecclesiastical Latin* simply lists:

Conjugális –*is* –*e*: conjugal, marital[50]

Translated properly, *coniugale commercium* means "marital intercourse," "marital congress," or "marital exchange." This fits
with Paul VI's overarching theme in the encyclical of the regu-
lation of births in marriage—a theme that appears as early as its
first sentence:

The transmission of human life is a most serious role in
which married people [Latin, *coniuges*] collaborate freely
and responsibly with God the Creator (*Humanae Vitae* 1).

If Paul VI wanted to indicate sexual intercourse in general, all
he would have had to do was write *commercium* and the context
would indicate it was sexual intercourse (or he could have used
coitus, a common word for sex). What *coniugale* does is specify the
kind of intercourse in question.[51]

309. The reason Paul VI used this phrase is because the question under discussion was whether there were circumstances in
which married couples could responsibly use contraception. The
Church already condemned all sexual activity outside marriage,
and the question of contraception outside of marriage was not
what the encyclical set out to answer.

310. Subsequent magisterial documents have followed the same
line. As noted earlier (§287), the *Catechism* deals with contraception only in the section titled "The fecundity of marriage"
(CCC 2366–2372), and it only mentions contraception between
a husband and a wife:

The innate language that expresses the total reciprocal self-giving *of husband and wife* [*coniugium*, lit., "of the spouses"] is overlaid, through contraception, by an objectively contradictory language, namely, that of not giving oneself totally to the other (CCC 2370).

Contraception is not discussed in the section "Offenses against chastity," which deals with sexual sins more broadly—e.g., masturbation, pornography, prostitution, rape (CCC 2351–2356).

311. A common view in orthodox Catholic circles is that contraception should not be used in *any* cases, and it's natural to want to find *Humanae Vitae* or the *Catechism* confirming that. The anonymous translator's own beliefs in this regard may have caused him not to note the difference between "conjugal intercourse" and "sexual intercourse." But a precise reading of the text is important because failing to note the difference can lead to bewilderment, shock, and charges of infidelity to Catholic teaching regarding other statements and actions of the Magisterium.

312. Although the major question in Catholic circles in the 1960s was whether married couples could use contraception, the subject was discussed in other contexts. A famous example concerns a group of nuns living in a part of the Congo where rapes were common. Since the nuns were not married, could they use contraception as a defense against becoming pregnant by rape? It is often misreported that Paul VI gave the nuns permission to use contraception for these purposes, though the facts are more complex. John Allen reports:

> In December 1961, the influential Italian journal *Studi Cattolici* ("Catholic Studies") published an issue in which three Catholic moral theologians agreed that in the Congo case, contraception could be justified.
> The future Paul VI, at that stage, was still the Archbishop of Milan, and close to the currents that shaped *Studi Cattolici*. It was assumed the conclusions reflected his

thinking. That appeared to be confirmed later when Paul VI made one of the authors, Pietro Palazzini, a cardinal.

Paul became pope in 1963, and never issued any edict writing that position into law. Thus, when pressed about it some years later, a Vatican spokesman could accurately say, "I am not aware of official documents from the Holy See in this regard."

Still, the Vatican never repudiated the 1961 position, so the takeaway [for Italians] was that it remained a legitimate option.[52]

The fact Paul VI took no action in the "Congo nuns" case makes it impossible to draw any firm conclusions from it. However, cases like this may be part of why he refrained from making a broader statement in *Humanae Vitae*.

313. More certain is a position taken by the U.S. bishops in *Ethical and Religious Directives for Catholic Health Care Services* (6th ed., 2018), which states:

Compassionate and understanding care should be given to a person who is the victim of sexual assault. Health care providers should cooperate with law enforcement officials and offer the person psychological and spiritual support as well as accurate medical information. *A female who has been raped should be able to defend herself against a potential conception from the sexual assault. If, after appropriate testing, there is no evidence that conception has occurred already, she may be treated with medications that would prevent ovulation, sperm capacitation, or fertilization.* It is not permissible, however, to initiate or to recommend treatments that have as their purpose or direct effect the removal, destruction, or interference with the implantation of a fertilized ovum (dir. 36, emphasis added).

This understands contraception *in cases of rape* not as the frustration of what should be the total act of self-giving between spouses, as in the *Catechism*, but as a legitimate defense against "potential conception from the sexual assault." It thus allows Catholic health-care workers to provide certain means of contraception to rape victims, provided precautions are taken to ensure that an abortion does not result. The common view that Paul VI condemned contraception in all circumstances could lead the faithful to charge the U.S. bishops with infidelity to Catholic teaching in this document (which was prepared in consultation with the CDF), but a careful reading of *Humanae Vitae* does not preclude this view.

314. A similar situation arose in 2010, with the release of *Light of the World*, a book-length interview Benedict XVI gave to Peter Seewald. In it, Pope Benedict said the use of a condom by prostitutes infected with the AIDS virus could be "a first step in the direction of a moralization" even though condoms are "not really the way to deal with the evil of HIV infection."[53]

People holding that *Humanae Vitae* condemned contraception in all cases expressed amazement that Benedict XVI could describe the use of a condom in these situations as a step toward "moralization," seemingly implying it could lessen rather than aggravate the immorality of the situation. Responding to the controversy, the CDF issued a *Note on the Banalization of Sexuality*, which stated:

> Those involved in prostitution who are HIV-positive and who seek to diminish the risk of contagion by the use of a condom may be taking the first step in respecting the life of another—even if the evil of prostitution remains in all its gravity. This understanding is in full conformity with the moral theological Tradition of the Church.

In other words, the use of a condom in these situations would mitigate the evil of endangering the life of another but would not mitigate the evil of prostitution.

Benedict's comments are based on an ongoing discussion at the Holy See regarding the use of contraception in situations like this. John Allen reports:

> Beyond the question of prostitution, many mainstream Catholic moral theologians have also argued for the moral acceptability of condoms in the case of a married hetero-sexual couple where one partner is HIV-positive and the other is not. In that set of circumstances, theologians have argued, condoms would be acceptable since the aim is not to prevent new life, but to prevent infection.
>
> Back in 2006, Benedict asked the Pontifical Council for the Health Care [Workers] under Cardinal Javier Lozano Barragán, who has since retired, to examine precisely that question. Having polled the doctors and other health care professionals, as well as theologians, who consult with the council, Barragán presented the pope with a tentatively positive response—that in the case of couples where one partner is infected with HIV and the other is not, condoms could be justified.
>
> To date that position has not been officially codified, and some Vatican officials have said on background that they worry doing so would be seen publicly as a blanket endorsement of condoms. Yet Benedict's comments to Seewald suggest that the pope himself is at least positively inclined to such a development.[54]

The fact that Benedict asked for the question to be studied indicates he sees more potential complexities to this issue than the popular understanding of *Humanae Vitae* would suggest.

315. None of the cases we've looked at involve official, magisterial statements on the use of condoms or other means of contraception in these situations.[55] However, a careful reading of *Humanae Vitae* and the *Catechism* reveal how churchmen could take the positions they have without being unfaithful.

The Importance of Genre

316. One of the most important things to know about a document is its genre. Genres are styles of writing or literature. They obey different rules and are used for different purposes. For example, in the Old Testament we find books that are legal, historical, poetic, and prophetic, whereas the New Testament contains biographies of Jesus, a history (Acts), letters, and prophecy (Revelation). Modern documents, including magisterial ones, also belong to different genres. A papal homily does not belong to the same genre as an encyclical.

There are important differences between the genres of Church documents. If you want to know what Church teaching requires you to believe, you want to look in a teaching document like the *Catechism of the Catholic Church* or an encyclical. If you want to know what Church law requires, you want to look in a legal document like the *Code of Canon Law*. There is some overlap: the *Code* contains provisions that express Church teaching, and the *Catechism* sometimes quotes from the *Code*. However, it's the *Code* that establishes legal obligations, whereas the *Catechism* documents doctrinal obligations.

The genre of the *Catechism*—as a catechism—is important. By nature, it provides only a *basic* summary of Catholic teaching. It doesn't explore every question—even about the doctrines it covers. Consequently, if you want a deeper look at a particular teaching, you need to dig into other documents.

Introductions and Norms

317. Within a given document there are often sections that obey their own rules, establishing a subgenre. Knowing the rules these sections obey and how they differ is important.

Some documents mix doctrinal and legal sections. For example, John Paul II's motu proprio *Apostolos Suos* (2002) begins with remarks of a doctrinal and pastoral nature about episcopal conferences and then shifts to give a series of "complementary norms" that establish legal requirements. This structure is common in recent documents establishing or modifying laws.

It is also followed in Benedict XVI's motu proprio *Omnium in Mentem* (2009) and in Pope Francis's motu proprio *Mitis Iudex Dominus Iesus* (2015), both of which modified the *Code of Canon Law.*

318. The same basic structure is found in the doctrinal decrees of some councils, including Trent. These often begin with a lengthy introductory section on doctrine and conclude with a series of canons that establish the legal penalty of anathema (a kind of excommunication) for those denying specific points of doctrine. The introduction/canon distinction is particularly important because the infallible definitions are found among the canons (see §§483–488).

Subgenres in the Catechism

319. Sometimes a document explains the subgenres it uses. The *Catechism of the Catholic Church* contains a section titled "Practical Directions for Using this Catechism" (CCC 18–22), which tells us several noteworthy things, including:

- The use of smaller, non-italic type in the *Catechism* signifies material of secondary importance.

- Some of the material in these sections is of "an historical or apologetic nature" rather than a doctrinal nature, though sometimes these sections offer "supplementary doctrinal explanations."

- The "IN BRIEF" sections in small, italic type summarize "the essentials of that unit's teaching in condensed formulae," meaning that they pick out the more essential points.

Textual Notes

320. A subgenre that deserves special attention is the textual note, which includes footnotes, endnotes, and inline citations (i.e., instances where a series of biblical or other documents are briefly cited in a parenthetical remark). Textual notes generally contain one of four things:

- Citations of biblical documents
- Citations of historic Christian documents (e.g., Church Fathers, theologians)
- Citations of magisterial documents
- Explanatory or supplemental comments

321. The fact these are presented in the form of brief notes indicates their contents are of lesser importance. If they were of primary importance, they would be part of the main text. However, in determining their weight, there are two extremes to be avoided: attributing too much or too little significance to them.

322. Sometimes a citation is given to tell you where a quotation in the main text comes from. For example, paragraph 227 of the *Catechism* cites this prayer from St. Teresa of Avila:

Let nothing trouble you / Let nothing frighten you
Everything passes / God never changes
Patience / Obtains all
Whoever has God / Wants for nothing
God alone is enough

The footnote at the end of this quotation reads:

St. Teresa of Jesus, *Poesías* 30, in *The Collected Works of St. Teresa of Avila*, vol. III, tr. by K. Kavanaugh, OCD, and O. Rodriguez, OCD (Washington DC: Institute of Carmelite Studies, 1985), 386 no. 9, tr. by John Wall.

The function of this footnote is simply to document the source of the quotation. It has no other purpose.

323. However, sometimes a note will give a citation or string of citations to documents that are not quoted. In this case, the note indicates the author thought the cited passages are relevant to his topic and examining them could be valuable. But he did not think it crucial or he would have quoted the documents. Thus paragraph 19 of the *Catechism* states:

> The texts of Sacred Scripture are often not quoted word for word but are merely indicated by a reference (cf.). For a deeper understanding of such passages, the reader should refer to the scriptural texts themselves.

324. Does the fact that a Church document cites a biblical passage create a *doctrine* that the passage proves a teaching discussed in the main text?

The answer appears to be no. In the last century the Magisterium has given biblical scholars extraordinary freedom to explore the many possible meanings of Scripture. Frequently, even the main texts of Church documents (not just the notes) discuss theories proposed by these scholars without imposing them as matters of doctrine. Thus the audiences of John Paul II and Benedict XVI refer to the idea that Genesis is composed of *Yahwist* and *Elohist* sources and that Isaiah was composed by more than one prophet (e.g., "Proto-Isaiah," "Deutero-Isaiah," and "Trito-Isaiah"). Yet it isn't Church doctrine that one must accept these views (see §373). Given this, it isn't plausible to think the Magisterium intends to create a doctrine that one must interpret a biblical passage a certain way just by citing it. Something more is needed.

What *is* binding are the doctrines the passages discuss. But Scripture citations generally have an illustrative rather than doctrinal force. Just as popes may propose ideas from biblical scholarship as helpful things for their audience to consider, yet not make them doctrines, so they may propose biblical passages as helpful ones to consider in relation to a point of doctrine they are discussing.

325. The same goes for citations of historic Christian documents, such as the writings of a Church Father or theologians living in different periods. Without the use of authoritative language attributing doctrinal force to them, they generally should be considered useful illustrations.

326. What about citations of previous magisterial documents? It's certain that authors think the prior document is relevant to the subject under discussion, but the fact that it's cited without being quoted indicates it's of secondary importance.

Often citations of previous magisterial documents are given to illustrate the history of a doctrine. Consequently, they have to be understood in light of doctrinal development. It would be mistaken to hold that, just because a previous document is cited, no doctrinal development has occurred.

327. The final type of material one finds in textual notes are explanatory and supplemental comments. These can clarify a point discussed in the main text or add a new point it does not mention but that is related. As always, this material is of secondary nature, but that doesn't mean it can be ignored.

Case Study: Footnotes in *Amoris Laetitia*

328. In 2016, Pope Francis issued an apostolic exhortation titled *Amoris Laetitia*, which followed two meetings of the Synod of Bishops (in 2014 and 2015) on the subject of the family. Much of the document consisted of well-established doctrinal and pastoral reflections, but portions proved controversial because of what they said about people in irregular marital situations. These remarks are found in its footnotes.

329. First, some background: based on Jesus' teachings regarding the permanence of marriage (Mark 10:1–12; cf. Rom. 7:2–3), the Church holds that Catholics cannot simply get a civil divorce and contract a new marriage. Such unions constitute an objective state of ongoing adultery. Since adultery is gravely sinful (Exod. 20:14), the Church prohibits such Catholics from receiving the Eucharist (cf. 1 Cor. 11:27) and from being absolved in confession unless they repent and address their adulterous situation.

This can be done in a number of ways, including separating from the current, civil spouse, by obtaining an annulment for the first marriage and then having the current union convalidated, or by refraining from having sex with the current partner and living "as brother and sister." In these cases, the person can go to confession, receive the Eucharist, and lead a normal sacramental life. Thus, in his exhortation *Familiaris Consortio* (1980), John Paul II wrote:

> The Church reaffirms her practice [*consuetudo,* "custom, usage, habit"], which is based upon Sacred Scripture, of not admitting to eucharistic Communion divorced persons who have remarried. They are unable to be admitted thereto from the fact that their state and condition of life objectively contradict that union of love between Christ and the Church which is signified and effected by the Eucharist. Besides this, there is another special pastoral reason: if these people were admitted to the Eucharist, the faithful would be led into error and confusion regarding the Church's teaching about the indissolubility of marriage.
>
> Reconciliation in the sacrament of penance which would open the way to the Eucharist, can only be granted to those who, repenting of having broken the sign of the covenant and of fidelity to Christ, are sincerely ready to undertake a way of life that is no longer in contradiction to the indissolubility of marriage. This means, in practice, that when, for serious reasons, such as for example the children's upbringing, a man and a woman cannot satisfy the obligation to separate, they take on themselves the duty to live in complete continence, that is, by abstinence from the acts proper to married couples (*Familiaris Consortio,* 84).

This discipline was reaffirmed on a number of occasions, including in the *Catechism of the Catholic Church* (n. 1650), in a 1994 letter from the Congregation for the Doctrine of the Faith entitled *Annus Internationalis Familiae,* and in Benedict XVI's 2007 apostolic exhortation *Sacramentum Caritatis* (n. 29).

330. From the beginning of his pontificate, Pope Francis signaled a desire to find a way to modify this discipline to allow the sacraments to be administered to at least some divorced and civilly remarried Catholics. This was discussed at the 2014 and 2015 synods, and when the pope announced his solution in *Amoris Laetitia,* he did not go as far as many progressives wished.

The approach he described is based on the fact that, although such unions are objectively adulterous and thus gravely sinful, the persons in them may not be in a state of mortal sin. Church teaching holds:

> For a sin to be mortal, three conditions must together be met: mortal sin is sin whose object is grave matter and which is also committed with full knowledge and deliberate consent (CCC 1857).

Ongoing sexual relations in an invalid marriage provide the grave matter, but they don't mean the knowledge and deliberation conditions are met. A person could, through inadequate catechesis, lack a proper understanding of the sinfulness of these acts. Alternately, due to various psychological factors, he could lack the deliberate consent needed to make the sins mortal. Consequently, some divorced and civilly remarried Catholics who continue to have sexual relations would not be committing mortal sin, and, in Pope Francis's judgment, it could be legitimate to admit these individuals to the sacraments in some situations.

331. Cardinal Gerhard Muller—former head of the CDF and a strong defender of the Church's teaching on marriage—affirmed the fundamental orthodoxy of this line of thought, stating:

> It is evident that *Amoris Laetitia* (art. 300–305) does not teach and does not propose to believe in a binding way

that the Christian in a condition of a present and habitual mortal sin can receive absolution and Communion without repentance for their sins and without formulating the intention of not sinning any more. . . .

An accurate analysis shows that the pope in *Amoris Laetitia* has not proposed any doctrine to be believed in a binding way that is in open or implicit contradiction to the clear doctrine of the Sacred Scripture and to the dogmas defined by the Church on the sacraments of marriage, penance, and Eucharist. . . .

It is possible that the tension that occurs here between the public-objective status of the "second" marriage and subjective guilt can open, under the conditions described, the way to the sacrament of penance and Holy Communion, passing through a pastoral discernment in [the] internal forum. . . .

What is at issue is an objective situation of sin which, due to mitigating circumstances, is subjectively not imputed.[56]

332. With this as background, it is instructive to look at two footnotes. The first is appended to *Amoris Laetitia* 298, which states:

The Church acknowledges situations "where, for serious reasons, such as the children's upbringing, a man and woman cannot satisfy the obligation to separate."[329]

The footnote reads:

[329]John Paul II, apostolic exhortation *Familiaris Consortio* (22 November 1981), 84: AAS 74 (1982), 186. In such situations, many people, knowing and accepting the possibility of living "as brothers and sisters" which the Church offers them, point out that if certain expressions of intimacy are lacking, "it often happens that faithfulness is endangered and the good of the children suffers" (Second Vatican Ecumenical Council, Pastoral Constitution on the Church in the Modern World *Gaudium et Spes*, 51).

333. Some have pointed out that this footnote uses a potentially misleading translation of a key phrase from *Gaudium et Spes* ("good of the children" suggesting children's *well-being* when in fact the Latin *bonum prolis* typically refers to the good that children themselves are in marriage), which is another reminder of the need to be careful about translations and to check original language documents.

Footnote 329 also cites *Familiaris Consortio* 84—the famous passage, quoted above, where John Paul II affirmed the discipline of not allowing divorced and civilly remarried Catholics to go to confession or receive the Eucharist. This raises the question of whether an earlier magisterial document can be cited in a footnote without reaffirming everything that document said. In fact, a key purpose of *Amoris Laetitia* was to modify *something* about the Church's practice, though there is a question of what.

Some have held that John Paul II did not mention any exceptions for administering the sacraments in cases where an objectively adulterous situation did not constitute mortal sin, and therefore there were to be no exceptions. By contrast, *Amoris Laetitiae* allows their administration in some cases *if* the sin is not mortal. (see §335). On this understanding, *Amoris* modified the substance of the Church's sacramental discipline by creating exceptions that previously were not to be made.

Others have argued that for centuries the Church's moral and pastoral theology has allowed certain subjectively guiltless couples to receive the sacraments, provided the danger of scandal is avoided (cf. St. Alphonsus Liguori, *Guide for Confessors*, ch. 1), and thus that these exceptions have always existed—though that is *not* to say that they are at all common.

On this understanding, *Amoris* merely called attention to such exceptions and thus did not modify the substance of the Church's discipline. Instead, one might argue, it encouraged greater awareness of the exceptions and thus more frequent administration of the sacraments in such circumstances.

Whether *Amoris* modified the substance of the Church's discipline or merely called attention to the existence of traditionally recognized exceptions, this illustrates the need to be aware that the citation of a prior document doesn't necessarily show everything it said is still in force.

334. Some authors argued that footnote 329 lacked force because it was a footnote. Fr. Regis Scanlon commented:

> Since footnotes are not part of the text, footnote 329 is probably not the work of the pope or the Magisterium.[57]

To which canonist Edward Peters responded:

> Come again? Footnotes are *not* part of this duly published papal text? How is that, I wonder.
>
> Granted, footnotes usually supply bare references to the sources underlying the assertions made in the main body of a text and so are not typically used for making substantive assertions on their own. But does such an adjectival footnote convention mean that footnotes *cannot* make assertions if that is in fact how they read?
>
> Looking at, say, the documents of the Second Vatican Council, one sees that, while most conciliar footnotes were merely informational in nature, some did make substantive assertions of their own and a few even carried legal consequences.[58]

Peters went on to provide examples of substantive footnotes, and he is certainly correct that they can have important consequences for how a text is understood and applied. Also, the suggestion that footnote 329 might not be "the work of the pope" is immaterial. Papal documents are regularly ghostwritten and edited by others. Regardless of how the language in a papal text originates, the pope signs off on it and issues it by his own authority.

335. An even more controversial footnote was appended to *Amoris Laetitia* 305, which states:

Because of forms of conditioning and mitigating factors, it
is possible that in an objective situation of sin—which may
not be subjectively culpable, or fully such—a person can
be living in God's grace, can love and can also grow in the
life of grace and charity, while receiving the Church's help
to this end.[351]

The footnote reads:

[351]In certain cases, this can include the help of the sacraments. Hence, "I want to remind priests that the confes-
sional must not be a torture chamber, but rather an encounter with the Lord's mercy" (apostolic exhortation *Evangelii
Gaudium* [24 November 2013], 44: AAS 105 [2013], 1038).
I would also point out that the Eucharist "is not a prize for
the perfect, but a powerful medicine and nourishment for
the weak" (ibid., 47: 1039).

This was controversial because it indicates that "the Church's
help" to the divorced and civilly remarried "can include the help
of the sacraments," with confession and the Eucharist listed as
examples. It thus indicates these two sacraments can be administered "in certain cases" because of "conditioning and mitigating
factors" that make it possible for a person in "an objective situation of sin" nevertheless to "be living in God's grace" (i.e., a state
of grace). On this understanding, *Amoris Laetitia* thus does not
change Church teaching regarding the possibility of receiving
the sacraments in a state of ongoing, unrepented *mortal* sin, but
takes an approach whose fundamental orthodoxy was affirmed
by Cardinal Muller. For our purposes, it indicates how footnotes
in magisterial documents can carry important implications.

CHAPTER 12

The Spectrum of Authority

336. In this chapter, we begin looking at the levels of authority Church teachings can have and how this can be assessed.

As we saw in chapters eight and nine, some magisterial documents have more weight than others: encyclicals are more authoritative than apostolic exhortations, apostolic exhortations are more authoritative than homilies, etc. Regardless of the overall weight a document has, the weight of an individual statement in it must be individually assessed. The document type colors the authority of a statement, but even highly authoritative documents like encyclicals can contain statements that aren't even expressions of doctrine, such as this one from Pope John Paul II's encyclical *Evangelium Vitae* (1995):

> The Church's canonical discipline, from the earliest centuries, has inflicted penal sanctions on those guilty of abortion (n. 62).

This statement is historical rather than doctrinal. It isn't a *teaching* of the Church that canon law has inflicted penalties for abortion. That's a fact of history, not a fact derived from the deposit of faith Christ gave to the apostles.

This doesn't mean the statement is unrelated to doctrine. The fact that abortion is contrary to Catholic teaching explains *why* canon law has imposed penalties on it, and John Paul II wrote the sentence to illustrate the continuity of the Church's teaching on abortion as part of the justification for the following statement:

Therefore, by the authority which Christ conferred upon Peter and his successors, in communion with the bishops—who on various occasions have condemned abortion and who in the aforementioned consultation, albeit dispersed throughout the world, have shown unanimous agreement concerning this doctrine—I declare that direct abortion, that is, abortion willed as an end or as a means, always constitutes a grave moral disorder, since it is the deliberate killing of an innocent human being (ibid.).

This is a highly authoritative statement, as indicated by the invocation of his Christ-given authority as the successor of Peter and the fact he's issuing this teaching in communion with the bishops, who have "shown unanimous agreement concerning this doctrine." Although the teaching on abortion was already infallible by virtue of the ordinary magisterium, this statement is only one step away from being a new infallible definition. All it would need would be for John Paul II to have said "I declare and define" instead of "I declare" (see §§489–495).

If a single encyclical can contain non-doctrinal statements and statements one step away from being new infallible definitions, it's clear we must proceed carefully when assessing where a statement falls on the spectrum of doctrinal authority.

So how can we describe that spectrum?

Theological Notes

337. Scholastic theologians developed an unofficial way of ranking different doctrinal propositions. These ranks were called "theological notes." Cardinal Avery Dulles explains:

The recognition that not all conclusions were equally certain [was characteristic of Scholastic theology]. Each thesis had to have a theological note attached to it, indicating the degree of its certitude or probability, as the case might be. Reasons were given for the note in question: for example, the definitions of popes and councils, the clear teaching of

Scripture, theological reasoning, the general consent of the fathers or of the theologians.[59]

At the top end of the spectrum were propositions *de fide definita* ("defined as being of the faith"). These were dogmas—things that the Church had infallibly defined as revealed by God. Below this were a variety of notes, which stretched all the way down to *propositio haeretica* ("heretical proposition")—i.e., the rejection of a dogma. The spectrum of notes had two halves. The first consisted of positive notes indicating a proposition was certain, probable, etc. This was mirrored in the second half, where the notes—known as censures—indicated how problematic a proposition was.

338. A sample of the positive theological notes is given by Ludwig Ott in his book *Fundamentals of Catholic Dogma*:

1. The highest degree of certainty appertains to the immediately revealed truths. The belief due to them is based on the authority of God Revealing (*fides divina* [divine faith]), and if the Church, through its teaching, vouches for the fact that a truth is contained in revelation, one's certainty is then also based on the authority of the infallible teaching authority of the Church (*fides catholica* [catholic faith]). If truths are defined by a solemn judgment of faith (definition) of the pope or of a general council, they are "*de fide definita*" [defined as of faith].

2. Catholic truths or Church doctrines, on which the infallible teaching authority of the Church has finally decided, are to be accepted with a faith which is based on the sole authority of the Church (*fides ecclesiastica* [ecclesiastical faith]). These truths are as infallibly certain as dogmas proper.

3. A teaching proximate to faith (*sententia fidei proxima* [opinion proximate to faith]) is a doctrine, which is regarded by theologians generally as a truth of revelation, but which has not yet been finally promulgated as such by the Church.

4. A teaching pertaining to the Faith, i.e., theologically certain (*sententia ad fidem pertinens* [opinion pertaining to the faith], i.e., *theologice certa* [theologically certain]) is a doctrine, on which the teaching authority of the Church has not yet finally pronounced, but whose truth is guaranteed by its intrinsic connection with the doctrine of revelation (theological conclusions).

5. Common teaching (*sententia communis* [common opinion]) is doctrine, which in itself belongs to the field of the free opinions, but which is accepted by theologians generally.

6. Theological opinions of lesser grades of certainty are called probable, more probable, well-founded (*sententia probabilis* [probable opinion], *probabilior* [more probable], *bene fundata* [well-founded]). Those which are regarded as being in agreement with the consciousness of faith of the Church are called pious opinions (*sententia pia*). The least degree of certainty is possessed by the tolerated opinion (*opinio tolerata*), which is only weakly founded, but which is tolerated by the Church.[60]

339. By contrast, Ott describes the negative notes as follows:

The usual censures are the following: a heretical proposition (*propositio haeretica*). This signifies that the proposition is opposed to a formal dogma; a proposition proximate to heresy (*propositio heresi proxima*) which signifies that the proposition is opposed to a truth which is proximate to the Faith (*Sent. fidei proxima*); a proposition savoring of or suspect of heresy (*propositio haeresim sapiens* or *de haeresi suspecta*); an erroneous proposition (*prop. erronea*), i.e., opposed to a truth which is proposed by the Church as a truth intrinsically connected with a revealed truth (*error in fide ecclesiastica*) or opposed to the common teaching of theologians (*error theologicus*); a false proposition (*prop. falsa*), i.e., contradicting a dogmatic fact; a temerarious proposition (*prop. temeraria*), i.e., deviating without reason from the general teaching; a proposition offensive to pious ears (*prop. piarum aurium offensiva*), i.e., offensive to religious feeling; a proposition badly expressed (*prop. male sonans*), i.e., subject to misunderstanding by reason of its method of expression; a captious proposition (*prop. captiosa*), i.e., reprehensible because of its intentional ambiguity; a proposition exciting scandal (*prop. scandalosa*).[61]

340. The censures were the first to appear in Church history. They arose because of the need to warn the faithful against problematic ideas and to indicate the nature of the problem. The positive notes became popular only later.

> Post-Tridentine theologians showed a tendency to elaborate and define precisely the various notes and censures. Here the great names are M. Cano, F. Suarez, O. de Castro, J. de Lugo, and the Salmaticenses (cf. J. Cahill). Catholics engaged in controversial theology (Veronius, Holden, etc.) tried to bring out as clearly as possible the essential truths of faith in contrast to theological opinions . . . in order to confine the debate with Protestants to certain formulas, and ultimately to serve the purpose of reunion. Systematic presentations of theological notes and censures began to appear at the beginning of the seventeenth century. In 1709 Antonius Sessa (Panormitanus) listed a total of sixty-nine theological notes.[62]

Because the notes were unofficial, their number and definition varied from author to author. One of the most influential recent books dealing with them is the 1951 volume by Sixtus Cartechini, *De Valore Notarum Theologicarum et de Criteriis ad Eas Dignoscendas* ("On the Value of Theological Notes and on the Criteria by Which They Will Be Discerned").

The notes were applied by individual theologians to indicate their estimation of how a proposition should be ranked, though they are occasionally used in older magisterial documents.

341. The notes largely fell out of use after Vatican II, which turned away from the neo-Scholastic theology of the early twentieth century. Cardinal Dulles explains:

> One of the central questions at Vatican II was whether the council would reaffirm the scholastic tradition or accept a measure of philosophical pluralism. Most of the preparatory schemas of 1962 [i.e., the draft documents prepared for the bishops to consider], drawn up principally by Roman professors, were strictly scholastic in thought and expression. But when the bishops assembled they rejected many of the schemas and established new commissions to write their documents. . . .
>
> In the end, the council documents were not written in scholastic style. Care was taken, in fact, not to adopt any philosophical option. The council chose to focus on pastoral aims and to avoid hard theoretical questions.[63]

Although the council refrained from using Scholastic language, it acknowledged the legitimacy of the notes in principle. Thus *Lumen Gentium* carries an appendix because a question had arisen "regarding the precise theological note which should be attached to the doctrine that is set forth in the *Schema de Ecclesia* [i.e., *Lumen Gentium*] and is being put to a vote."[64]

At the time, theologians often wrote manuals dividing theology into individual propositions, each of which would be assigned a note. But following the council, they strove to present organic discussions of theology in prose form, like the authors in the Patristic age.

Three Levels of Teaching in the New Profession of Faith

342. Though the use of theological notes has fallen off in recent years, a need for rankings remains, and the Magisterium has begun employing a similar system.

In 1998, John Paul II issued a new profession of faith to be used when someone assumes certain offices (e.g., bishop or seminary rector). This profession consists of the Nicene Creed, followed by three concluding paragraphs, which read:

> With firm faith, I also believe everything contained in the word of God, whether written or handed down in Tradition, which the Church, either by a solemn judgment or by the ordinary and universal magisterium, sets forth to be believed as divinely revealed.
>
> I also firmly accept and hold each and everything definitively proposed by the Church regarding teaching on faith and morals.
>
> Moreover, I adhere with religious submission of will and intellect to the teachings which either the Roman pontiff or the college of bishops enunciate when they exercise their authentic magisterium, even if they do not intend to proclaim these teachings by a definitive act.

These paragraphs refer to teachings with three different levels of doctrinal authority. They were discussed in a very informative document issued by Joseph Ratzinger and Tarcisio Bertone titled the *Doctrinal Commentary on the Concluding Formula of the Professio Fidei*. Although its authors were, respectively, the head and the secretary of the CDF, it is an unofficial commentary rather than an act of the Magisterium, as it does not contain a note of papal approval (cf. §§50, 361).

Dogmas

343. The truths referred to in the first concluding paragraph are dogmas. These are truths that the magisterium has infallibly taught to be divinely revealed (see §271). The paragraph thus refers to the truths that "the Church, either by a solemn judgment or by the ordinary and universal magisterium, sets forth to be believed as divinely revealed."

Although the first paragraph doesn't make explicit that these are infallibly proposed, this is presupposed by the terms "solemn judgment" and "ordinary and universal magisterium"—

both of which are terms of art. Ratzinger and Bertone state:

> These doctrines are contained in the word of God, written
> or handed down, and defined with a solemn judgment as
> divinely revealed truths either by the Roman pontiff when
> he speaks *"ex cathedra,"* or by the college of bishops gath-
> ered in council, or *infallibly proposed* for belief by the ordi-
> nary and universal Magisterium (*Doctrinal Commentary,* 5,
> emphasis altered).

344. The fact that something is a dogma has implications for the
way it is to be received:

> These doctrines require *the assent of theological faith* by all
> members of the faithful (ibid.)

The response here referred to as "theological faith" is referred
to in other documents as "divine and catholic faith" (e.g., CIC
750 §1). Ludwig Ott explains:

> Dogma in its strict signification is the object of both divine
> faith (*fides divina*) and catholic faith (*fides catholica*); it is the
> object of the divine faith (*fides divina*) by reason of its divine
> revelation; it is the object of catholic faith (*fides catholica*) on ac-
> count of its infallible doctrinal definition by the Church. . . .
>   If, despite the fact that a truth is not proposed for belief by
> the Church, one becomes convinced that it is immediately
> revealed by God, then, according to the opinion of many
> theologians (Suarez, De Lugo), one is bound to believe it
> with divine faith (*fide divina*). However, most theologians
> teach that such a truth prior to its official proposition of the
> Church is to be accepted with theological assent (*assensus
> theologicus*) only, as the individual may be mistaken.[65]

A converging explanation is offered by the *New Commentary
on the Code of Canon Law*:

The faith is called "divine" because it responds to God's self-revelation, and "catholic" because it is proposed by the Church as divinely revealed.[66]

Other Infallible Teachings

345. A step down from dogmas are the truths referred to in the second concluding paragraph. Like dogmas, they have been infallibly taught, but the magisterium has not infallibly taught them *to be divinely revealed.*

Although the Magisterium's primary mission is to teach divine revelation, it is also able to infallibly teach certain additional things connected with divine revelation (see §§428–450). This allows it to protect revealed truths. For example, to protect a dogma the Church might need to infallibly settle whether a pope or council that defined it was a valid pope or a genuine ecumenical council. The Church also may need to define points of a more directly doctrinal nature. Ratzinger and Bertone explain:

> The object taught by this formula includes all those teachings belonging to the dogmatic or moral area, which are necessary for faithfully keeping and expounding the deposit of faith, even if they have not been proposed by the Magisterium of the Church as formally revealed. . . .
>
> The truths belonging to this second paragraph can be of various natures, thus giving different qualities to their relationship with revelation. There are truths which are necessarily connected with revelation by virtue of an *historical relationship*, while other truths evince a *logical connection* that expresses a stage in the maturation of understanding of revelation which the Church is called to undertake (*Doctrinal Commentary*, 6–7).

To be infallible, they must be defined through one of the ways that the Church exercises its infallibility:

Such doctrines can be defined solemnly by the Roman

pontiff when he speaks *"ex cathedra"* or by the college of bishops gathered in council, or they can be taught infallibly by the ordinary and universal Magisterium of the Church as a *"sententia definitive tenenda"* (Latin, "an opinion to be definitively held") (n. 6).

346. This response—definitively holding a view—is different from the theological faith that is called for by dogmas since only divine revelation calls for the response of theological faith. Truths of another nature don't. The Church thus expresses this distinction by saying that such truths must be "definitively held":

> Every believer, therefore, is required to give firm and definitive assent to these truths, based on faith in the Holy Spirit's assistance to the Church's Magisterium, and on the Catholic doctrine of the infallibility of the Magisterium in these matters (n. 6).

The *Doctrinal Commentary* later states:

> With regard to the *nature* of the assent owed to the truths set forth by the Church as divinely revealed (those of the first paragraph) or to be held definitively (those of the second paragraph), it is important to emphasize that there is no difference with respect to the full and irrevocable character of the assent which is owed to these teachings. The difference concerns the supernatural virtue of faith: in the case of truths of the first paragraph, the assent is based directly on faith in the authority of the word of God (doctrines *de fide credenda* ["to be believed concerning the Faith"]); in the case of the truths of the second paragraph, the assent is based on faith in the Holy Spirit's assistance to the Magisterium and on the Catholic doctrine of the infallibility of the Magisterium (doctrines *de fide tenenda* ["to be held concerning the Faith"]) (n. 8).

This distinction dates back more than a century. Cardinal Avery Dulles explains:

> In saying "hold" rather than "believe" the profession of faith here follows the language of Vatican I, which distinguished between *credenda* (doctrines "to be believed" in the strict sense of the word, [DH 3011]) and *tenenda* (doctrines "to be held," [DH 3074]).[67]

347. The validity of a papal election or the fact that a council was ecumenical could never be a dogma since these truths are not part of the original revelation given by Christ. However, revealed truths that have not yet been defined as such can be elevated to the rank of dogma. Ratzinger and Bertone explain:

> It cannot be excluded that at a certain point in dogmatic development, the understanding of the realities and the words of the deposit of faith can progress in the life of the Church, and the Magisterium may proclaim some of these doctrines as also dogmas of divine and catholic faith (*Doctrinal Commentary*, n. 7).

For that to happen, a new infallible definition would be needed. The original definition guaranteed the particular teaching is *true*, and a new one could guarantee it is *divinely revealed*. Therefore, one should not characterize the truths in this category as *non-revealed* infallible truths. Some may belong to divine revelation, but the Church has not yet infallibly defined that they do.

The *Doctrinal Commentary* gives papal infallibility as an example of a truth that once belonged to this category but later went on to become a dogma:

> Although its character as a divinely revealed truth was defined in the First Vatican Council, the doctrine on the infallibility and primacy of jurisdiction of the Roman pontiff was already recognized as definitive in the period before

the council. History clearly shows, therefore, that what was accepted into the consciousness of the Church was considered a true doctrine from the beginning, and was subsequently held to be definitive; however, only in the final stage—the definition of Vatican I—was it also accepted as a divinely revealed truth (n. 11).

The commentary also points to the impossibility of ordaining women to the priesthood as a truth that currently belongs to this category and that might one day become a dogma:

A similar process can be observed in the more recent teaching regarding the doctrine that priestly ordination is reserved only to men. The supreme pontiff, while not wishing to proceed to a dogmatic definition, intended to reaffirm that this doctrine is to be held definitively, since, founded on the written word of God, constantly preserved and applied in the Tradition of the Church, it has been set forth infallibly by the ordinary and universal Magisterium. As the prior example illustrates, this does not foreclose the possibility that, in the future, the consciousness of the Church might progress to the point where this teaching could be defined as a doctrine to be believed as divinely revealed (ibid.).

Other Teachings

348. The third concluding paragraph deals with non-infallible teachings of the Magisterium. They are "the teachings which either the Roman pontiff or the college of bishops enunciate when they exercise their authentic Magisterium, even if they do not intend to proclaim these teachings by a definitive act." Ratzinger and Bertone explain:

To this paragraph belong all those teachings—on faith and morals—presented as true or at least as sure, even if they have not been defined with a solemn judgment or proposed as definitive by the ordinary and universal Magisterium (n. 10).

They go on to explain:

They are set forth in order to arrive at a deeper understanding of revelation, or to recall the conformity of a
teaching with the truths of faith, or lastly to warn against
ideas incompatible with those truths or against dangerous
opinions that can lead to error (ibid.).

349. Since they are not dogmas, these teachings do not require
the response of theological faith, and since they are not infallible
and could change, they are not to be held definitively.

Such teachings are, however, an authentic expression of
the ordinary Magisterium of the Roman pontiff or of the
college of bishops and therefore require *religious submission
of will and intellect* (ibid.).

The meaning of this response was elaborated by Msgr. Fernando Ocáriz Braña in an article published in the Vatican newspaper, *L'Osservatore Romano*:

Precisely because it is "religious" assent, such assent is not
based purely on rational motives. This kind of adherence
does not take the form of an act of faith. Rather, it is an act
of obedience that is not merely disciplinary, but is well-
rooted in our confidence in the divine assistance given to
the Magisterium, and therefore "within the logic of faith
and under the impulse of obedience to the faith" (Congregation for the Doctrine of the Faith, Instruction *Donum Veritatis*, 24 May 1990, n. 23). This obedience to the
Magisterium of the Church does not limit freedom but,
on the contrary, is the source of freedom. Christ's words:
"he who hears you hears me" (Luke 10:16) are addressed
also to the successors of the apostles; and to listen to Christ
means to receive in itself the truth which will make you
free (cf. John 8:32).[68]

Theological Opinions

350. In the *Doctrinal Commentary*, Ratzinger and Bertone stated that the third concluding paragraph referred to propositions that the magisterium has "presented as true or at least as sure." Magisterial documents don't always do this. Sometimes they propose theological opinions without indicating they are true or sure. Pope Benedict XVI did so when considering the nature of the "fire" of purgatory:

> Some recent theologians are of the opinion that the fire which both burns and saves is Christ himself, the Judge and Savior. The encounter with him is the decisive act of judgment. Before his gaze all falsehood melts away. This encounter with him, as it burns us, transforms and frees us, allowing us to become truly ourselves (*Spe Salvi,* 47).

He says "some recent theologians" have thought this.[69] He doesn't say that he—by his papal authority—mandates this view or that the Church does. Consequently, he proposes an idea from theology for the reader's consideration, without imposing it as Church teaching.

When a magisterial document proposes theological ideas this way, they have the favorable recommendation of the author, and we owe them respectful and appreciative consideration, in keeping with the hermeneutic of charity (§§296–298), but they do not require the "religious submission of will and intellect" that doctrines do.

Other Non-Doctrinal Statements

351. Msgr. Ocáriz's piece in *L'Osservatore Romano* grew out of the Holy See's dialogue with the traditionalist group known as the Society of St. Pius X. The dialogue today is conducted by the Pontifical Commission *Ecclesia Dei* under the auspices of the CDF and focuses on statements by Vatican II that the Society finds objectionable. It's therefore significant that Msgr. Ocáriz observes:

Documents of the Magisterium may contain elements that are not exactly doctrinal—as is the case in the documents of the Second Vatican Council—elements whose nature is more or less circumstantial (descriptions of the state of a society, suggestions, exhortations, etc.). Such matters are received with respect and gratitude, but do not require an intellectual assent in the strictest sense.[70]

We've already seen that magisterial documents can propose theological ideas for the reader's consideration, but what about the kinds mentioned here? An example might be a statement John Paul II made in this passage discussing the death penalty:

It is clear that, for these purposes to be achieved, the nature and extent of the punishment must be carefully evaluated and decided upon, and ought not go to the extreme of executing the offender except in cases of absolute necessity: in other words, when it would not be possible otherwise to defend society. Today however, as a result of steady improvements in the organization of the penal system, such cases are very rare, if not practically non-existent (*Evangelium Vitae,* 56).

The first statement—that the death penalty should be applied only in cases of necessity—could be taken as an expression of doctrine. However, the second statement seems to be one of the "descriptions of the state of a society" that is "not exactly doctrinal" and thus as a judgment that should be "received with respect and gratitude" but that does "not require an intellectual assent in the strictest sense."

This understanding is reflected in a 2004 memorandum by Cardinal Ratzinger, who wrote:

If a Catholic were to be at odds with the Holy Father on the application of capital punishment or on the decision to wage war, he would not for that reason be considered unworthy to present himself to receive Holy Communion. . . .

There may be a legitimate diversity of opinion even among Catholics about waging war and applying the death penalty (*Worthiness to Receive Holy Communion: General Principles,* 3).

Msgr. Ocáriz's observation that the Magisterium's non-doctrinal statements "are received with respect and gratitude" is in keeping with the hermeneutic of charity (§§296–298).[71]

The Positive Side of the Spectrum

352. From what we've seen, several kinds of statements can be found in magisterial documents:

KIND OF STATEMENT	NATURE	RESPONSE CALLED FOR
1. Dogma	Infallibly defined by the Church as divinely revealed	Theological faith (i.e., divine and catholic faith)
2. Other Infallible Statement	Infallibly defined by the Church but not defined as divinely revealed	Definitive assent
3. Other Doctrine	Authoritatively taught by the Church	Religious submission of will and intellect
4. Theological Opinion	Theological view proposed for our consideration	Respectful and appreciative consideration
5. Other Non-Doctrinal Statement	Non-theological view	Respectful and appreciative consideration

The Hierarchy of Truths

353. Vatican II observed:

When comparing doctrines with one another, [theologians] should remember that in Catholic doctrine there exists a "hierarchy" of truths, since they vary in their relation to the fundamental Christian faith (*Unitatis Redintegratio,* 11).

This hierarchy of truths is related to but distinct from the spectrum of authority that Church teachings have. At the top of the hierarchy of truths are the core teachings of the Christian faith, such as the existence of God, the Trinity, and the Incarnation of Christ. Doctrines surrounding these core truths are lower in the hierarchy. Thus the Marian doctrines—her Immaculate Conception, her perpetual virginity, her status as the Mother of God, and her Assumption—are lower than the Incarnation of Christ, to which they are oriented (CCC 487).

The hierarchy of truths is related to the spectrum of authority in that the highest truths tend to be infallibly defined dogmas. If something is a central teaching of the Christian faith, it will be defined as part of divine revelation. Less authoritative teachings tend to be lower in the hierarchy of truths. However, the hierarchy of truths is distinct from the spectrum of authority because a teaching does not have to be a central truth to be a dogma or to be infallible. Even minor points of revelation can be proclaimed dogmas, and some non-revealed truths can be taught infallibly (see §§428–430, 434–450). Thus teachings lower in the hierarchy of truths can rank high on the spectrum of authority, as with the Marian dogmas. Similarly, items that are divinely revealed and that one day could be proclaimed as dogmas may not have been taught infallibly at this point.

Sometimes people ask why they should believe a truth if it's lower in the hierarchy, and the answer is because it is true. Other times people ask why a truth was defined as a dogma if it's lower in the hierarchy. The historical reasons may vary, but the ability of the Church to define such matters is not in question. If God thought a truth important enough to reveal it to mankind, it's the potential subject of a definition.

The Negative Side of the Spectrum

354. When doctrinal notes were in common use, the positive notes were often paired with corresponding negative ones. Thus, the denial of a dogma was a heresy.

Some older magisterial documents use these negative notes, or censures. Pope Pius V's bull *Exsurge Domine* (1520), which concerned the errors of Martin Luther, stated:

All and each of the above-mentioned articles or errors, as set before you, we condemn, disapprove, and entirely reject as respectively heretical or [*aut*] scandalous or [*aut*] false or [*aut*] offensive to pious ears or [*vel*] seductive of simple minds and in opposition to Catholic truth (DH 1492).

This employs six censures:

• Heretical

• Scandalous

• False

• Offensive to pious ears

• Seductive of simple minds

• Opposed to Catholic truth

These censures are not all synonyms. In fact, some of them don't even imply that an idea is false. "Offensive to pious ears" means that a proposition is offensively phrased but not that it is technically false.

Latin has more than one way of saying "or." *Aut* tends to be an exclusive "or" (this or that, but not both), whereas *vel* tends to be an inclusive "or" (this or that, maybe both). When contrasted with *vel,* the use of *aut* in *Exsurge Domine* means that *some* of Luther's claims are heretical (opposed to dogma[72]) though others are scandalous (tending to lead people to sin), others false (untrue but not opposed to dogma), and others offensive to pious ears (offensively phrased). The shift to *vel* then indicates that these ideas, and others, *are also* seductive of simple minds (tending to deceive the uneducated) and opposed to Catholic truth (in the ways indicated).

355. The Magisterium still needs to indicate when an idea is problematic and what the nature of the problem is. Ratzinger and Bertone briefly list the problems associated with denying truths belonging to the three added paragraphs. Concerning the first paragraph, which dealt with dogmas, they explain:

Whoever obstinately places them in doubt or denies them falls under the censure of heresy, as indicated by the respective canons of the Codes of Canon Law (*Doctrinal Commentary,* n. 5).

This corresponds to the modern use of the term "heresy" (see §264).
Concerning the second paragraph, which dealt with other infallible teachings, they said:

Whoever denies these truths would be in a position of rejecting a truth of Catholic doctrine and would therefore no longer be in full communion with the Catholic Church (n. 6).

A key term in this statement is "full communion." Someone who rejects an infallible teaching of the Church is not thereby put entirely out of the Church but is rather in a state of impaired communion (i.e., a form of communion which is not "full"). This concept is further explained by the fathers of Vatican II (see §§575–577), who mention charity as an element necessary for full incorporation in the Church. Applying this to truths of the second paragraph, to deny an infallible doctrine that is not a dogma impairs one's communion with the Church. If done willfully, the result can be a loss of charity and thus a mortal sin.
Concerning the third paragraph, which dealt with non-infallible teachings, they said:

A proposition contrary to these doctrines can be qualified as *erroneous* [Latin, *falsum*, literally "false"] or, in the case of teachings of the prudential order, as rash or dangerous and therefore "*tuto doceri non potest*" [Latin, "not able to be taught safely"] (n. 10).

Here a distinction is drawn between doctrines of a more theological nature and those "of the prudential order," as in the

Church's social teaching. A proposition contrary to the former would be labeled as *false*, whereas a proposition contrary to the latter could be labeled in a number of ways that correspond to the older system of censures. Ratzinger and Bertone mention a proposition could be termed "rash" (*temerarium*, reckless) or "dangerous" (*periculosum*, having the potential to cause harm), meaning it is "not able to be safely taught." Notice that the latter qualifications don't mean the idea is necessarily false but that it carries unacceptable risk.

The *Doctrinal Commentary* doesn't deal with theological opinions and other non-doctrinal statements found in magisterial documents. Since these do not require assent, there would be no censure for disagreeing with them. However, if rejected out of ill will toward the Magisterium, one could be faulted for a failure of charity and an improperly filial attitude toward the pastors of the Church.

KIND OF STATEMENT	CENSURE FOR CONTRARY PROPOSITION
1. Dogma	Heresy
2. Other Infallible Statement	Infallibly defined by "Rejecting a truth of Catholic doctrine," "no longer . . . in full communion"
3. Other Doctrine (theological nature)	False
4. Other Doctrine (prudential order)	Rash, dangerous, not able to be safely taught
5. Theological Opinion	None
6. Other Non-Doctrinal Statement	None

Conclusion

356. How can we know to which category a statement in a magisterial document is to be assigned? It can be tricky, because over the centuries the Magisterium has used different methods of signaling the weight of a teaching. Today the matter is mostly discussed by experts, and the experts do not always agree. Yet there are indicators, which we will discuss in coming chapters.

CHAPTER 13

Non-Doctrinal Statements

Reasons for Non-Doctrinal Statements

357. Magisterial documents contain a surprising number of non-doctrinal statements, and it is important to spend time surveying them to become aware of when they are made.

You might wonder why they're there in the first place. Shouldn't Church documents confine themselves to matters of doctrine? The answer is no. The bishops aren't commissioned just to be teachers but to be pastors of the faithful. They need to provide pastoral care, including helping people understand the history and reasons for Church teachings and how to implement them. They need to communicate in an effective and winning way, so Church documents need to communicate organically, not simply list propositions or offer logical demonstrations like we find in Euclid's *Elements*.

We see this in the very first Church documents: the writings of the New Testament. The Gospels and Acts contain many doctrinal statements (e.g., Jesus' teachings), but they set them in an organic, historical context. Even St. Paul—the greatest theologian among the apostles—writes in a pastoral way. He tells his readers he is praying for them, discusses his travel plans, and conveys personal greetings. It is no surprise that the documents of subsequent eras have followed the same pattern.

Identifying Non-Doctrinal Statements

358. For a statement in a Church document to be an expression of doctrine, it must meet the following criteria:

1) It must occur in a document that carries magisterial authority.
2) It must state a matter pertaining to faith or morals.
3) It must state this matter in a way that places the authority of the Church behind it and creates an obligation for the faithful to respond at least with "religious submission of will and intellect" (see §348–349).

The first condition exists because bishops and popes are capable of issuing unofficial documents, and Church bodies such as bishops conferences or Vatican dicasteries are capable of issuing documents that don't meet the criteria for exercising the Magisterium (§§33–34, 50, 147, 153–154, 188–191).

The second condition exists because the Magisterium is commissioned to announce truths known by divine revelation. It also has the ability to teach certain related matters "without which that deposit cannot be rightly preserved and expounded" (CDF, *Mysterium Ecclesiae*. 3). Though these truths are not part of the deposit of faith, they nevertheless *pertain to* it and thus pertain to faith and morals (see §§428–430). Other truths—e.g., from geometry, physics, chemistry, history—don't fall within the sphere of the Church's teaching authority.

The third condition exists because the Magisterium is capable of proposing ideas for consideration without imposing them as matters the faithful are obligated to believe (§§350–351).

359. If the first and second conditions are met, they generally entail the third. That is, if a statement pertains to faith or morals and is made in a document that carries magisterial authority, the faithful generally are expected to believe it. The document doesn't have to go out of its way to say, "This is authoritative teaching."

However, even in a magisterial document, that presumption doesn't hold if (1) the statement doesn't pertain to faith or morals or (2) if the document indicates it isn't a matter of authoritative teaching. These two situations can be used as a guide for identifying non-doctrinal statements in magisterial documents.

Statements Not Pertaining to Faith or Morals

Introductory and Concluding Statements

360. Magisterial documents frequently contain non-doctrinal statements at their beginnings and ends. Here is how Pope John Paul II's encyclical *Dominum et Vivificantem* (1986) begins:

Ioannes Paulus PP. II
DOMINUM ET VIVIFICANTEM
On the Holy Spirit in the Life of the Church
and the World
INTRODUCTION
Venerable Brothers, Beloved Sons and Daughters,
Health and the Apostolic Blessing!

This tells us the document's author, title, subject, and audience (the bishops and the Catholic faithful). Also, as an expression of pastoral concern, John Paul II wishes the audience health and imparts his apostolic blessing.

At the end of the document, we find:

Given in Rome, at St. Peter's, on May 18, the Solemnity of Pentecost, in the year 1986, the eighth of my pontificate.

This situates the document in space and time, telling us where it was issued (from St. Peter's in Rome, which underscores its authority) and when (Pentecost of 1986, an appropriate day given its subject matter).

361. Although not statements of doctrine, introductory and concluding texts provide important information about a document. Introductory texts frequently tell us what kind of document we are reading, which has a bearing on the level of authority it carries. We also typically find notices of authorization either at the beginning or the end of texts. Here is the end of the CDF's instruction *Dignitas Personae*:

> *The sovereign pontiff Benedict XVI, in the audience granted to the undersigned cardinal prefect on 20 June 2008, approved the present instruction, adopted in the ordinary session of this congregation, and ordered its publication.*
> Rome, from the offices of the Congregation for the Doctrine of the Faith, 8 September 2008, Feast of the Nativity of the Blessed Virgin Mary.
> William Card. Levada
> *Prefect*
> + Luis F. Ladaria, S.I.
> Titular Archbishop of Thibica
> *Secretary*

The italicized sentence—which is italicized in the original to underscore its importance—indicates that the document has been authorized by the pope and thus participates in his personal magisterium. Without that authorization, it might be an interesting and informative study, but it wouldn't be a document of the Magisterium (§50).

Statements of Gratitude/Praise

362. Documents based on speeches frequently begin with statements of gratitude or praise for those being addressed. Thus John Paul II once told the Pontifical Academy of Sciences:

> I am very grateful to the Pontifical Academy of Sciences and to its president, Professor Carlos Chagas, for having arranged this interesting Study Week on the subject of "The Impact of Space Exploration on Mankind" being held in the Casina of Pius IV.
>
> For me it is a source of great satisfaction to meet you, the members of the Pontifical Academy and scientists from all over the world. The present assembly gives me an opportunity to express my admiration at the exceptional developments which have taken place in space technology (*Address to Scientists*, October 2, 1984, n. 1).

These statements parallel St. Paul's expressions of praise and gratitude for his readers and serve a pastoral function. By expressing goodwill and appreciation, they encourage a favorable reception of the message.

Statements of Purpose

363. Introductions often contain a statement of purpose, which is important for identifying the authors' goals. Thus the *Catechism of the Catholic Church* states:

> This catechism aims at presenting an organic synthesis of the essential and fundamental contents of Catholic doctrine, as regards both faith and morals, in the light of the Second Vatican Council and the whole of the Church's Tradition. Its principal sources are the sacred scriptures, the Fathers of the Church, the liturgy, and the Church's Magisterium. It is intended to serve as a point of reference for the catechisms or compendia that are composed in the various countries.
>
> This work is intended primarily for those responsible for catechesis: first of all the bishops, as teachers of the faith and pastors of the Church. It is offered to them as an instrument in fulfilling their responsibility of teaching the people of God. Through the bishops, it is addressed to redactors of catechisms, to priests, and to catechists. It will also be useful reading for all other Christian faithful (CCC 11–12).

This statement lets us know the *Catechism*:

- provides "the essential and fundamental contents of Catholic doctrine," not every point of Church teaching
- reflects both Vatican II and "the whole of the Church's Tradition," so it shouldn't be dismissed as either out of date or detached from Tradition
- is meant to help with composing or revising other catechisms, not to supplant them

- is meant for use by many, including the lay faithful, so it shouldn't be dismissed as just for bishops

Structural Statements

364. Magisterial documents sometimes contain statements indicating the structure of the document. These allow the reader to know what to expect and how to situate material in the context of its overall design. For example, the *Catechism of the Catholic Church* states:

> The plan of this catechism is inspired by the great tradition of catechisms which build catechesis on four pillars: the baptismal profession of faith (the Creed), the sacraments of faith, the life of faith (the Commandments), and the prayer of the believer (the Lord's Prayer) (CCC 13).

Directions for Use

365. The early parts of documents sometimes contain instructions for use, such as this statement from the *Catechism*:

> The texts of Sacred Scripture are often not quoted word for word but are merely indicated by a reference (cf.). For a deeper understanding of such passages, the reader should refer to the scriptural texts themselves. Such biblical references are a valuable working-tool in catechesis (CCC 19).

Definitions and Etymologies

366. Once we move past the introductory sections of a document, we continue to find non-doctrinal statements, including definitions and etymologies that shed light on the use of key terms. For example, John Paul II's apostolic exhortation *Catechesi Tradendae* (1979) explains:

> Catechesis is an education in the faith of children, young people, and adults which includes especially the teaching of Christian doctrine imparted, generally speaking, in an

organic and systematic way, with a view to initiating the hearers into the fullness of Christian life (n. 18).

Statements About History

367. To situate Church teaching in its historical context, magisterial documents frequently make statements about history, such as this one from the *Catechism*:

> The social doctrine of the Church developed in the nineteenth century when the gospel encountered modern industrial society with its new structures for the production of consumer goods, its new concept of society, the state and authority, and its new forms of labor and ownership (CCC 2421).

Statements About Science

368. Sometimes Church documents comment on matters of science, as with the *Catechism*'s statement:

> The question about the origins of the world and of man has been the object of many scientific studies which have splendidly enriched our knowledge of the age and dimensions of the cosmos, the development of life-forms, and the appearance of man (CCC 283).

Pope Francis's encyclical *Laudato Si'*, which focuses on environmental concerns, contains more scientific statements than any other recent Church document. For example:

> At the global level, [the climate] is a complex system linked to many of the essential conditions for human life. A very solid scientific consensus indicates that we are presently witnessing a disturbing warming of the climatic system. In recent decades this warming has been accompanied by a constant rise in the sea level and, it would appear, by an increase of extreme weather events, even if a scientifically determinable cause cannot be assigned to each particular

phenomenon. Humanity is called to recognize the need for changes of lifestyle, production and consumption, in order to combat this warming or at least the human causes which produce or aggravate it. It is true that there are other factors (such as volcanic activity, variations in the earth's orbit and axis, the solar cycle), yet a number of scientific studies indicate that most global warming in recent decades is due to the great concentration of greenhouse gases (carbon dioxide, methane, nitrogen oxides and others) released mainly as a result of human activity. As these gases build up in the atmosphere, they hamper the escape of heat produced by sunlight at the earth's surface. The problem is aggravated by a model of development based on the intensive use of fossil fuels, which is at the heart of the worldwide energy system. Another determining factor has been an increase in changed uses of the soil, principally deforestation for agricultural purposes (n. 23).

Statements About Technology

369. Modern magisterial documents often contain statements about technology, such as this one from John Paul II:

One of the biggest tasks that can be carried out by the use of satellites is the elimination of illiteracy. About one billion people are still illiterate. Again, satellites can be used for a wider spreading of culture in all the countries of the world, not only in those where illiteracy has already been eliminated but also in those where many can still not yet read or write, for culture can be spread with the use of pictures alone (*Address to Scientists*, October 2, 1984, n. 6).

Statements About Society

370. In his *L'Osservatore Romano* piece, Msgr. Ocáriz noted that magisterial documents contain statements about the state of societies (see §351). Examples include these statements by John Paul II:

The call for Christian unity made by the Second Vatican Ecumenical Council with such impassioned commitment is finding an ever greater echo in the hearts of believers, especially as the year 2000 approaches, a year which Christians will celebrate as a sacred jubilee, the commemoration of the Incarnation of the Son of God, who became man in order to save humanity (*Ut Unum Sint, 1*).

It is undeniable that this time of rapid and complex change can leave especially the younger generation, to whom the future belongs and on whom it depends, with a sense that they have no valid points of reference (*Fides et Ratio, 6*).

Statements About Philosophy

371. Philosophy interacts with faith in several ways (e.g., proofs of the existence of God, discussions of morality, metaphysical ideas about creation and the afterlife). Philosophical ideas thus can become the subject of doctrinal statements. However, the Church doesn't endorse any one philosophical system, and magisterial documents sometimes merely describe such systems, as in this passage from the *Catechism*:

Ancient religions and cultures produced many myths concerning origins. Some philosophers have said that everything is God, that the world is God, or that the development of the world is the development of God (Pantheism). Others have said that the world is a necessary emanation arising from God and returning to him. Still others have affirmed the existence of two eternal principles, Good and Evil, Light and Darkness, locked, in permanent conflict (Dualism, Manichaeism). According to some of these conceptions, the world (at least the physical world) is evil, the product of a fall, and is thus to be rejected or left behind (Gnosticism). Some admit that the world was made by God, but as by a watch-maker who, once he has made a watch, abandons it to itself (Deism). Finally, others reject any transcendent origin for the world, but see it as merely the interplay of matter that has always existed (Materialism) (CCC 285).

None of these views are compatible with the Catholic faith, though that isn't indicated in the sentences just quoted. Instead, it's indicated in the preceding sentence ("Since the beginning the Christian faith has been challenged by responses to the question of origins that differ from its own"). This illustrates how non-doctrinal statements interlock with doctrinal ones. Merely describing what non-Christians believe doesn't create a statement of Catholic doctrine, but such a description can be paired with statements that are binding on the faithful and cast new light on the description.

Statements About Biblical Studies

372. The history of how the Magisterium interacts with biblical studies is complex. Scripture is a repository of divine revelation, and a major goal of biblical studies is explaining the meaning of scriptural texts. The Magisterium thus may need to teach authoritatively on ideas proposed by biblical scholars.

This includes theories about the origins of the sacred texts. Ideas popular in the last two centuries include proposals that the Pentateuch was composed after the time of Moses from four principal sources (the Yahwist, Elohist, Priestly, and Deuteronomic sources) and that Isaiah was composed by several individuals in different periods (Proto-Isaiah, Deutero-Isaiah, and Trito-Isaiah).

When these ideas were first proposed, it was thought they might undermine the inspiration and authority of Scripture, and in the early twentieth century the Pontifical Biblical Commission—then an organ of the Magisterium (§54)—prohibited them from being taught. Pope Benedict XVI commented on this period:

Let us take, for example, the book of Isaiah. When the exegetes discovered that from chapter forty on the author was someone else—Deutero-Isaiah, as he was then called—there was a moment of great panic for Catholic theologians. Some thought that in this way Isaiah would be destroyed and that at the end, in chapter fifty-three, the vision of the Servant of God was no longer that of Isaiah who lived almost 800 years before Christ. "What shall we do?" people wondered (*Lenten Meeting with the Clergy of Rome*, February 22, 2007).

373. However, the Magisterium subsequently took a different view and allowed them to be taught (§§217–218). Today, the Church regards how the biblical books were composed as a historical question that doesn't affect their inspiration or authority. Such proposals even appear in magisterial statements, such as these by John Paul II:

> From the point of view of biblical criticism, it is necessary to mention immediately that the first account of man's creation [Gen. 1:1–2:4a] is chronologically later than the second [Gen. 2:4b–25], whose origin is much more remote. This more ancient text is defined as "Yahwist" because the term "Yahweh" is used to name God. . . . In comparison with this description, the first account, that is, the one held to be chronologically later, is much more mature both as regards the image of God, and as regards the formulation of the essential truths about man. This account derives from the priestly and "Elohist" tradition, from "Elohim," the term used in that account for God (*General Audience*, September 12, 1979).
>
> The book of the great prophet Isaiah, who lived in the eighth century B.C., also contains the voices of other prophets who were his disciples and successors. This is the case of the one whom biblical scholars have called "Deutero-Isaiah," the prophet of Israel's return from the Babylonian exile which took place in the sixth century B.C. His work forms the chapters 40–55 of the book of Isaiah (*General Audience*, November 20, 2002).

By including ideas from modern biblical studies in their texts, recent popes haven't made them part of Catholic doctrine. The

Magisterium does not have authoritative teachings on these matters, and they fall into the realm of free opinion (§324). Hypothetically, these matters could one day be judged necessary for defending and explaining the deposit of faith, at which time the Church might authoritatively address them, but this isn't presently the case. Consequently, when one sees ideas like this discussed in Church documents, they should be regarded as non-doctrinal statements.

Aspirational Statements

374. There are several types of aspirational statements, and they often occur at the end of documents, when authors express their desires for the future. Some are *statements of hope*. These nudge the readers in the direction the author wants and reveal information about his author's intentions in writing, as in this example from John Paul II:

> It is my hope that this pastoral visit to the Church in New Zealand will further the cause of ecumenism and draw us all closer to our one Lord and Savior (*Homily*, November 22, 1986).

375. Some documents contain *suggestions* (§351). These invite people to do something, making them more direct than the nudges given in statements of hope, but they do not have a sense of urgency, as in this suggestion from Benedict XVI:

> To conclude, dear friends, today I would like to suggest that you keep the Holy Bible within reach, during the summer period or in your breaks, in order to enjoy it in a new way by reading some of its books straight through, those that are less known and also the most famous, such as the Gospels, but without putting them down (*General Audience*, August 3, 2011).

376. A step up from suggestions are *requests*. Here people are directly asked to do something, as in this example from John Paul II:

I ask *everyone* to look more deeply at man, whom Christ has saved in the mystery of his love, and at the human being's unceasing search for truth and meaning (*Fides et Ratio,* 107).

377. Stronger yet are *exhortations.* These are urgent requests, as in this example from John Paul II:

I, John Paul, *servus servorum Dei* [Latin, "servant of the servants of God"], venture to make my own the words of the apostle Paul, whose martyrdom, together with that of the apostle Peter, has bequeathed to this See of Rome the splendor of its witness, and I say to you, the faithful of the Catholic Church, and to you, my brothers and sisters of the other Churches and ecclesial communities: "Mend your ways, encourage one another, live in harmony, and the God of love and peace will be with you. . . . The grace of the Lord Jesus Christ and the love of God and the fellowship of the Holy Spirit be with you all" (2 Cor. 13:11, 13) (*Ut Unum Sint,* 103).

378. A final kind of aspirational statement is the *prayer*—in which aspirations are directed heavenward. In recent times it has become common to end important Church documents with a prayer, and frequently a prayer to the Virgin Mary.

Statements of Regret or Condemnation

379. The opposite of aspirational statements are expressions of regret and condemnation. Some documents are written specifically to express regret. Whenever a notable tragedy occurs in the world, the Holy See may send a telegram expressing the pope's concern and his prayers for those involved. This serve as a form of pastoral care and evangelization. For example:

It was with great sadness that His Holiness Pope Francis learned of the tragic loss of life following the recent earthquake in Papua New Guinea. Commending the souls of the deceased to the mercy of almighty God, he sends his heartfelt condolences to their families, and he assures all those affected by this disaster of his closeness in prayer. Upon all those who mourn at this difficult time, and upon the emergency personnel involved in the important relief efforts, Pope Francis willingly invokes the divine blessings of strength and consolation (*Telegram*, March 7, 2018).

Other times, the pastors of the Church express regret concerning longstanding problems, as in this example from Pope Paul VI:

We ourself share the suffering of seeing prolonged on the African continent the conflicts in which there are bleeding or starving so many human beings called to the joy of life. We deplore the precarious conditions of life which, despite many efforts, prevail among so many urban and rural peoples in Africa, with limitations opposed to their development and their dignity. Of even greater concern it seems to us is the situation of the young African who becomes discouraged and exasperated, faced with uncertainty about his professional future (*Address to the New Ambassador of Senegal*, April 22, 1969).

380. Misfortunes are often caused by sin, and John Paul II was noted for a series of expressions of regret concerning historical sins committed by Catholics.[73] These culminated in a "day of pardon" in 2000, when he asked forgiveness for faults committed by Christians in the past:

Let us forgive and ask forgiveness! While we praise God who, in his merciful love, has produced in the Church a wonderful harvest of holiness, missionary zeal, total dedication to Christ and neighbor, we cannot fail to recognize *the infidelities to the gospel committed by some of our brethren*, especially during the second millennium. Let us ask pardon for the divisions which have occurred among Christians, for the violence some have used in the service of the truth and for the distrustful and hostile attitudes sometimes taken toward the followers of other religions (*Homily for the "Day of Pardon,"* March 12, 2000).

381. Expressions of condemnation are stronger than those of regret. They do not just express sorrow at an unfortunate occurrence; they also censure it as a moral evil. Thus, after the U.S. priestly sexual abuse scandal broke into the news in 2002, John Paul II stated:

The abuse which has caused this crisis is by every standard wrong and rightly considered a crime by society; it is also an appalling sin in the eyes of God. To the victims and their families, wherever they may be, I express my profound sense of solidarity and concern (*Address*, April 23, 2002).

All these statements—whether concerning unavoidable tragedies or crimes committed by churchmen—play a pastoral function as Church leaders seek to care for souls and to rebuild bridges when they have been at fault.

Statements of Pastoral Solidarity

382. Church documents also contain statements of pastoral solidarity indicating the Church's concern for people facing particular trials, as in this example from the *Catechism*:

Couples who discover that they are sterile suffer greatly. "What will you give me," asks Abraham of God, "for I continue childless?" and Rachel cries to her husband Jacob, "Give me children, or I shall die!" (CCC 2374).

Metadoctrinal Statements

383. A final category of non-doctrinal statements are what could be called "metadoctrinal" statements, or statements *about* doctrinal statements, as in this example from Pope Francis:

It is my hope that this encyclical letter, which is now added to the body of the Church's social teaching, can help us to acknowledge the appeal, immensity, and urgency of the challenge we face (*Laudato Si'*, 15).

Formally speaking, the reference to the encyclical being added to the Church's social teaching is unnecessary. The fact it's an encyclical indicates it's a teaching document, and the fact that it deals with society's impact on the environment places it in the realm of social doctrine. However, this statement makes it explicit that *Laudato Si'* contains doctrine, so it cannot be dismissed as simply dealing with non-doctrinal matters. Metadoctrinal statements also are found in other documents to indicate that a teaching is authoritative or to indicate the level of authority it has.

Statements Not Creating an Obligation

Questions

384. Some statements in magisterial documents do pertain to faith or morals but nevertheless don't generate an obligation for the faithful to respond with "religious submission of will and intellect." For example, some don't make assertions but merely ask questions, as in this passage from the *Catechism*:

> Is the universe governed by chance, blind fate, anonymous necessity, or by a transcendent, intelligent, and good Being called "God"? and if the world does come from God's wisdom and goodness, why is there evil? Where does it come from? Who is responsible for it? Is there any liberation from it? (CCC 284).

The Church has answers to these questions—found elsewhere in the *Catechism*—but since they aren't given here, this passage doesn't teach any doctrines.

Issues Expressly Set Aside

385. Sometimes a magisterial figure will raise an issue and then expressly set it aside. Though not framed in the form of a question, this type of statement functions as an open-ended question. Thus in one of his audiences, Benedict XVI raised and then set aside the issue of who the beloved disciple is in John's Gospel:

> According to tradition, John [the son of Zebedee] is the "disciple whom Jesus loved," who in the fourth Gospel laid his head against the teacher's breast at the Last Supper (cf. John 13:23), stood at the foot of the cross together with the Mother of Jesus (cf. John 19:25) and lastly, witnessed both the empty tomb and the presence of the risen one himself (cf. John 20:2; 21:7).
>
> We know that this identification is disputed by scholars today, some of whom view him merely as the prototype of a disciple of Jesus. Leaving the exegetes to settle the matter, let us be content here with learning an important lesson for our lives: the Lord wishes to make each one of us a disciple who lives in personal friendship with him (*General Audience*, July 5, 2006).

By deferring the matter to exegetes (biblical scholars) to settle, Benedict XVI indicates he does not regard it as settled by Catholic doctrine.

Statements Flagged as the Author's Opinion

386. Statements dealing with faith and morals also can fail to generate an obligation when they are flagged as matters of the author's opinion rather than doctrines. Thus when Pope Francis was asked, in 2017, why he took a more negative tone toward nations maintaining nuclear arsenals as deterrents than John Paul II had in 1982, he replied:

> In thirty-four years, nuclear [development] has gone further and further and further. Today we are at the limit. This can be argued; it is my opinion, but my staunch opinion: I am convinced of it. We are at the limit of what's licit in regard

to having and using nuclear weapons. Why? Because today, with so sophisticated a nuclear arsenal, we risk the destruction of humanity, or at least of a large part of humanity. . . . We are at the limit, and since we are, I ask myself this question—not as papal magisterium, but it is the question a pope asks—today is it licit to maintain nuclear arsenals, as they are, or today, to save creation, to save humanity, is it not necessary to go back? (*Press Conference*, December 2, 2017).

Whether it's legitimate for nations to maintain a nuclear deterrent is a moral question, but here no obligation to believe the pope's opinion is created. Aside from the fact this is an interview rather than a magisterial document, Pope Francis flags what he says as "his opinion," "not as papal magisterium," and as a "question a pope asks."

387. Pope Francis's response contains multiple indicators that it's his opinion, but statements sometimes signal the same thing in subtler ways, as with this example from John Paul II:

The New Testament provides no information on the circumstances of Mary's death. This silence leads one to suppose that it happened naturally, with no detail particularly worthy of mention. If this were not the case, how could the information about it have remained hidden from her contemporaries and not have been passed down to us in some way?

As to the cause of Mary's death, the opinions that wish to exclude her from death by natural causes seem groundless (*General Audience*, June 25, 1997).

Here he indicates his own at least tentative opinion that Mary died a natural death (cf. §307). But instead of saying, "this is my opinion," he uses subtler language, saying the silence of the New Testament "leads one to suppose" it was a natural death and opinions to the contrary "seem groundless." Such tentativeness indicates we are in the realm of opinion rather than doctrine.

388. The same is indicated when an issue is framed in terms of probability, as in this discussion of the authorship of Hebrews by Benedict XVI:

> Tertullian attributes to him [Barnabas] the letter to the Hebrews. This is not improbable. Since he belonged to the tribe of Levi, Barnabas may have been interested in the topic of the priesthood; and the letter to the Hebrews interprets Jesus' priesthood for us in an extraordinary way (*General Audience,* January 31, 2007).

"This is not improbable" signals a permitted opinion, though not necessarily one Benedict holds since "not improbable" indicates a notable but not an absolute degree of probability.

Statements Flagged as the Opinion of Others

389. Statements can also be flagged as the opinion of some person or group. When these are raised for our consideration without being endorsed or condemned, they do not create a doctrine. Thus Benedict XVI discussed a theological proposal by Bl. John Duns Scotus (c. 1266–1308):

> Unlike many Christian thinkers of the time, [Duns Scotus] held that the Son of God would have been made man even if humanity had not sinned. He says in his *Reportatio Parisiensis* (Latin, "Parisian Report"): "To think that God would have given up such a task had Adam not sinned would be quite unreasonable! I say, therefore, that the fall was not the cause of Christ's predestination and that if no one had fallen, neither the angel nor man in this hypothesis Christ would still have been predestined in the same way" (in *III Sent.,* d. 7, 4). This perhaps somewhat surprising thought crystallized because, in the opinion of Duns Scotus the Incarnation of the Son of God, planned from all eternity by God the Father at the level of love is the fulfillment of creation and enables every creature, in Christ

and through Christ, to be filled with grace and to praise and glorify God in eternity. Although Duns Scotus was aware that in fact, because of original sin, Christ redeemed us with his passion, death, and resurrection, he reaffirmed that the Incarnation is the greatest and most beautiful work of the entire history of salvation, that it is not conditioned by any contingent fact but is God's original idea of ultimately uniting with himself the whole of creation, in the person and flesh of the Son (*General Audience*, July 7, 2010).

Scotists have favored this proposal, whereas Thomists have been skeptical of it, but the Magisterium has not weighed in. Benedict XVI flags it as Scotus's opinion but neither endorses nor criticizes it.

390. The same thing happens with ideas proposed by groups, as when Benedict XVI stated "some recent theologians are of the opinion" that the fire of purgatory is Christ himself (§350). It isn't necessary for the word "opinion" to be used. The mere attribution of a view to a person or group—without further magisterial comment—is enough. For example, after mentioning that it is "not improbable" that the author of Hebrews was Barnabas, Benedict XVI went on to say:

> After returning to Ephesus, Apollos resisted Paul's invitation to return to Corinth immediately, postponing the journey to a later date of which we know nothing (cf. 1 Cor. 16:12). We have no further information about him, even though some scholars believe he is a possible author of the letter to the Hebrews which Tertullian believed Barnabas had written (*General Audience*, January 31, 2007).

Here the view that Apollos was the author is attributed to "some scholars," and the pope makes no judgment on the matter.

391. In identifying statements of this type, the following factors are key:

1. Discussion of a view
2. The naming of a person (Bl. John Duns Scotus, St. Thomas Aquinas, Bl. John Henry Newman) or group (scholars, theologians, exegetes)
3. Language that attributes a view to them ("according to," "tell us," "are of the opinion," "have proposed," "consider")
4. Absence of an authoritative magisterial evaluation of the view

Sometimes the author of the document will make a tentative evaluation. For example, a pope might say that the view of a theologian or scholar is probable or improbable. But since neither judgment is definite, it would leave the matter in the realm of opinion. He might even endorse or reject the view wholeheartedly, stating it explicitly as a matter of *his own* opinion, without making an authoritative pronouncement.

392. However, an author may make an authoritative judgment on the opinion of others. For example, John Paul II discussed the proposal of various theologians that the Holy Spirit may be understood in a special way, as a divine Person, as the mutual love of the Father and the Son:

> [St. Augustine's] reflections developed the concept of the Holy Spirit as the mutual love and the bond of unity between the Father and the Son in the communion of the Trinity. He wrote: "As we appropriately call the sole Word of God "Wisdom," even though generally speaking the Holy Spirit and the Father himself are Wisdom, the Spirit also is given Love as a proper name, even though the Father and the Son are love as well in a general sense" (*General Audience*, November 14, 1990).

In the same audience, he went on to give an authoritative judgment on the matter stating:

> It is the doctrine of the East and West which Pope Leo XIII gathered from the tradition and synthesized in his encyclical

on the Holy Spirit, wherein we read that the Holy Spirit "is divine goodness and the mutual love of the Father and the Son" (citing Leo XIII *Divinum Illud Munus,* 3).

The understanding of the Holy Spirit as the mutual love of the Father and the Son thus is a matter of Church teaching rather than simply theological opinion.

How Non-Doctrinal Statements Relate to Doctrinal Ones

393. As we've seen, there are more non-doctrinal statements in magisterial documents than one might initially suppose. These play a variety of roles, including pastoral functions. Although they are not expressions of doctrine, they are still related to doctrine.

Statements of regret and condemnation concerning specific events presuppose the Church's moral teachings. So do statements of gratitude and praise.

It's sometimes possible to identify the doctrinal principles underlying a non-doctrinal statement, as when we saw (§371) how a single sentence in the *Catechism* ("Since the beginning the Christian faith has been challenged by responses to the question of origins that differ from its own") implied a rejection of numerous philosophical positions, though the description of those views was itself a collection of non-doctrinal sentences (see CCC 285).

Although it's sometimes possible to extract principles of Catholic doctrine from non-doctrinal statements, this must be done with care, and often the non-doctrinal statements are too ambiguous. If the pope makes a general expression of gratitude to some group, it's usually impossible to extract a specific set of moral propositions and say these are Church doctrines on the basis of his remarks.

There are thus two extremes to be avoided: saying non-doctrinal statements have *no* bearing on Church teaching and—in violation of the hermeneutic of precision—drawing incautious inferences about Church teaching from them.

CHAPTER 14

Non-Infallible Doctrines

The Nature of Non-Infallible Doctrines

394. Teachings that fall into this category are referred to several ways:

- They are called *non-infallible* because they don't belong to the category of infallible teachings.
- They are called *non-definitive* because they haven't been defined.
- They are called *non-irreformable* because they can be changed.

Each term involves a negation with respect to another category of teachings (those that are infallible, definitive, or reformable). To date, no non–negative way of referring to them (e.g., "ordinary" teachings) has become standard. Sometimes the term "fallible" is used, but the Magisterium studiously avoids this. One might wonder: if they aren't infallible, why not just call them fallible? That would seem preferable to the clunky double-negative "non-infallible."

The reason is that calling them fallible could undermine their authority by suggesting they are mistaken or likely to be mistaken. The truth is that, although the Holy Spirit has not (yet) guided the Church to infallibly define them, he has guided the Magisterium in a more general way in formulating and proclaiming them. This, along with their foundation in Scripture and Tradition, is why they call for the response of "religious

submission of will and intellect" (*Lumen Gentium,* 25). Msgr.
Fernando Ocáriz Braña comments:

> Even if the Magisterium proposes a teaching without di-
> rectly invoking the charism of infallibility, it does not fol-
> low that such a teaching is therefore to be considered "fal-
> lible"—in the sense that what is proposed is somehow a
> "provisional doctrine" or just an "authoritative opinion."
> Every authentic expression of the Magisterium must be
> received for what it truly is: a teaching given by pastors
> who, in the apostolic succession, speak with the "charism
> of truth" (*Dei Verbum,* n. 8), "endowed with the authority
> of Christ" (*Lumen Gentium,* n. 25), "and by the light of the
> Holy Spirit" (ibid.).[74]

395. Although there are understandable reasons for avoiding the
term "fallible," that expression contains a truth. Thus Ocáriz acknowledges they shouldn't be considered fallible "in the sense"
he goes on to describe. Taking the term in another sense, there
remains the possibility—however remote—of their involving
error, and in recent years the Magisterium has more frankly acknowledged this. The CDF explains:

> In order to serve the people of God as well as possible, in
> particular, by warning them of dangerous opinions which
> could lead to error, the Magisterium can intervene in ques-
> tions under discussion which involve, in addition to solid
> principles, certain contingent and conjectural elements. It
> often only becomes possible with the passage of time to
> distinguish between what is necessary and what is contin-
> gent (*Donum Veritatis,* 24).

396. The process of discerning what is solid and what is not occurs over the course of doctrinal development. Before Galileo
it was taken for granted (1) that Scripture is divinely inspired
and thus true and (2) that certain passages of Scripture imply the

earth is stationary and the sun moves around it. Many thus inferred it is a matter of Christian faith that the sun moves around the earth. Although premise (1) is an article of the Christian faith, the other is not. The discoveries of Galileo and others prompted a reexamination of premise (2), and it was realized that the passages in question didn't mandate the common interpretation.

The twentieth century saw many similar disentanglements as it was realized the inspiration, truth, and authority of Scripture didn't require its books to be written by known individuals living at known times (e.g., the book of Isaiah being written by a single prophet in the eighth century B.C.). This was not obvious at the beginning of the century, and the Pontifical Biblical Commission initially prohibited the teaching of non-traditional ideas about the authorship of these books. However, as the century progressed, awareness grew that the inspiration of the biblical books is a separate question than the details of how they were composed, and these prohibitions ceased (§§217–218, 324, 372–373).

397. The possibility of mixing solid principles with less certain ones is a particular risk in areas involving prudential reasoning, such as in the social doctrine of the Church. It uses contingent facts from fields such as sociology, economics, and even the physical sciences (cf. *Laudato Si'*). Consequently, the CDF states:

> When it comes to the question of interventions in the prudential order, it could happen that some magisterial documents might not be free from all deficiencies. Bishops and their advisors have not always taken into immediate consideration every aspect or the entire complexity of a question. But it would be contrary to the truth, if, proceeding from some particular cases, one were to conclude that the Church's Magisterium can be habitually mistaken in its prudential judgments, or that it does not enjoy divine assistance in the integral [i.e., complete, overall] exercise of its mission. In fact, the theologian, who cannot pursue his discipline well without a certain competence in history, is aware of

the filtering which occurs with the passage of time. This is
not to be understood in the sense of a relativization of the
tenets of the faith. The theologian knows that some judgments of the Magisterium could be justified at the time in
which they were made, because while the pronouncements
contained true assertions and others which were not sure,
both types were inextricably connected. Only time has permitted discernment and, after deeper study, the attainment
of true doctrinal progress (ibid.).

398. This degree of frankness about the possibility of error was
new. At the press conference presenting the document, Cardinal
Joseph Ratzinger stated:

> [*Donum Veritatis*] states—perhaps for the first time with such
> candor—that there are magisterial decisions which cannot
> be the final word on a given matter as such but, despite
> the permanent value of their principles, are chiefly also a
> signal for pastoral prudence, a sort of provisional policy.
> Their kernel remains valid, but the particulars determined
> by circumstances can stand in need of correction. In this
> connection, one will probably call to mind both the pon-
> tifical statements of the last century regarding freedom of
> religion and the anti-Modernist decisions of the beginning
> of this century, especially the decisions of the then Biblical
> Commission. As warning calls against rash and superficial
> accommodations, they remain perfectly legitimate: no less
> a personage than J. B. Metz, for example, has remarked that
> the anti-Modernist decisions of the Church performed the
> great service of saving her from foundering in the bour-
> geois-liberal world. Nevertheless, with respect to particular
> aspects of their content, they were superseded after having
> fulfilled their pastoral function in the situation of the time.[75]

In 2003, he was even more blunt about the early replies of the
Pontifical Biblical Commission, stating:

It is true that, with the above-mentioned decisions, the Magisterium overly enlarged the area of certainties that the Faith can guarantee; it is also true that with this, the credibility of the Magisterium was diminished and the space necessary for research and exegetical questions was excessively restricted (*On the 100th Anniversary of the Pontifical Biblical Commission*, May 10, 2003).

399. We thus see that the possibility of error in non-infallible teachings is a real one, and one about which the Magisterium is becoming increasingly frank. However, the Holy Spirit still guides the Magisterium when formulating such teachings. Although he does not guarantee complete freedom from error in the Church's non-definitive teaching, he ensures the content of the deposit of faith is preserved and its essential principles remain present in the Church's teaching—even if there is an admixture of ideas that needs to be purified through doctrinal development, which also takes place under his guidance. Consequently, one cannot infer "that the Church's Magisterium can be habitually mistaken in its prudential judgments," and its non-infallible teachings ordinarily require the "religious assent of will and intellect" (§349).

Identifying Non-Infallible Doctrines

400. Showing that a statement in a Church document expresses a non-infallible teaching consists of two steps:

1. Showing it expresses a doctrine
2. Showing the doctrine has not been infallibly defined

The first is accomplished using the principles in §§358–359, and the second is the default assumption concerning Church teachings. The *Code of Canon Law* provides:

No doctrine is understood as defined infallibly unless this is manifestly evident (can. 749 §3).

The conditions needed for this presumption to be overcome will be discussed in chapter sixteen.

401. When evaluating whether a doctrine is infallible, it isn't enough to look at a single passage and apply the tests for infallibility. Consider this statement from the *Catechism* on the Assumption of Mary:

> Finally, the Immaculate Virgin, preserved free from all stain of original sin, when the course of her earthly life was finished, was taken up body and soul into heavenly glory, and exalted by the Lord as queen over all things, so that she might be the more fully conformed to her Son, the Lord of lords and conqueror of sin and death. The Assumption of the Blessed Virgin is a singular participation in her Son's resurrection and an anticipation of the resurrection of other Christians (CCC 966).

This passage doesn't use the right language to create a new infallible definition. However, though the Assumption of Mary isn't defined here, it *is* defined in Pope Pius XII's apostolic constitution *Munificentissimus Deus* (1950). Therefore, to verify a teaching isn't infallible, you may need to look at more than one document.

For famous infallible teachings (the Assumption of Mary, the real presence of Christ in the Eucharist, the dogma of the Trinity), this may not be necessary. You may already know the doctrine is infallible. But what if you're not sure? There are several options:

- Look at chapter fifteen and see if it's among the doctrines listed as infallible. However, this list isn't exhaustive or itself definitive.

- Look it up in a manual of theology that uses doctrinal notes (e.g., Ludwig Ott's *Fundamentals of Catholic Dogma*). However, these doctrinal notes are largely unofficial and represent the personal view of the theologian.

- Look up the Church documents listed to support it in the manual of theology and apply the tests for infallibility. The relevant passages will almost always be found in Denzinger's *Enchiridion Symbolorum* (§§234–236). Given its long history and the careful, scholarly work done on it, it's unlikely an infallible doctrinal definition won't be in Denzinger.
- Look in Denzinger's extensive doctrinal index, check the passages it lists, and apply the tests for infallibility.

Be very wary of online sources discussing infallibility. The wild and woolly world of the internet is filled with authors who are not experts, who don't understand the criteria for infallibility, and who either dramatically *under*estimate the number of infallible doctrines (in the case of progressive authors) or who dramatically *over*estimate their number (in the case of traditionalist authors).

These procedures offer a generally reliable way of determining whether the Church's extraordinary magisterium has defined a matter. Verifying infallible teachings by the ordinary and universal magisterium presents additional challenges that will be discussed in chapter fifteen.

402. There are many instances of non-infallible Church teachings, particularly among those that have only been recently articulated. The U.S. bishops' Committee on Doctrine notes:

> An example of teaching that is non-definitive and calls for *obsequium religiosum* [Latin, "religious submission"] is the teaching of the instruction *Donum Vitae* against such practices as artificial insemination, surrogate motherhood, and *in vitro* fertilization (*The Teaching Ministry of the Diocesan Bishop*, fn. 25).

Evaluating the Weight of Non-Infallible Doctrines

403. Once a doctrine has been identified as a non-infallible teaching, there is more to say about its doctrinal weight. Based on principles articulated in *Lumen Gentium* 25, the CDF has identified three criteria for evaluating the weight of non-definitive teachings:

> [These teachings] require degrees of adherence differentiated according to the mind and the will manifested; this is shown especially by the nature of the documents, by the frequent repetition of the same doctrine, or by the tenor of the verbal expression (*Doctrinal Commentary*, 11).

Since *Lumen Gentium* establishes that these teachings are to be received with "religious submission of will and intellect," the different "degrees of adherence" are best understood as degrees of the intensity of such submission. Highly authoritative teachings require a more intense submission of will and intellect than more tentative ones. Unfortunately, the Magisterium hasn't worked out a way of describing these degrees, though it might one day do so, perhaps based on the formerly common doctrinal notes. In the meantime, it's still possible to apply the three criteria to determine relative weight.

The Nature of the Documents

404. The first criterion is the nature of the documents in which a teaching appears. Thus a papal encyclical is more authoritative than a weekly papal audience, and the dogmatic constitutions of Vatican II are more authoritative than its decrees.

It is difficult to apply this criterion because the relative weights of different documents are only loosely defined, as discussed in chapters eight and nine. The Holy See has not published an explanation of their weights, and it often isn't clear why a document was issued in one form rather than another. Despite the fuzziness of the system, it can still be said that if a doctrine is mentioned in high-level documents, this adds weight it wouldn't have if it were mentioned only in lower-level documents.

The Frequency of Repetition

405. The second criterion is the frequency with which the Magisterium repeats a doctrine. If it is mentioned only rarely (perhaps not even in centuries), it has a lower level of authority; if the Magisterium repeats it frequently, it is more authoritative. There are a number of reasons why a doctrine may be mentioned frequently:

1. It is a fundamental teaching of the Faith.
2. It is a popular idea.
3. It is an unpopular idea.
4. Doctrinal development is occurring.

Fundamental Teachings

406. It's obvious that fundamental teachings of the Faith will be mentioned frequently. The fact that Jesus is the Christ is mentioned in document after document, giving it enormous authority. Fundamental teachings of the Faith naturally are infallible at least by virtue of the ordinary and universal magisterium. Consequently, this specific reason why doctrines can be mentioned frequently doesn't apply for determining the weight of *non-infallible* doctrines. However, the others can.

Popular Teachings

407. The substance of the Faith is the same in every age, but particular ideas about it rise and fall in popularity. During periods when an idea is popular, it may be repeated with some frequency in Church documents, and this gives it added weight in those periods. However, as doctrinal development progresses, an idea's popularity may recede, causing it to lose weight. For example, see §§568–570 on the view that infants dying without baptism could not go to heaven.

Unpopular Teachings

408. In every age there are ideas that are unpopular, and this can lead the Magisterium to frequently repeat its teaching on them. Today, the Church's teachings on abortion, contraception, and reserving the priesthood to men are unpopular in society. Consequently, the Magisterium has reiterated them on numerous occasions. At present, the Vatican website (vatican.va) has hundreds of references to these teachings. Nothing like that number of references would be found in the documents of a prior century, when there was no public controversy on them.

Doctrinal Development

409. A teaching may be mentioned frequently in Church documents because doctrinal development is taking place. For example, although it's always been recognized that the Church is "the pillar and bulwark of the truth" (1 Tim. 3:15), the implications of this for its infallibility have undergone significant development in the last two centuries. This led to more frequent discussions in Church documents of the infallibility of the pope, ecumenical councils, and the ordinary and universal Magisterium of the Church.

The Tenor of the Verbal Expression

410. The third criterion for assessing the weight of a teaching is the tenor of the words used to express it. If it is proposed briefly and tentatively, it will have less authority, whereas if it is expounded at length and emphatically, it will have more.

411. Consider this statement by Pope John Paul II:

> Wherefore, in order that all doubt may be removed regarding a matter of great importance, a matter which pertains to the Church's divine constitution itself, in virtue of my ministry of confirming the brethren (cf. Luke 22:32) I declare that the Church has no authority whatsoever to confer priestly ordination on women and that this judgment is to be definitively held by all the Church's faithful (*Ordinatio Sacerdotalis,* 4).

The doctrine in question was already infallible by the ordinary and universal Magisterium of the Church, which is what the pope is saying. However, he doesn't make a new, papal definition (i.e., an *ex cathedra* statement), as later confirmed by Joseph Ratzinger and Tarcisio Bertone, who stated, "the supreme pontiff, while not wishing to proceed to a dogmatic definition, intended to reaffirm that this doctrine is to be held definitively" (*Doctrinal Commentary,* 11).

Note how forceful the language can be without creating a new definition, with multiple elements stressing the importance of the teaching:

- "that all doubt may be removed"
- "a matter of great importance"
- "a matter which pertains to the Church's divine constitution itself"
- "my ministry of confirming the brethren"
- "I declare"
- "no authority whatsoever"
- "this judgment is to be definitively held by all the Church's faithful"

The only thing keeping this from being a new, papal definition is the fact he didn't use the verb "I define" (see §489–495).

412. On the other hand, consider this statement from John Paul II:

Can it perhaps be said that, after the failure of Communism, capitalism is the victorious social system, and that capitalism should be the goal of the countries now making efforts to rebuild their economy and society? Is this the model which ought to be proposed to the countries of the Third World which are searching for the path to true economic and civil progress?

The answer is obviously complex. If by "capitalism" is meant an economic system which recognizes the fundamental and positive role of business, the market, private property, and the resulting responsibility for the means of production, as well as free human creativity in the economic sector, then the answer is certainly in the affirmative, even though it would perhaps be more appropriate to speak of a "business economy," "market economy," or simply "free economy." But if by "capitalism" is meant a system in which freedom in the economic sector is not circumscribed within a strong juridical framework which places it at the service of human freedom in its totality, and which sees it as a particular aspect of that freedom, the core of which is ethical and religious, then the reply is certainly negative (*Centissimus Annus*, 42).

Notice the tentativeness of the language: if you understand capitalism one way, the answer is yes, but if you understand it another way, the answer is no. This is definite enough to establish a teaching, but the tentativeness of the language indicates the teaching has less authority. If the language of a statement is tentative enough, it will not express a doctrine but only an opinion (§188–190, 386–392).

CHAPTER 15

Understanding the Church's Infallibility

413. Infallible teachings are referred to a number of ways:

- They are called *infallible* because they are taught in a way that is not fallible (capable of resulting in error).

- They are called *definitive* because they bring all legitimate discussion completely (Latin, *de-*) to an end (*finis*)—thus an act that teaches a proposition definitively is called a *definition*.

- They are called *irreformable* because they are not capable of being "reformed" or changed in substance, though they can be supplemented or clarified.

The Basis of the Church's Infallibility

414. Jesus told Peter: "You are Peter, and on this rock I will build my church, and the powers of death [lit., "gates of hades"] shall not prevail against it" (Matt. 16:18). This means the Church won't pass out of existence but will remain until the Second Coming. Theologians call this quality *indefectibility* since the Church can never defect (Latin *deficere*, "to fail or fall away"). Jesus also declared:

All authority in heaven and on earth has been given to me. Go therefore and make disciples of all nations, baptizing them in the name of the Father and of the Son and of the Holy Spirit, teaching them to observe all that I have commanded you; and lo, I am with you always, to the close of the age (Matt. 28:18–20).

Here Jesus commissions the Church to preach the whole of the Faith—"all that I have commanded you"—and assures it he will be with it until the end of the world, guiding it using the authority he has been given. He thus backs the teaching mission of the Church with his own authority. As he said on another occasion, "He who hears you hears me, and he who rejects you rejects me, and he who rejects me rejects him who sent me" (Luke 10:16). He further promised the Holy Spirit would lead his disciples "into all the truth" (John 16:13), and that the Holy Spirit will "be with you forever" (John 14:16). Therefore, as down through the ages the Church proclaims "the faith which was once for all delivered to the saints" (Jude 3), its teaching mission is backed by the authority of and guided by Christ and the Holy Spirit.

415. Authority can be exercised in different degrees, which raises the question of what happens when the Church uses its teaching authority to definitively settle a question and irrevocably bind the faithful to believe its teaching.

Theologians perceived that the Church wouldn't be indefectible if it could definitively teach a false proposition, for then it would defect from the true faith and fall away from Christ. Therefore, the divine guidance it is given would prevent it from definitively binding the faithful to believe something false. The divine guidance and indefectibility of the Church thus mean it is protected from teaching error—or infallible— in at least some circumstances.

416. Some ask how any man or group of men could teach infallibly. As the popular saying has it, "To err is human," and as Scripture says, "we all make many mistakes" (James 3:2). Surely only God is infallible. This objection contains a measure of truth: only God is intrinsically and absolutely infallible. However, he can protect men from error. He obviously did so with the men who wrote Scripture, for "all Scripture is inspired of God" (2 Tim. 3:15) and therefore guaranteed to be true. The gift of inspiration entails the lesser qualities of infallibility and inerrancy—at least while one is working under its influence (§§141–143). Thus Peter could write two inspired documents (1 and 2 Peter) and yet make mistakes on other occasions.

Church documents are not inspired (§140), but in his omnipotence God can certainly stop a man from teaching something false.

417. The Church's infallibility is subject to limitations. Just because a defined proposition is guaranteed to be true doesn't mean it is also guaranteed to be:

- phrased well
- a complete expression of the truth on a matter
- given at an opportune time
- given at all

It's thus possible for the Church to express a truth in an imperfect or incomplete way, to define it earlier or later than would be prudent, or not to define it at all. Despite these limitations, the Church's infallibility is an asset that serves its teaching mission and indefectibility.

The Subjects of Infallibility

God

418. When scholars discuss the Church's infallibility, they frequently speak of both the *subjects* and the *objects* of infallibility. The first refer to the subjects—the people—who are capable of teaching infallibly, whereas the latter refers to the objects—the propositions—that can be taught.

Ultimately, God alone is absolutely infallible, so he is the first and primary subject of infallibility.

The Church

419. People think of the pope as infallible, but he isn't the only one possessing a gift of infallibility. The Church as a whole does. In 1973, the CDF stated:

> God, who is absolutely infallible, thus deigned to bestow upon his new people, which is the Church, a certain shared infallibility, which is restricted to matters of faith and morals, which is present when the whole people of God unhesitatingly holds a point of doctrine pertaining to these matters, and finally which always depends upon the wise providence and anointing of the grace of the Holy Spirit, who leads the Church into all truth until the glorious coming of her Lord.
>
> Concerning this infallibility of the people of God the Second Vatican Council speaks as follows: "The body of the faithful as a whole, anointed as they are by the Holy One (cf. 1 John 2:20, 27), cannot err in matters of belief. Thanks to a supernatural instinct of faith which characterizes the people as a whole, it manifests this unerring quality when, from the bishops down to the last member of the laity, it shows universal agreement in matters of faith and morals" (*Mysterium Ecclesiae*, 2, quoting *Lumen Gentium*, 12).

Though the people of God as a whole have a gift of infallibility, the Church doesn't speak of them "teaching" infallibly. That term is reserved for the Magisterium, which God has commissioned to teach in a special way.

420. Nevertheless, the sense of the faithful (Latin, *sensus fidelium*) is infallible when they, together with the Magisterium, "show universal agreement in matters of faith and morals." Examples of teachings that have been infallibly held this way, from the beginning, include the fact God exists and that Jesus is the Messiah. No one would, in the proper sense, be a member of the Christian faithful if he did not hold these teachings.

421. This brings up an important point: not all who profess to be Christian are genuinely faithful. Many professing Christians hold the Faith imperfectly and don't lead lives open to the promptings of divine grace. Consequently, they have an impaired sense of the faith (Latin, *sensus fidei*). The International Theological Commission notes:

> In the history of the people of God, it has often been not the majority but rather a minority which has truly lived and witnessed to the faith. The Old Testament knew the "holy remnant" of believers, sometimes very few in number, over against the kings and priests and most of the Israelites. Christianity itself started as a small minority, blamed and persecuted by public authorities. . . . In many countries today, Christians are under strong pressure from other religions or secular ideologies to neglect the truth of faith and weaken the boundaries of ecclesial community. It is therefore particularly important to discern and listen to the voices of the "little ones who believe" (Mark 9:42) (*Sensus Fidei in the Life of the Church,* 118).

The Bishops

422. Because it is difficult to discern the voice of the true faithful from those who make a compromised profession of the Faith, we can't identify the *sensus fidelium* with popular opinion among Christians (see §600). Therefore, apart from particularly clear cases like the existence of God and the fact Jesus is the Messiah, it is difficult to determine when a teaching is infallible because it is held by the faithful as a whole. We thus need a more clearly identifiable voice capable of speaking with infallibility.

This is found in the next subject of infallibility, the bishops. Because of their divine commission as authoritative teachers, they teach infallibly when "maintaining the bond of communion among themselves and with the successor of Peter, and authentically teaching matters of faith and morals, they are in agreement on one position as definitively to be held" (*Lumen Gentium,* 25).

This infallibility is exercised only in communion with each other, for "the individual bishops do not enjoy the prerogative of infallibility" (ibid.), and only in communion "with the successor of Peter," the head of the college of bishops.

423. The bishops can teach infallibly "even though dispersed through the world" (ibid.), in which case a matter is said to be defined by the "ordinary and universal Magisterium of the Church." But when they are dispersed it can be difficult to verify that they have the kind of agreement needed.

424. Consequently, the infallibility of their teaching is "more clearly verified when, gathered together in an ecumenical council, they are teachers and judges of faith and morals for the universal Church, whose definitions must be adhered to with the submission of faith" (ibid.).

The Pope

425. Ecumenical councils are massive and difficult undertakings, and during a time of pressing need—such as an outbreak of heresy—it may not be possible for an ecumenical council to meet in a timely manner. Or, if a council does meet, it may not be able to reach a consensus on what response to give. This creates a need for recourse to an infallible voice that can address issues definitively without the encumbrances involved in an ecumenical council.

That need is met by the fourth and final subject of infallibility—the pope, the head of the college of bishops and thus the head of the Magisterium.

426. Because of the need for the pope to be able to teach infallibly on an independent basis, apart from the other bishops, his teachings don't require the approval of others:

His definitions, of themselves, and not from the consent of the Church, are justly styled irreformable, since they are pronounced with the assistance of the Holy Spirit, promised to him in blessed Peter, and therefore they need no approval of others, nor do they allow an appeal to any other judgment. For then the Roman pontiff is not pronouncing judgment as a private person, but as the supreme teacher of the universal Church, in whom the charism of infallibility of the Church itself is individually present, he is expounding or defending a doctrine of catholic faith (*Lumen Gentium,* 25).

This doesn't mean the pope shouldn't consult the world's bishops or even the body of the faithful more broadly when possible. It also doesn't mean he shouldn't study a matter diligently and consult theological experts. To attempt an infallible definition without proper preparation would be dangerous and imprudent (§§416–417).

427. Because the pope occupies the "Chair of Peter" (i.e., exercises Peter's teaching authority), his infallible definitions are referred to as *ex cathedra* statements (Latin, "from the chair").

The Objects of Infallibility

428. Simply put, a truth is an object of infallibility if the Church can infallibly define it. According to Vatican I, the pope is capable of defining "a doctrine regarding faith or morals" (*doctrina fidei et morum*) (*Pastor Aeternus,* 4). Similarly, Vatican II stated:

This infallibility, with which the divine Redeemer willed his Church to be endowed in defining doctrine of faith and morals (*doctrina de fide vel moribus*), extends as far as the deposit of revelation extends, which must be religiously guarded and faithfully expounded (*Lumen Gentium,* 25).

429. Two things need to be clarified about this statement. The first concerns the phrase "faith and morals." The Latin word *mores* (singular, *mos*) is notoriously difficult to translate in this context and doesn't mean exactly the same thing as "morals" in English. Instead, *mos* means "custom, manner, action"[76] or "an established practice, custom, or usage."[77] Francis Sullivan explains:

> *Mores* includes far more than what we would call "morals"; actually it includes everything that the gospel reveals about the Christian way of life: how to live, how to pray, how to worship God. . . . Perhaps the English word that comes closest to the Tridentine sense of *mores* is "practices," so that *res fidei et morum* would be better translated "matters pertaining to (Christian) faith and practice."[78]

This opens the range of possible infallible definitions to more than what would at first glance count as points of faith or morals.

430. The second clarification concerns the statement that infallibility "extends as far as the deposit of revelation extends, which must be religiously guarded and faithfully expounded." It is *not* obvious, but the statement refers to two distinct bodies of truth: (1) "the deposit of revelation" and (2) the things needed to religiously guard and faithfully expound it. We know this because the Doctrinal Commission at Vatican II issued a clarification, stating:

> The object of infallibility extends to all those things, and only to those, which either directly pertain to the deposit itself or are required in order that the same deposit may be religiously safeguarded and faithfully expounded.[79]

Afterward, this explanation was echoed by the CDF:

> According to Catholic doctrine, the infallibility of the Church's Magisterium extends not only to the deposit of faith but also to those matters without which that deposit cannot be rightly preserved and expounded (*Mysterium Ecclesiae* 3).

Consequently, scholars divide the object of infallibility in two and distinguish between two kinds of truths it covers. These are called the "primary" and "secondary" objects of infallibility.

The Primary Object of Infallibility

431. According to the Vatican II Doctrinal Commission, the primary object of infallibility consists of those things which "directly pertain to" the deposit of faith. The primary object of infallibility thus consists of truths that have been divinely revealed. It is called the *primary* object because God gave the Church its teaching mission so that it might proclaim these truths. These truths may have been revealed explicitly or implicitly, but they must be part of the deposit of faith.

432. When the Church defines that one of these truths is divinely revealed, the resulting teaching is known as a *dogma* (§§343–344). Dogmas require the response of "theological faith" (*Doctrinal Commentary*, 5), which the *Code of Canon Law* refers to as "divine and catholic faith" (can. 750 §1).

433. Dogmas are referred to in the first added paragraph of the profession of faith (§342). Joseph Ratzinger and Tarcisio Bertone provide examples of dogmas:

To the truths of the first paragraph belong:

- the articles of faith of the Creed;
- the various Christological dogmas and Marian dogmas;
- the doctrine of the institution of the sacraments by Christ and their efficacy with regard to grace;
- the doctrine of the real and substantial presence of Christ in the Eucharist and the sacrificial nature of the eucharistic celebration;
- the foundation of the Church by the will of Christ;

- the doctrine on the primacy and infallibility of the Roman pontiff;
- the doctrine on the existence of original sin;
- the doctrine on the immortality of the spiritual soul and on the immediate recompense after death;
- the absence of error in the inspired sacred texts;
- the doctrine on the grave immorality of direct and voluntary killing of an innocent human being (*Doctrinal Commentary,* 11).

The Secondary Object of Infallibility

434. Experience has shown that the Church also needs the ability to define certain truths closely connected with divine revelation. Because these truths aren't revealed, they aren't part of the Church's primary teaching mission. For this reason, they are referred to as the *secondary* object of infallibility. According to the Vatican II Doctrinal Commission, the secondary object of infallibility consists of truths that "are required in order that [the deposit of faith] may be religiously safeguarded and faithfully expounded" (§430).

435. It's significant that Vatican II's Doctrinal Commission restricted the secondary object "to all those things, and only to those, which . . . are required" to guard and expound the deposit of faith. Similarly, the CDF limited it to things "without which that deposit cannot" be guarded and expounded. This differs from some earlier authors who held that the Church could infallibly define things more loosely connected with the deposit of faith. By stressing that it includes "only those" things "required" and without which revealed truth "cannot" be properly proclaimed, the Magisterium is taking a narrower view of the secondary object.

436. Because truths belonging to the secondary object of infallibility are not defined as divinely revealed, they do not call for the response of divine and catholic faith. Instead, they are to be "held definitively" (§346). Ratzinger and Bertone state:

> The fact that these doctrines may not be proposed as formally revealed, insofar as they add to the data of faith *elements that are not revealed or which are not yet expressly recognized as such*, in no way diminishes their definitive character, which is required at least by their intrinsic connection with revealed truth (*Doctrinal Commentary,* 7).

437. Some authors refer to all truths that belong to the secondary object of infallibility as *dogmatic facts* because they are non-revealed facts that pertain in one way or another to dogma.[80] Other authors restrict the term "dogmatic facts" to a subset of truths within the secondary object.[81] When the more restricted use is employed, dogmatic facts are generally said to be truths of a historical nature such as the validity of a pope's election, the fact that a council was ecumenical, or the meaning of the words in a theological text.

438. Regarding the nature of truths belonging to the secondary object, Ratzinger and Bertone explain:

> [These truths] can be of various natures, thus giving different qualities to their relationship with revelation. There are truths which are necessarily connected with revelation by virtue of a *historical relationship*; while other truths evince a *logical connection* that expresses a stage in the maturation of understanding of revelation which the Church is called to undertake (ibid.).

Truths with a Historical Connection to Revelation

439. The classic examples of dogmatic facts in the narrow sense have a *historical connection* with revealed truth, and it is easy to see why the Church needs the ability to infallibly define them.

Suppose a heresy arises and, to deal with it, the pope calls an ecumenical council, which infallibly defines a dogma. In response, the heretics argue the pope who called the council was not validly elected, the council was not truly ecumenical, or the language it used did not actually constitute an infallible definition. Doubt about these matters then spreads among the faithful. To end the doubt, the Church needs the ability to authoritatively assert the key facts: the pope *was* validly elected, the council *was* ecumenical, and it *did* issue an infallible definition on the matter. These facts are not themselves part of the deposit of revelation, which closed with the death of the last apostle. However, they are closely connected with the dogma issued by the council. They thus count as dogmatic facts and belong to the secondary object of infallibility.

A historical controversy in which something like this happened began in 1653, when Innocent X infallibly condemned as heretical five propositions from the posthumously published book *Augustinus* by Cornelius Jansen. In response, Jansen's followers argued that the condemned propositions were heretical but that they weren't actually taught in *Augustinus*. Consequently, in 1656, Alexander VII defined that they were contained in it (DH 2010–2012). Although the first definition dealt with revealed truth, the second dealt with the dogmatic fact that these propositions were taught in a particular book (see §514).

Ratzinger and Bertone also list "the declaration of Pope Leo XIII in the apostolic letter *Apostolicae Curae* on the invalidity of Anglican ordinations" as belonging to this category (ibid., 11).

440. The understanding that the secondary object of infallibility includes "only those" things "required" and without which revealed truth "cannot" be properly proclaimed (§435) raises a question about the infallibility of the canonization of saints. That a particular person is a saint—at least those born after biblical times—couldn't be defined as a dogma since it isn't part of the deposit of faith and doesn't belong to the primary object of infallibility. However, many authors have held that the sainthood of a postbiblical person is part of the secondary object of infallibility. Cardinal Dulles explains:

Among other non-revealed matters that have frequently been seen as falling within the secondary object of infallibility is the solemn canonization of saints. . . . Although the common teachings of theologians gives some support for holding infallibility in these cases, it is difficult to see how they fit under the object of infallibility as defined by the two Vatican Councils.[82]

Presumably, the basis of this view would be that the proposition that a particular man or woman died in a state of grace does not seem "required" to properly guard and expound revealed truths or a proposition without which the Church "cannot" do so. Opinion is presently mixed among theologians regarding whether saint canonizations are infallible, though Ratzinger and Bertone support the view that they are (ibid.).

This question is significant for assessing the number of truths the Church has infallibly proclaimed. If saint canonizations are infallible then both the number of infallible pronouncements and the number of infallibly defined truths would be dramatically higher. During his pontificate Pope John Paul II didn't infallibly define any truths of a doctrinal nature, but he made 51 canonizations concerning 482 saints. That would mean 51 infallible pronouncements and 482 infallible truths.

Truths with a Logical Connection to Revelation

441. Non-revealed truths that can be defined because they have a *logical connection* with the deposit of faith include certain philosophical truths. Cardinal Dulles explains:

It is generally agreed that the Magisterium can infallibly declare the "preambles of faith," that is, naturally knowable truths implied in the credibility of the Christian message, such as the capacity of the human mind to grasp truth about invisible realities, to know the existence of God by reasoning from the created world ([DH 3004, 3026, 3538]), and to grasp the possibility of revelation ([DH 3027]) and miracles ([DH 3033–34]).[83]

442. Various moral matters also fall into this category. Another example of a non-revealed truth that one day could be defined is the moral impermissibility of *in vitro* fertilization. This technique of reproductive technology was not dreamed of in Jesus' day, but it has a logical connection to Scripture's teaching on God, family, and life that could one day warrant an infallible definition of the matter as a way of "religiously guarding and faithfully expounding" those teachings.

443. Similarly, Ratzinger and Bertone list euthanasia as a subject falling into this category:

> The doctrine on the illicitness of euthanasia, taught in the encyclical letter *Evangelium Vitae*, can also be recalled. Confirming that euthanasia is "a grave violation of the law of God," the pope declares that "this doctrine is based upon the natural law and upon the written word of God, is transmitted by the Church's Tradition and taught by the ordinary and universal Magisterium." It could seem that there is only a logical element in the doctrine on euthanasia, since Scripture does not seem to be aware of the concept. In this case, however, the interrelationship between the orders of faith and reason becomes apparent: Scripture, in fact, clearly excludes every form of the kind of self-determination of human existence that is presupposed in the theory and practice of euthanasia (*Doctrinal Commentary*, 11).

444. The relationship between divine law and the secondary object of infallibility became controversial following Pope Paul VI's encyclical *Humanae Vitae* (1968). Some argued its teaching on contraception was infallibly taught by the ordinary and universal Magisterium of the Church, and a few argued that

Humanae Vitae itself defined the matter. Others argued it was not infallible, and some argued it *could not* be infallibly defined because the subject lay beyond the scope of the Church's infallibility. Those taking the latter position fell into a number of camps:

1. The most extreme seemed to hold that the Church is unable to define any teaching regarding morals.
2. Another school held that the Church can define only divinely revealed moral truths but not those known only by natural law.
3. A final school held that the Church can define certain truths of natural law but not others (e.g., it could infallibly teach fundamental principles contained in natural law but not their application to particular situations).

445. Few authors subscribed to the first position. Both Vatican I and Vatican II taught that the Church's infallibility extends to matters of faith *and morals*.[84] Therefore, if a particular moral truth is included in divine revelation (as in the Ten Commandments or the Sermon on the Mount), the Church would be able to infallibly define it.

446. Moral truths not contained in the deposit of faith would not fall under the primary object of infallibility but they would fall under the secondary object if they are "matters without which that deposit cannot be rightly preserved and expounded" (CDF, *Mysterium Ecclesiae*, 3).

The Church hasn't yet said whether everything that belongs to natural law falls into this category. However, representatives of the CDF, including Joseph Ratzinger, were asked for clarification on this point in a 1999 meeting with several national doctrinal commissions. Their response involved a distinction between what are known as the positive and negative norms of natural law. The former are commandments ("do this") and the latter prohibitions ("don't do this"). Concerning the negative norms, they said:

Given that the observance of all negative moral norms that concern intrinsically evil acts (*intrinsece mala*) is necessary for salvation, it follows that the Magisterium has the competence to teach infallibly and make obligatory the definitive assent of the members of the faithful with regard to the knowledge and application in life of these norms. This judgment belongs to the Catholic doctrine on the infallibility of the Magisterium.[85]

Note that the CDF representatives addressed only natural law prohibitions "that concern intrinsically evil acts," or acts which by their nature are always evil. They didn't say the Church can infallibly define it when an act is *extrinsically* evil—i.e., when it is rendered evil due to circumstances. To determine an act is extrinsically evil, one must apply general principles to a concrete circumstance, and the CDF representatives indicated that it hasn't been defined that the Magisterium can infallibly teach on those cases:

With regard to the particular application of the norms of the natural moral law that do not have a necessary connection with revelation—for example, numerous positive moral norms that are valid *ut in pluribus* ["in most cases"]—it has not been defined nor is it binding that the Magisterium can teach infallibly in such matters.[86]

There thus remain questions regarding the extent to which the Magisterium can define some matters known by natural law.

447. *Humanae Vitae* 14 doesn't use the language needed to create a new infallible definition. Paul VI merely says "we declare" not "we declare and define" (see §§489–495). However, some argue that the teaching is infallible based on the ordinary and universal magisterium.

Ratzinger and Bertone do not mention contraception in their *Doctrinal Commentary*, and the CDF hasn't yet addressed its infallibility. In 1986, the CDF sent a letter to Fr. Charles E. Curran, who dissents from *Humanae Vitae*, but although the letter both noted that he rejects the teaching on contraception and discussed the subject of infallible teachings, it refrained from addressing whether the teaching on contraception is infallible (*Letter to Fr. Charles Curran*, July 25, 1986).

At the press conference for the encyclical's release in 1968, the man chosen to introduce the document—Msgr. Ferdinando Lambruschini—stated:

> The decision has been given . . . and it is not infallible. But it does not leave the question of the regulation of birth in a state of vague uncertainty. Only definitions strictly so-called command the assent of theological faith. But a pronouncement of the authentic Magisterium requires a full and loyal assent—internal and not merely external—in proportion to the importance of the authority that issues it (in this case the supreme pontiff), and the matter with which it deals (in the present case a matter of the greatest importance, treating as it does of the vexed question of the regulation of birth).[87]

He thus held that it was a non-infallible teaching, since it does not demand "theological faith," but that it was nevertheless highly authoritative and demands "a full and loyal assent—internal and not merely external."

Others have held that it is infallible. In 1997, the Pontifical Council for the Family stated:

> The Church has always taught the intrinsic evil of contraception, that is, of every marital act intentionally rendered unfruitful. This teaching is to be held as definitive and irreformable (*Vademecum for Confessors*, 2:4).

This document did not carry the approval needed to make it part of the papal magisterium (§§50, 361). The Holy See thus has yet to address the question of the teaching's infallibility in a magisterial document.

On the Way to Becoming Dogma?

448. Truths initially recognized as belonging *at least* to the secondary object of infallibility may—by doctrinal development—eventually be discerned to belong to its primary object and be elevated to the status of dogmas. Ratzinger and Bertone comment:

> It cannot be excluded that at a certain point in dogmatic development, the understanding of the realities and the words of the deposit of faith can progress in the life of the Church, and the Magisterium may proclaim some of these doctrines as also dogmas of divine and catholic faith (*Doctrinal Commentary*, 7).

449. As an example, Ratzinger and Bertone offer papal infallibility:

> With reference to those connected with revelation by a logical necessity, one can consider, for example, the development in the understanding of the doctrine connected with the definition of papal infallibility, prior to the dogmatic definition of the First Vatican Council. The primacy of the successor of Peter was always believed as a revealed fact, although until Vatican I the discussion remained open as to whether the conceptual elaboration of what is understood by the terms "jurisdiction" and "infallibility" was to be considered an intrinsic part of revelation or only a logical consequence. On the other hand, although its character as a divinely revealed truth was defined in the First Vatican Council, the doctrine on the infallibility and primacy of jurisdiction of the Roman pontiff was already recognized as definitive in the period before the council. History clearly shows, therefore, that what was accepted into the consciousness of the Church was considered a true doctrine from the beginning, and was subsequently held to be definitive; however, only in the final stage—the definition of Vatican I— was it also accepted as a divinely revealed truth (ibid., 11).

450. They argue the same thing may presently be occurring with respect to the reservation of the priesthood to men:

A similar process can be observed in the more recent teaching regarding the doctrine that priestly ordination is reserved only to men. The supreme pontiff [i.e., John Paul II], while not wishing to proceed to a dogmatic definition, intended to reaffirm [in *Ordinatio Sacerdotalis*] that this doctrine is to be held definitively, since, founded on the written Word of God, constantly preserved and applied in the Tradition of the Church, it has been set forth infallibly by the ordinary and universal Magisterium. As the prior example illustrates, this does not foreclose the possibility that, in the future, the consciousness of the Church might progress to the point where this teaching could be defined as a doctrine to be believed as divinely revealed (ibid.).

Several things are worth noting here, because there has been confusion on this matter. When John Paul II released *Ordinatio Sacerdotalis* in 1994, some thought it was a new *ex cathedra* statement, and thus that we had a new infallible truth and a dogma. However, what he said was:

I declare that the Church has no authority whatsoever to confer priestly ordination on women and that this judgment is to be definitively held by all the Church's faithful (n. 4).

This lacks the language needed for a new *ex cathedra* statement (see §§489–495). John Paul II says only "I declare," not "I declare and define." It thus is not a definition but a solemn confirmation of a truth *already* infallibly taught by the ordinary and universal Magisterium. Also, it isn't being presented as a dogma. John Paul II does not say that this is a matter of divine revelation but that it is a truth "to be definitively held." That places it in the category of infallible truths but not in the category of dogma (see §§496–499).

This understanding was confirmed by Ratzinger and Bertone's statement that John Paul II was "not wishing to proceed to a dogmatic definition," though they noted that future doctrinal development might lead to it being defined as a dogma. The same understanding was confirmed, in a magisterial act, when the CDF issued a 1995 *Dubium* stating:

> This teaching requires definitive assent, since, founded on the written Word of God, and from the beginning constantly preserved and applied in the Tradition of the Church, it has been set forth infallibly by the ordinary and universal Magisterium (cf. Second Vatican Council, Dogmatic Constitution on the Church *Lumen Gentium* 25:2). Thus, in the present circumstances, the Roman pontiff, exercising his proper office of confirming the brethren (cf. Luke 22:32), has handed on this same teaching by a formal declaration, explicitly stating what is to be held always, everywhere, and by all, as belonging to the deposit of the Faith (*Responsum Concerning the Teaching Contained in Ordinatio Sacerdotalis*, October 28, 1995).

This English version contains a potentially misleading translation when it says the reservation of priestly ordination to men is something "belonging to the deposit of faith." That could suggest it has been divinely revealed, but the Ratzinger-Bertone commentary indicates that the Church has not yet established this (see quotation above). The phrase "belonging to the deposit of faith"/"pertaining to the deposit of faith" (*ad fidei depositum pertinens*) thus may only indicate a truth required to guard and expound the deposit of faith (the secondary object of infallibility) rather than a revealed truth (the primary object of infallibility).

This phrase also occurs in other magisterial documents, and it illustrates why it's necessary to read Church documents carefully, and be aware of technical meanings.

The Exercise of Infallible Teaching

451. Ratzinger and Bertone explain that—whether a teaching being defined is a dogma or merely an infallible truth—it will be proclaimed by one of two kinds of acts—either a "defining" act or a "non-defining" one:

> In the case of a *defining* act, a truth is solemnly defined by an *"ex cathedra"* pronouncement by the Roman pontiff or by the action of an ecumenical council. In the case of a *non-defining* act, a doctrine is taught *infallibly* by the ordinary and universal magisterium of the bishops dispersed throughout the world who are in communion with the successor of Peter (*Doctrinal Commentary*, 9).

452. When the pope or an ecumenical council issues an infallible definition, it is an extraordinary act of teaching, and so the term "extraordinary magisterium" is used (§13). In both cases, there is a moment when the Magisterium articulates a truth in an infallible way, thus bringing legitimate discussion of the question to an end. It is thus referred to as a definition (§413), and Ratzinger and Bertone refer to this intervention as "a defining act."

453. Other acts of teaching are not extraordinary, so they are referred to as "ordinary magisterium" (§13). However, when the bishops of the whole world (i.e., universally) agree that a truth must be held, they also are capable of teaching it infallibly. In this case there is no single, concrete statement in which the teaching is defined, so Ratzinger and Bertone refer to it being infallibly taught by a "non-defining act" through the emergence of a consensus of the bishops, together with the pope.

454. In *Ordinatio Sacerdotalis* and *Evangelium Vitae*, John Paul II confirmed teachings that had been infallibly taught by the ordinary and universal magisterium. Ratzinger and Bertone comment:

> *Such a doctrine can be confirmed or reaffirmed by the Roman pontiff, even without recourse to a solemn definition,* by declaring explicitly that it belongs to the teaching of the ordinary

and universal magisterium as a truth that is divinely revealed (first paragraph [added to the profession of faith]) or
as a truth of Catholic doctrine (second paragraph). Consequently, when there has not been a judgment on a doctrine
in the solemn form of a definition, but this doctrine, belonging to the inheritance of the *depositum fidei* [deposit of
faith], is taught by the ordinary and universal magisterium,
which necessarily includes the pope, such a doctrine is to
be understood as having been set forth infallibly. The declaration of *confirmation or reaffirmation* by the Roman pontiff
in this case is not a new dogmatic definition, but a formal
attestation of a truth already possessed and infallibly transmitted by the Church (ibid.).

CHAPTER 16

Identifying Infallible Teachings

455. Sometimes people ask, "Is this document infallible?" The question is problematic because the Magisterium doesn't issue documents whose teaching is infallible from beginning to end. Instead, it issues documents that contain *individual propositions* that are infallible. In *Ineffabilis Deus* (1854) and *Munificentissimus Deus* (1950)—the documents that defined the Immaculate Conception and Assumption of Mary—only a single sentence in each document was infallible (i.e., the definitions themselves). The rest of the documents provided context for the definitions.

456. A better question would be, "Is this *teaching* infallible?"[88] The initial presumption is that it's not: "No doctrine is understood as defined infallibly unless this is manifestly evident" (CIC 749 §3). Note the forcefulness of the language: it mustn't just be evident that a doctrine is infallible; it must be *manifestly* (clearly) evident. This places a weighty burden of proof on one wishing to claim that a teaching is infallible.

Neglect of this principle is a frequent source of problems. Many people casually assume a prior teaching is infallible and then encounter difficulties squaring it with a more recent one. But the Church has always been careful about what it defines, and the rule has always been that a teaching is not to be regarded as infallible unless the contrary is clear.

So what factors overcome the presumption of non-infallibili-
ty? This depends on how the Magisterium teaches it.

The Ordinary and Universal Magisterium

457. The first appearance of the term "ordinary magisterium" in
a Church document was in Pope Pius IX's letter *Tuas Lebenter*
(1863), to the archbishop of Munich:

> [Divine faith] would not have to be limited to those matters
> that have been defined by explicit decrees of ecumenical
> councils or by the Roman pontiffs and by the Apostolic See,
> but would also have to be extended to those matters trans-
> mitted as divinely revealed by the ordinary magisterium of
> the whole Church dispersed throughout the world and, for
> that reason, held by the universal and constant consensus of
> Catholic theologians as belonging to the Faith (DH 2879).

By the time of Vatican I (1870), the qualifier "universal" had
been added to this phrase to make it clear that the whole episcopate
had to be in agreement. The ordinary magisterium exercised by
an individual bishop or pope wouldn't be enough. Vatican I stated:

> All those things are to be believed with divine and catho-
> lic faith that are contained in the word of God, written or
> handed down, and which by the Church, either in solemn
> judgment or through her ordinary and universal magisteri-
> um are proposed for belief as having been divinely revealed
> (*De Filius* 3; DH 3011).

458. Vatican II then provided what is currently the most doctrinally developed and authoritative explanation of the conditions in
which the ordinary and universal magisterium teaches infallibly:

> Although the individual bishops do not enjoy the prerogative
> of infallibility, they nevertheless proclaim Christ's doctrine
> infallibly whenever, even though dispersed through the

world, but still maintaining the bond of communion among themselves and with the successor of Peter, and authentically teaching matters of faith and morals, they are in agreement on one position as definitively to be held (*Lumen Gentium*, 25; cf. CIC 749 §2).

Vatican II thus indicates the following criteria must be met for the ordinary and universal magisterium to define a teaching:

1. The bishops of the world maintain communion among themselves.
2. They maintain communion with the successor of Peter.
3. They teach authentically (i.e., authoritatively).
4. They teach on a matter of faith and morals.
5. They are in agreement on one position as definitively to be held.

The first two conditions require that the bishops not be in a state of schism, which is "the refusal of submission to the supreme pontiff or of communion with the members of the Church subject to him" (CIC 751).

The third condition requires that they must teach on a matter authoritatively. It wouldn't be enough for them to privately believe an opinion among themselves. It must be communicated to the faithful as an authoritative teaching.

The fourth condition requires the matter to concern "faith and morals." That is, it must either be a revealed truth or one required to properly guard and explain revealed truth (§§428–450). Bear in mind that "morals" (Latin, *mores*) includes aspects of Christian life that go beyond the principles of moral theology (§429).

The final condition requires three specific things:

a) It requires the bishops be in agreement. This is generally understood as a moral unanimity among them. It wouldn't be enough if only a portion or even a mere majority were in agreement, but it needn't be every single bishop in the world.

b) The bishops must agree on one position. It isn't enough if
   they consider a range of positions legitimate. They must
   agree on a single, specific truth.
c) They must agree this truth is "definitively to be held" by
   the faithful, thereby bringing all legitimate discussion to
   an end. If the bishops merely agreed that it *should* be held
   then the teaching would be authoritative but non-infallible. It is only when they agree a teaching is *absolutely man-
   datory* that infallibility is engaged. (Note: The possibility of
   the bishops defining non-revealed truths is why the phrase
   "definitively to be held" is used rather than "definitively to
   be believed"; see §346).

459. Sometimes people state that teachings defined by the ordinary magisterium must have always been held. This is not the
case. Vatican II taught that the bishops teach infallibly *when/
whenever* (Latin, *quando*) the above conditions are met. If, at a
given moment in history, the bishops arrive at the needed consensus, then *from that moment forward* the teaching is infallible.
It is possible a consensus previously didn't exist or that the idea
hadn't even occurred to prior generations of bishops (as with
truths implicit in the deposit of faith or many truths belonging
to the secondary object of infallibility).

460. Similarly, it isn't sufficient for a teaching always to have existed.
An idea may have been present in the consciousness of the Church
from the beginning, but it may have been viewed as one of a number of legitimate opinions or as a teaching of a lesser order. It is only
when the bishops arrive at a morally unanimous consensus that it is
"*definitively* to be held" that the teaching becomes infallible.

It thus isn't sufficient to produce a catalogue of quotations
from churchmen spanning many centuries to show that a teaching is infallible by the ordinary and universal magisterium. For
that, the quotations must indicate that the teaching is definitively to be held. If, in their own day, the churchmen only taught in
a way that required "religious assent of will and intellect" then

the matter would be a longstanding teaching but not an infallible one. As in every other exercise of magisterium, definitiveness—not length of time—is the key to infallibility.

Thus the non-definitive understanding that prevailed for many centuries that certain passages of Scripture entail a geocentric understanding of the cosmos did not make this teaching infallible (see §396).

461. Recently Pope John Paul II confirmed four truths as having been infallibly taught in this way: the reservation of priestly ordination to men (*Ordinatio Sacerdotalis,* 4) and the moral impermissibility of the direct and voluntary killing of an innocent human being, of direct abortion, and of euthanasia (*Evangelium Vitae,* 57, 62, 65). Joseph Ratzinger and Tarcisio Bertone also state:

> Other examples of moral doctrines which are taught as definitive by the universal and ordinary Magisterium of the Church are the teaching on the illicitness of prostitution and of fornication (*Doctrinal Commentary,* 11).

462. The difficulty of ascertaining whether the needed consensus exists among the bishops, without taking a vote, is one of the key difficulties in establishing whether the ordinary and universal magisterium has taught a truth infallibly. It is also one of the key reasons ecumenical councils are held.

Ecumenical Councils

463. *Lumen Gentium* states that the conditions for infallibility are "even more clearly verified" when the bishops meet in an ecumenical council (n. 25). According to the *Code of Canon Law*:

> The college of bishops also possesses infallibility in teaching when the bishops gathered together in an ecumenical council exercise the Magisterium as teachers and judges of faith and morals who declare for the universal Church that a doctrine of faith or morals is to be held definitively (CIC 749 §2).

This formulation indicates the following criteria must be jointly met for an ecumenical council to define a teaching:

1. The college of bishops is gathered together in an ecumenical council.
2. They exercise their magisterium.
3. They exercise it concerning a matter of faith and morals.
4. They issue a declaration for the universal Church.
5. The declaration indicates that the matter is to be held definitively.

464. The first condition requires that an ecumenical council meet. The conditions governing ecumenical councils are specified in the *Code of Canon Law* (cann. 337–341). Today, only the pope can convoke an ecumenical council (can. 338 §1), though this wasn't the case in all of Church history. The first seven ecumenical councils were called by emperors.

465. The second condition requires the bishops exercise their teaching authority. This is significant because not everything found in the documents of an ecumenical council involves the exercise of magisterium. They can contain non-doctrinal statements, such as expressions of pastoral concern (§351).

The *Code of Canon Law* provides a special requirement for an ecumenical council to exercise its teaching authority:

The decrees of an ecumenical council do not have obligatory force unless they have been approved by the Roman pontiff together with the council fathers, confirmed by him, and promulgated at his order (can. 341 §1).

This is because the college of bishops can't teach apart from its head, the pope. His approval gives the decrees of a council ecumenical status. The pope was barely involved in some early councils, and not involved at all in the case of Constantinople I (381), yet they are reckoned as ecumenical councils because later popes approved them. "A council is never ecumenical unless it is confirmed or at least accepted as such by the successor of Peter" (*Lumen Gentium,* 22). Popes don't have to accept the decrees of councils, and they haven't always done so. Pope Martin V didn't approve all the decrees of Constance, though it elected him.

466. The third condition requires that the subject matter be "faith and morals," which we have already discussed (§§428–447).

467. The fourth condition requires the bishops issue a declaration for the whole Church. This doesn't mean the document in which a definition is found must be addressed to the whole Church, but it does mean it must somehow indicate the teaching is obligatory for the whole Church.

468. The final condition requires the bishops to declare the teaching "is to be held definitively." Again, the use of "held" rather than "believe" allows a non-revealed truth to be defined (§458), and the qualifier "definitively" is key: if the bishops don't teach that the truth must be held in a way that excludes all possibility of future debate, it's not infallible. The language must indicate absolute adherence to the proposition.

469. Some councils have defined many propositions and some have defined none. Trent (1545–1563) defined dozens of ideas as erroneous. Vatican I (1870) is famous for having defined the infallibility of the pope, though it also defined several other matters. Vatican II (1962–1965) didn't issue any new infallible teachings. Neither did several previous councils, such as Lateran I–III (1123, 1139, 1179).

Popes

470. Because of the difficulties in verifying the infallible teaching of the ordinary magisterium and holding an ecumenical council in a timely manner, it's possible for the pope—the head of the college of bishops and thus of the Magisterium—to teach infallibly. Vatican I proclaimed:

> We teach and define that it is a dogma divinely revealed: that the Roman pontiff, when he speaks *ex cathedra*, that is, when in discharge of the office of pastor and teacher of all Christians, by virtue of his supreme apostolic authority, he defines a doctrine regarding faith or morals to be held by the universal Church, is, by the divine assistance promised to him in blessed Peter, possessed of that infallibility with which the divine Redeemer willed that his Church should be endowed in defining doctrine regarding faith or morals (*Pastor Aeternus,* 4).

The same truth was articulated by the Second Vatican Council as follows:

> [The infallibility Christ willed his Church to have] is the infallibility which the Roman pontiff, the head of the college of bishops, enjoys in virtue of his office, when, as the supreme shepherd and teacher of all the faithful, who confirms his brethren in their faith, by a definitive act he proclaims a doctrine of faith or morals (*Lumen Gentium* 25; cf. CIC 749 §1).

471. The first of these formulations—which is itself an infallible definition—states, at its core, that "the Roman pontiff, when he speaks *ex cathedra* . . . is . . . possessed of that infallibility with which the divine Redeemer willed that his Church should be endowed."

Embedded within this is an explanation of what counts as an *ex cathedra* statement: one made "when in discharge of the office of pastor and teacher of all Christians, by virtue of his supreme apostolic authority, he defines a doctrine regarding faith or morals to be held by the universal Church." The criteria for an *ex cathedra* statement are thus:

1. The pope is exercising his office as pastor and teacher of all Christians.
2. He exercises his supreme apostolic authority.
3. He defines a doctrine.

4. The doctrine concerns faith or morals.
5. The doctrine is to be held by the universal Church.

472. The first condition requires the pope be acting in his official capacity, not simply as a private individual, as popes sometimes do (§§188–191).

The second condition requires not just that he be acting in his official capacity but that he be exercising the fullness of his authority. Any lesser degree will not result in an infallible definition.

The third condition requires that the pope define a doctrine, thus forever closing off legitimate debate about it.

The fourth condition requires the doctrine concern "faith or morals," which we have previously discussed (§§428–447).

The fifth condition requires that the doctrine is to be held by all of the faithful.

The formulation offered by Vatican II is simpler but conveys the same essential content. It expressly mentions conditions 1, 3, and 4, though it expresses the third condition by saying that the pope must proclaim the teaching "by a definitive act" (instead of "he defines"). Conditions 2 and 5 are omitted since they are implied by the nature of a definitive act of teaching. Such acts necessarily involve the fullness of the pope's authority and result in teachings to be held by all the faithful.

473. The number of papal definitions is debated among scholars, even if we set aside the question of saint canonizations (§440) and look strictly at definitions of a doctrinal nature. Though it doesn't claim to give an exhaustive list, the 1908 French *Dictionnaire de Théologie Catholique* lists about a dozen examples of documents that "are usually or fairly regarded as containing an infallible definition."[89] Other sources from the same period give similar lists.[90]

As the twentieth century progressed, scholars further studied these texts, and many concluded that some of them didn't meet the criteria for infallibility. Some took a minimalist position and concluded there are only two such documents: *Ineffabilis Deus* (1854) and *Munificentissimus Deus* (1950), which defined the Immaculate Conception and the Assumption. However, most scholars haven't taken such an extreme position. According to Cardinal Dulles:

> Except for the definition of the Immaculate Conception, there is little clarity about which papal statements prior to Vatican I [1870] are irreformable. Most authors would agree on about half a dozen statements. Among the clearest examples are the statement of Pope Benedict XII on the nature of the beatific vision (1336; [DH 1000–1002]) and the condemnation of five Jansenist propositions by Innocent X (1653; [DH 2001–2007]).[91]

Bear in mind this represents the number of documents containing infallible definitions, not the number of definitions. Some of these documents contain more than one definition, so the number of doctrines infallibly proclaimed by popes would be somewhat higher. For a case study of proposed papal definitions, see §§500–518.

Terms Indicating Infallibility

474. How can we recognize when a council is teaching a doctrine "is to be held definitively" or when a pope teaches one "by a definitive act"? The answer is by looking at the language used.

This is a complex issue, because the language has developed over time and there isn't a single, set form of words. At Vatican I, some bishops suggested the council should develop a specific formula popes must use when issuing an infallible definition, but this proposal was rejected. One reason was that there had been no set formula in the past; another was that councils can't bind popes.[92]

475. When recent magisterial documents discuss infallibility, they frequently use words like *define, definitive, definitively,* and *definition* rather than just "infallible." This is because there has been a development both of doctrine and of language concerning infallibility.

Before a certain stage, the Church's infallible teaching authority hadn't been explicitly formulated. Like original sin and the two wills of Christ, it's a truth that was originally implicit in the deposit of faith. Consequently, early popes and councils didn't think in terms of teaching under the charism of infallibility. Instead, they issued proclamations intending to make it absolutely clear that a given teaching *must* or *must not* be held by Christians—that it was *not* the subject of legitimate discussion. They thus sought to bring any controversy concerning it completely (Latin, *de-*) to an end (*finis*). By thus defining things, they used the fullness of their teaching authority, and later theological reflection made it clear that such definitions are infallible.

If you asked early popes or council fathers, "Have you used your teaching authority infallibly?" they would be puzzled by the expression, just as if you asked St. Paul, "Do you believe in original sin?" The relevant terms hadn't been coined. However, if—following a definition—you asked them, "Is there any possibility what you just taught is wrong?" they would answer there is absolutely none, the teaching is certain, and all Christians must adhere to it.

This historical development is why we don't find popes and councils saying, "We hereby infallibly teach . . ." Instead, a variety of expressions have been used.

Heresy

476. The term *heresy* (Greek, *hairesis*) originally meant "opinion" or "choice" (§270). However, the Church was quickly beset by people advocating false opinions, and *heresy* came to be applied to views contrary to the Christian faith. This led popes and councils to denounce various positions as heretical.

Because heresy is incompatible with the Christian faith, the term sometimes appears in infallible definitions and can serve as a signal that a definition is being made. Thus scholars commonly regard Pope Innocent X's 1653 constitution *Cum Occasione* (DH 2001–2007) as an infallible declaration, partly because it censures five propositions of Cornelius Jansen as "heretical."

As we have noted, heresy is rejection of a dogma (§264), and since the eighteenth-century dogmas have been understood as truths the Church has infallibly taught to be divinely revealed (§271). Heresies thus are opposed to infallible teachings, and the censure of heresy can infallibly indicate a proposition is false.

477. However, it doesn't do so in all cases. We need to sound three notes of caution. First, infallible teaching occurs in solemn, official acts (§§463, 471). Consequently, if a pope was giving an interview and said, "Oh! That's heretical!" or if he wrote a book as a private scholar and described a position as heretical, these wouldn't be definitions since he wouldn't be acting in his official capacity and exercising the fullness of his teaching authority.

478. Second, since no teaching is infallible unless this is "manifestly evident" (§456), definitions must deal with specific, identifiable propositions. But sometimes early councils say things like, "We condemn the views of so-and-so and his followers as heretical." This tells us that *something* the individual taught is being condemned, but not what. It thus isn't "manifestly evident" which propositions are to be rejected.

Similarly, the censure of heresy can be mixed in with other censures without it being clear to which propositions it applies. Thus most scholars don't regard Pope Leo X's 1520 bull *Exurge Domine* (DH 1451–1492) as infallible because, although it condemns many ideas of Martin Luther, it applies different censures to them (including "offensive to pious ears," which just means phrased in an offensive way but not necessarily false) and it doesn't indicate which ones are heretical (§354).

479. Third, and most problematic, the term *heresy* hasn't always had its modern sense. Francis Sullivan explains:

> The problem is that at Trent, and other councils before Trent, the term "heresy" had a broader meaning than it

has in modern canon law. It included not only the denial of a truth which must be believed with divine and catholic faith, but also ways of believing and acting which would endanger either one's own faith or that of the community. The fathers of Trent saw such danger to the faith of the Catholic people in many things which the reformers were saying and doing, over and above their denial of what Catholics held to be divinely revealed truth.[93]

This means earlier condemnations of propositions as heretical may not indicate they are contrary to divine revelation but are dangerous in some other way. A determination thus has to be made whether the issue involves divine revelation.

Anathema

480. The Greek term *anathema* originally had several meanings. In the New Testament, it could mean an offering devoted to God (Luke 21:5), something cursed (1 Cor. 12:3), and a curse itself (Acts 23:14).

481. In 1 Corinthians 16:22, St. Paul writes, "If anyone has no love for the Lord, let him be accursed [Greek, *anathema*]," and this formula began to be used in the early Church to condemn propositions. Thus, after teaching the divinity of Christ in the original version of the Nicene Creed, the fathers of I Nicaea state:

However, those who say: "There was a time when he [the Son] was not" and "Before he was born, he was not" and "He was made from nothing" or who say that God [the Son of God] may be of another substance or essence or may be subject to change and alteration, [such persons] the Catholic Church anathematizes (DH 126).

Other councils and popes copied St. Paul's formula "let him be anathema" exactly. Trent used it numerous times in its canons, such as this one:

> If anyone says that, without divine grace through Jesus Christ, man can be justified before God by his own works, whether they be done by his own natural powers or through the teaching of the law, let him be anathema (*Decree on Justification*, can. 1).

In Latin, the phrase "let him be anathema" (*anathema sit*) is so commonly used that some English versions leave it untranslated or simply abbreviate "*a.s.*"

482. As canon law developed, *anathema* came to be used for a specific penalty: a major excommunication performed with a special ceremony. This is the meaning it has in Trent. Contrary to a misunderstanding common in the Protestant community, it isn't a declaration a person is damned by God. Neither does it mean that Protestants are under anathema. It doesn't even mean Catholics who commit the offense in question are automatically anathematized.

In canon law, "let him be anathema" established a penalty to be applied by the authorities, just as civil law might say, for offenders of a certain type, "let him be fined $500" or "let him be incarcerated for one to three years." Penalties have to be applied by a judge, and in the case of anathemas, the judge was the local bishop. If a bishop determined a person in his diocese (e.g., a theologian) was teaching a condemned proposition and wouldn't desist after appropriate warnings, he could sentence him to excommunication by anathema, which involved performing a public ceremony. There was a parallel ceremony for lifting the anathema when the man repented.

Bishops wouldn't waste their time initiating judicial proceedings against people who made no pretense of being Catholic, so anathemas weren't applied to non-Catholics. In recent centuries, they became very rare, though the penalty was still on the books when the 1917 *Code of Canon Law* was released. It provided that excommunication "is called *anathema* especially when it is inflicted with the formalities that are described in the Roman Pontifical" (can. 2257 §2).

The penalty was abolished with the release of the 1983 *Code*, which didn't include the penalty and which abrogated "any universal or particular penal laws whatsoever issued by the Apostolic See unless they are contained in this Code" (can. 5 §1 °3). The penalty thus applies to no one today, although other forms of excommunication still exist (cf. CIC 1331).

483. The term *anathema* is significant for our purposes because it was often applied to heretics in solemn declarations, like the one above from Trent. There, the penalty is prescribed for one who says that "without divine grace through Jesus Christ, man can be justified before God by his own works, whether they be done by his own natural powers or through the teaching of the law." Establishing this penalty is a sign the proposition in question is heretical.

Trent's canons are the most solemn pronouncements it made. They distill the key points from its doctrinal decrees and indicate particular teachings are to be absolutely avoided by Christians. They thus can serve to infallibly define matters. Although the canonical penalty of anathema no longer exists, the canons retain their doctrinal force (and, even today, one who denies a dogma would be excommunicated on grounds of heresy; cf. CIC 1364 §1).

484. The use of *anathema* is an important clue to the presence of an infallible definition, but it isn't sufficient of itself. The cautions we mentioned above apply here: (1) unofficial or non-solemn uses of the term don't create definitions, (2) it must be applied to specific, identifiable propositions, and (3) we must take different ways the term is used into account.

485. For example, anathemas weren't *always* applied to doctrinal offenses. They were also applied to moral ones. Thus the Fourth Lateran Council (1215) issued this disciplinary canon:

Against magistrates and rulers of cities and others who strive to oppress churches and ecclesiastical persons with taxes and other exactions, the Lateran Council, desiring to protect ecclesiastical immunity, prohibited actions of this kind under penalty of anathema, commanding that transgressors and their abettors be punished with excommunication until they make suitable satisfaction (can. 46).

It subsequently decreed:

Furthermore, under penalty of anathema, we forbid all Christians for a period of four years to send their ships to oriental countries inhabited by the Saracens, in order that a greater number of ships may be available to those who wish to go to the aid of the Holy Land, and that to the Saracens may be denied the benefits that they usually reap from such commercial intercourse (*Holy Land Decrees*).

Neither of these is an infallible definition. They simply prescribe the penalty of anathema as punishment for actions such as oppressing churches with taxes or sending commercial ships to certain countries "for a period of four years."

486. In a related vein, Francis Sullivan states:

There is no doubt that a number of the canons of Trent pronounce the sentence of excommunication against those who reject beliefs or practice which, while traditional, are not part of the deposit of faith. In such cases, the "anathema" does not help us to identify a defined dogma. It is up to the theologian, then, to determine whether, in any particular case, the proposition to which the canon refers belongs to the primary object of magisterium—in other words, whether its denial would constitute heresy in the strict sense of modern canon law or in the broader sense the term had at Trent.[94]

487. Among the canons he cites as belonging to the latter category are the following:

If anyone denies that each and all of Christ's faithful of both sexes are bound, when they reach the age of reason, to receive Communion every year, at least during the Paschal Season, according to the precept of Holy Mother Church, let him be anathema (*Decree on the Eucharist,* can. 9; DH 1659).

If anyone says that confession of all sins as it is observed in the Church is impossible and is a human tradition that pious people must abolish; or that it is not binding on each and all of the faithful of Christ of either sex once a year in accordance with the constitution of the great Lateran Council and that for this reason the faithful of Christ are to be persuaded not to confess during Lent, let him be anathema (*Canons on Penance,* can. 8; DH 1708).

If anyone says that besides the priesthood there are in the Catholic Church no other orders, major and minor, by which, as by various steps, one advances toward the priesthood, let him be anathema (*Decree on the Sacrament of Orders,* can. 2; DH 1772).

If anyone says that marriage contracted but not consummated is not dissolved by the solemn religious profession of one of the spouses, let him be anathema (*Decree on the Sacrament of Marriage,* can. 6; DH 1806).

If anyone says that the prohibition of the solemnization of marriages at certain times of the year is a tyrannical superstition derived from pagan superstition; or condemns the blessing and other ceremonies that the Church uses in solemn nuptials, let him be anathema (*Decree on the Sacrament of Marriage,* can. 11; DH 1811).

Sullivan is correct that these canons deal with matters that aren't divinely revealed:

- The requirement to receive Communion once a year is a matter of canon law rather than divine law, as indicated in the text itself ("according to the precept of Holy Mother Church").

- Neither is the requirement to confess once a year a matter of divine law, as the text acknowledges ("in accordance with the constitution of the great Lateran Council").

- The minor orders weren't matters of divine law, and— since Pope Paul VI's 1972 motu proprio *Ministeria Quaedam* (which also renamed them "ministries")—they are no longer used to advance toward the priesthood.

- Unconsummated marriages are no longer dissolved by the religious profession of one of the parties (cf. CIC 1141–1150).

- The times at which marriages can be celebrated is a matter of canon law, and this has changed over time (presently they are not celebrated only on Good Friday and Holy Saturday; *Paschales Solemnitatis* 61, 75).

488. Since these matters are not divinely revealed, they don't fall within the primary object of infallibility and can't be the subject of dogmas. However, do they fall within the secondary object? A case can be made that they do—i.e., that they dealt with points needed to properly guard and expound revealed truths.

Although it isn't a matter of divine law that the faithful receive Communion once a year, the Church established this rule to guard a revealed truth: "Unless you eat the flesh of the Son of man and drink his blood, you have no life in you" (John 6:53). Further, it was true that in the 1500s (as today) the faithful were required to receive Communion once a year. Therefore, one could understand this and similar canons as dealing with *dogmatic facts* that existed at the time of Trent and thus were capable of being infallibly defined.

That doesn't mean the dogmatic facts apply to all ages. Today unconsummated marriages aren't dissolved by religious profession, but as long as the law held they were, this was a dogmatic fact, and the Church could define it was true in that age.

One could thus argue that if the council intended to teach these matters definitively that they would count as infallible definitions. The fact many of the other canons are definitions, and that they are phrased the same way ("If anyone says . . . let him be anathema"), at least suggests the council intended to define them. This conclusion is arguable and would need to be made on a canon-by-canon basis, but it should be considered.

Define/Definitive/Definitively/Definition

489. Finally, we come to the group of terms based on the word *define*. It should be no surprise these can be clues for infallible definitions:

- In particular, if a pope or council says "I/we define," this is a major indicator a definition is being given.
- If the words "definitive," "definitively," or "definition" are used then they can indicate the authors regard an infallible teaching as *already* given. Thus Vatican I refers to a definition given by the Council of Florence (*Pastor Aeternus,* 3; DH 3059), and John Paul II indicates that the reservation of priestly ordination to men is a truth "to be definitively held" due to the ordinary and universal magisterium (*Ordinatio Sacerdotalis,* 4; DH 4983).

490. The standard cautions apply: (1) unofficial or non-solemn uses of these terms don't create definitions, (2) they must be applied to specific, identifiable propositions, and (3) we must take different ways the terms are used into account.

491. The last is particularly important because these terms have multiple meanings, and frequently don't indicate an infallible definition: they didn't acquire their modern, technical meanings for some time. Therefore, particularly in early magisterial statements, they may not indicate an infallible definition by a pope or council.[95] Even today they are used other ways:

- Sometimes magisterial documents employ "define" and "definition" as they're used in ordinary speech (i.e., as explanations of the meanings of words or concepts). Thus John Paul II writes:

For a correct moral judgment on euthanasia, in the first place a clear definition is required. Euthanasia in the strict sense is understood to be an action or omission which of itself and by intention causes death, with the purpose of eliminating all suffering (*Evangelium Vitae*, 65).

- In this statement, the "definition" simply explains the meaning of the term *euthanasia*, as a dictionary would. Here, John Paul II doesn't say anything about how Catholics are to regard it or whether it is compatible with Christian moral principles (he does that later).

- In 2006 the Pontifical Council for Promoting Christian Unity issued a statement on why Pope Benedict XVI chose to drop the papal title "Patriarch of the West" and said the term *West* cannot "be understood as the definition of a territory belonging to a patriarchate" (DH 5106). Here the term means something like "specification" or "description."

- Church documents sometimes refer to people "defining" something even though the person is not a pope and thus can't make an infallible definition, as when Benedict XVI referred to how St. Augustine "defines the essence of the Christian religion" (*Address to the Pontifical Academy of Sciences*, April 19, 2005). In such cases, the term could have been translated "describes" or "explains."

- Sometimes the Latin term *definitio* so clearly means something else that it's rendered with a different English word, as when the translation of Benedict XVI's encyclical *Deus Caritas Est* (2005) discusses ways of understanding the concept of love and says, "There are other, similar classifications [*definitiones*], such as the distinction between possessive love and oblative love" (n. 7; DH 5101).

Ultimately, the definition-related terms in magisterial documents can have the full range of meaning they do in ordinary language. Thus the Latin verb *definio* means "solve, define, determine, limit," and the noun *definitio* means "definition, determination, measure.""⁹⁶ This puts us on notice that the use of these terms doesn't automatically mean that an infallible definition is being given.

492. How can we tell when the terms do signal an infallible definition? We need to look at the context and see if the other conditions are met. For example, here are the two papal definitions that everyone agrees are infallible:

Definition of the Immaculate Conception
To the honor of the holy and undivided Trinity, to the glory and distinction of the Virgin Mother of God, for the exaltation of the Catholic faith and the increase of the Christian religion, by the authority of our Lord Jesus Christ, of the blessed apostles Peter and Paul and our own, we declare, pronounce, and define: that the doctrine that maintains that the Most Blessed Virgin Mary, at the first instant of her conception, by the singular grace and privilege of almighty God and in view of the merits of Jesus Christ, the Savior of the human race, was preserved immune from all stain of original sin, is revealed by God and, therefore, firmly and constantly to be believed by all the faithful.

Therefore, if any people (which God forbid!) will presume in their hearts to think otherwise than what has been defined by us, let them henceforth know and understand that they are condemned by their own judgment, and they have made shipwreck of their faith and defected from the unity of the Church; moreover, if they should dare to express in words or in writings, or by any other outward means, these errors that they think in their hearts, they subject themselves ipso facto to the penalties established by law (*Ineffabilis Deus;* DH 2803-2804).

Definition of the Assumption of Mary
To the glory of almighty God, who has lavished his special affection upon the Virgin Mary, for the honor of her Son, the immortal King of the Ages and the Victor over sin and

death, for the increase of the glory of that same august Mother, and for the joy and exultation of the entire Church; by
the authority of our Lord Jesus Christ, of the blessed apostles
Peter and Paul, and by our own authority, we pronounce,
declare, and define it to be a divinely revealed dogma: that
the Immaculate Mother of God, the ever Virgin Mary, having completed the course of her earthly life, was assumed
body and soul into heavenly glory.

Hence, if anyone, which God forbid, should dare willfully to deny or to call into doubt that which we have
defined, let him know that he has fallen away completely from the divine and catholic faith (*Munificentissimus
Deus*, 44–45; DH 3903–3904).

Notice the elements these have in common:

a) The respective popes (Pius IX and Pius XII) both begin by
   using exalted language to build up the significance of the
   definition.
b) They invoke the authority of Jesus Christ.
c) They invoke the authority of Peter and Paul, the founding
   apostles of Rome.
d) They invoke their own authority.
e) They pile up verbs: "declare," "pronounce," and most cru-
   cially "define."
f) They indicate that the matter is to be believed by all the
   faithful, either by saying so directly (in the case of *Ineffibilis Deus*) or at least by saying that anyone who rejects the
   teaching has "made a shipwreck of"/"fallen away completely from" the Faith.
g) After making the definition, they refer to "what has been
   defined by us"/"that which we have defined."

All of this makes it "manifestly evident" that the popes are (1)
exercising their offices as pastor and teacher of all Christians (b,
c, d, f), (2) exercising the full extent of their authority (a, b, c, d,

e), (3) defining a doctrine (e, g), (4) concerning faith or morals (f), (5) to be held by the universal Church (f).

493. Now that these precedents have been established, future papal definitions may follow their model as a way of making it clear what the pope is doing. At a minimum, since Vatican I and II spoke of the pope defining or teaching "by a definitive act," we would expect future definitions to use the word "define" or another member of this family (e.g., "I teach by a definitive act," "I teach definitively," "I proclaim the following definition").

494. These two definitions shed light on other statements by recent popes. We *know* the kind of language Pius IX and Bl. Pius XII used when they wanted to make infallible definitions. Therefore, language of a lesser order should be presumed non-infallible. The same is true of other recent popes. Thus when John Paul II refrained from using the verb "define" in *Ordinatio Sacerdotalis* and *Evangelium Vitae*, the relevant statements shouldn't be understood as new definitions (as the CDF confirmed).

495. Of course, we can't expect the popes and councils of earlier times to follow the same model. However, one way or another, it must be "manifestly evident" that the conditions for infallibility spelled out by Vatican I and II are met.

Identifying Dogmas

496. Once an infallible statement has been identified, the question remains of whether it represents a dogma (§271). Cardinal Dulles explains:

> In current Catholic usage, the term "dogma" means a divinely revealed truth, proclaimed as such by the infallible teaching authority of the Church.[97]

For an infallible definition to create a dogma, *the definition* must indicate that the matter is divinely revealed. It is not sufficient that the matter itself is divinely revealed. The infallibility of the pope was always part of divine revelation, though it took time for it to be made explicit. As Ratzinger and Bertone indicated (*Doctrinal Commentary*, 11), it only became a dogma when Vatican I defined it *as a matter of revelation* (§§448–449). If the matter at hand appears to be divinely revealed, but the definition doesn't say it is, you might conjecture it could one day become a dogma, but that hasn't happened yet and it's only an infallible teaching.

497. What language indicates the presence of a dogma? Sometimes the definition will be explicit. *Munificentissimus Deus* says the Assumption is "a divinely revealed dogma." Without using the word *dogma*, the definition in *Ineffabilis Deus* says the Immaculate Conception "is revealed by God."

498. Two additional terms—*heresy* and *faith*—may also indicate the presence of a dogma. Today, *heresy* refers to the rejection of a dogma (§264), and *faith* indicates that matters of divine revelation are under discussion (§§344–346). However, care must be taken when evaluating these terms in centuries when they had broader meanings. Francis Sullivan remarks:

> What is true of the broader meaning of "heresy" in earlier councils is also true of the correlative term "faith." This denoted an attitude of fidelity to the Christian tradition, which meant not only the acceptance of revealed truth, but also the acceptance of truths connected with revelation, and the rejection of whatever could endanger one's faith. Earlier councils sometimes defined as doctrines of faith, truths that were merely connected with revelation, and condemned as heretics those who denied them. An example of this is the definition by the Council of Vienne (1311-1312) that the soul is the "form" of the body. . . .
>
> At that time, it was sufficient that the doctrine "pertained" to the faith, in the sense that the council saw a *danger* to the faith in its denial.[98]

The idea of the soul as the "form" of the body borrows a concept from philosophy, and neither Scripture nor the early Fathers speak of the soul this way. It's thus plausible that this represents a *dogmatic fact* that is "connected with revelation by a logical necessity" (*Doctrinal Commentary,* 11) rather than a truth drawn from revelation. If so, it would be part of the secondary object of infallibility, and Vienne's definition that the soul is the form of the body would be an infallible truth but not a dogma.

499. Authors also commonly recognize as a dogmatic fact the fittingness of the term *transubstantiation* to describe the miraculous transformation that takes place in the Eucharist. Writing in 1896, Sylvester Hunter, S.J., stated:

> In the same way [as other dogmatic facts had been defined], the Council of Trent (Sess. 13, can. 2; [DH 1652]) defined that the word *transubstantiation* was most fit to apply to the change of the elements in the Eucharist.[99]

The canon in question is interesting, because it appears to shift between the primary and secondary objects of infallibility:

> If anyone says that in the most holy sacrament of the Eucharist the substance of bread and wine remains together with the body and blood of our Lord Jesus Christ and denies that wonderful and unique change of the whole substance of the bread into his body and of the whole substance of the wine into his blood while only the species of bread and wine remain, a change which the Catholic Church very fittingly calls transubstantiation, let him be anathema (*Decree on the Eucharist,* can. 2; DH 1652).

Sullivan points out:

> Here what is defined as a dogma of faith is the "wonderful and unique change of the whole substance of bread," etc.

On the other hand, that the Church "very fittingly" calls this change of substance by the name "transubstantiation" is hardly something that God has revealed.[100]

The term *transubstantiation* was not coined until the 1000s (§82), and thus the truth that it fittingly describes the conversion of the bread and wine into the body, blood, soul, and divinity of Jesus is seen as a dogmatic fact. However, the reality of the change is contained in Scripture and Tradition and is therefore divinely revealed and part of the primary object of infallibility. The canon thus defines both a dogma (the reality of the change) and a dogmatic fact needed to properly guard and expound that dogma (the fittingness of the term *transubstantiation*).

Case Study: Proposed Papal Definitions

500. The infallible definitions made by councils are too numerous to cover, but we will take a brief look at proposed papal definitions. The most extensive contemporary discussion of them I'm aware of is by Francis Sullivan.[101]

Our starting point will be the passages the 1908 *Dictionnaire de Théologie Catholique* (§473) lists as examples that "are usually or fairly regarded as containing an infallible definition." These are not presented as an exhaustive list, but they certainly include the most commonly proposed ones.

Leo I, *Lectis Dilectionis Tuae* (449; DH 290-295)

501. This letter—also known as the Tome of Leo (or First Tome of Leo)—deals with the fact that Christ is one Person who has two distinct natures. Its teaching on this point is infallible, though Leo doesn't use language suggesting a definition, and modern scholars often hold that its teaching is infallible because it was subsequently defined by the Council of Chalcedon in 451 (DH 301).

Agatho, *Consideranti Mihi* (680; DH 542-545)

502. This letter deals with the two wills of Christ. Its teaching on this point is infallible, though, as with the Tome of Leo, scholars often hold this is because it was subsequently defined by the Third Council of Constantinople in 680 (DH 553-559) rather than because of the language it uses.

Boniface VIII, *Unam Sanctam* (1302; DH 875)

503. This bull dealt with the relationship of Church and state. It contains the statement "Furthermore we declare, state, and define that it is absolutely necessary for the salvation of all human creatures that they submit to the Roman pontiff" (DH 875). This is often regarded as an infallible definition, though that has been challenged because of the ambiguity of what it means to "submit" to the Roman pontiff. Given the Church-state issues being discussed, must they submit politically? Politically and spiritually? Only spiritually? In a separate and non-infallible statement Boniface indicated he meant they need to submit to the pope's spiritual power "with respect to sins." Whether or not *Unam Sanctam* qualifies as a definition in the modern sense, the teaching "outside the Church there is no salvation" is regarded as a dogma (Holy Office, *Letter to the Archbishop of Boston*, August 8, 1949; DH 3866), even if this has been set in a broader context than in Boniface's day (§§568-569).

Benedict XII, *Benedictus Deus* (1336; DH 1000-1002)

504. This constitution defines various aspects of the beatific vision, including the fact that the saints don't have to wait until the end of the world to experience it. It also defines that those who die in mortal sin go to hell and experience its sufferings before the Day of Judgment. Both of these were denied by Benedict's predecessor, John XXII. The infallibility of this document is widely accepted.

Leo X, *Exsurge Domine* (1520; DH 1451-1492)

505. This bull condemns errors of Martin Luther, saying they are "respectively heretical or scandalous or false or offensive to pious ears or seductive of simple minds and in opposition to Catholic truth" (DH 1492). Not all of these censures indicate falsity (scandalous means having a tendency to lead into sin, offensive to pious ears means offensively phrased, and seductive of simple minds means misleading). Because Leo X didn't indicate which propositions had which censures, the faithful couldn't know what attitude to take toward individual propositions (e.g., is this one heretical or only offensively phrased?). Consequently, the document is not widely regarded today as infallible (§§354, 478).

Innocent X, *Cum Occasione* (1653; DH 2001-2007)

506. This constitution deals with errors taught by bishop and theologian Cornelius Jansen in a book titled *Augustinus*, which was published after his death in 1638. The errors have to do with grace and free will. Each proposition is censured as heretical. Given the solemnity of the proclamation, its infallibility is widely acknowledged.

Innocent XI, *Caelestis Pastor* (1687; DH 2201-2269)

507. This constitution condemned sixty-eight errors of the Spanish mystic Miguel de Molinos, which were of a Quietistic nature. (Quietism was a tendency to regard perfection as achievable on earth through contemplation.) Like *Exurge Domine*, this document condemned the errors with a variety of censures, not all of which indicated falsity. Consequently, since it didn't indicate which were heretical, it is not widely regarded today as infallible.[102]

Innocent XII, *Cum Alias* (1699; DH 2351-2374)

508. This papal brief condemned twenty-three errors of Francois de Fenelon, the archbishop of Cambrai. They deal with the love of God and have a Quietistic character. As with *Exsurge Domine* and *Caelestis Pastor*, the censures attached to them don't all indicate falsity, they are not attached to specific propositions, and heresy isn't even listed as one of the censures. Consequently, this document is not widely regarded today as infallible.[103]

Clement XI, *Unigenitus* (1713; DH 2400-2502)

509. This constitution dealt with errors of Pasquier Quesnel, which were similar to those of Cornelius Jansen. Although 101 errors are condemned, specific censures are not applied to specific propositions. Consequently, this document is not widely regarded today as infallible.

Pius VI, *Auctorem Fidei* (1794; DH 2600-2700)

510. This constitution condemns errors committed by the Synod of Pistoia (in Tuscany) in 1786. Eighty-five passages from the synod are condemned, and the document tells us which censures apply to which propositions. Those passages that state a proposition is heretical are widely understood as infallible definitions.

Pius IX, *Ineffibilis Deus* (1854; DH 2800-2804)

511. This is the constitution in which Pius IX defined the Immaculate Conception of Mary. It is universally acknowledged as containing an infallible definition of dogma (DH 2803).

Pius IX, *Quanta Cura* (1864; DH 2890-2896)

512. This encyclical condemns various errors, including ones related to naturalism, socialism, and the proper relationship of Church and state. It concludes with Pius IX stating, "by our apostolic authority, we reject, proscribe, and condemn all the singular and evil opinions and doctrines severally mentioned in this letter and will and command that they be thoroughly held by all children of the Catholic Church as rejected, proscribed, and condemned" (DH 2896). Although Pius IX invokes his authority and tells Catholics to reject the "evil opinions and doctrines" he has mentioned, he doesn't provide us with a specific list of these, doesn't tell us which count as evil opinions and which are false doctrines, and doesn't apply specific censures to them. Furthermore, he had a decade earlier provided an example of the kind of language he used in making infallible definitions. This is a step down from that. Also, although the *Dictionnaire de Théologie Catholique* says that "many theologians and canonists would gladly add the famous encyclical *Quanta Cura*" to the list of documents containing a definition, this phrasing (only "many" theologians and canonists; not a majority?) suggests significant doubts about its status even in 1908. Consequently, this document is not widely regarded today as containing an infallible definition.

513. To the documents suggested in the *Dictionnaire de Théologie Catholique*, we must add a few more for consideration:

Alexander VII, *Ad Sanctam Beati Petri Sedem* (1656; DH 2010-2012)

514. After Innocent X condemned the errors of Jansen (§506), the latter's followers argued that, although the condemned propositions could be understood in a heretical sense, this wasn't the sense in which Jansen taught them. Sullivan comments:

> To meet this objection, Pope Alexander VII, in 1656, defined that those five propositions were found in [the book] *Augustinus*, and were condemned in the sense intended by the author. Now this is obviously not a truth revealed by God, but one deemed necessary for the defense of the truths previously defined by Pope Innocent X. Theologians speak of this as an example of a "dogmatic fact," that is, a fact that is connected with dogma in such a way as to justify its infallible definition. Thus, there are two definitions involved, but only that of Innocent X resulted in defined dogma.[104]

The constitution *Ad Sanctam Beati Petri Sedem* thus contains a new infallible definition, though not a new definition of dogma since the truths being defined belong to the secondary object of infallibility.

Leo XIII, *Apostolicae Curae* (1896; DH 3315-3319)

515. This apostolic letter teaches that Anglican orders are invalid. It is sometimes proposed as an infallible definition. However, this also is challenged. The key sentence reads: "Therefore, . . . confirming and, as it were, renewing [the decrees of previous pontiffs], by virtue of our authority, of our own initiative, and with sure knowledge, we proclaim and declare that the ordinations carried out according to the Anglican rite have been and are absolutely null and utterly void" (DH 3319). Although Leo invokes his authority and uses strong language, he says only "we proclaim and declare," not "we define"—language that had already become standard in definitions through its use by Pius IX and Vatican I. Further, this document is an apostolic letter, which is typically seen as less authoritative than an encyclical and certainly less authoritative than the apostolic constitutions normally used for infallible definitions. On the other hand, Ratzinger and Bertone propose this as an example of a papal definition of a dogmatic fact (*Doctrinal Commentary*, 11; but see also Dulles, *Magisterium*, 91).

Pius XII, *Munificentissimus Deus* (1950; DH 3903)

516. This is the constitution that defined the Assumption of Mary. This is widely acknowledged as the only infallible papal definition of a dogmatic nature in the twentieth century.

517. In surveying the range of scholarly opinion on the number of papal documents containing infallible definitions, we can distinguish several trends:

- Some scholars, particularly in the early twentieth century, such as the authors of the *Dictionnaire* or Ludovico Billot in his *Tractatus de Ecclesia Christi* (1903), propose about a dozen examples.

- Others, in the late twentieth century, have taken a minimalist approach and only acknowledged two—*Ineffibilis Deus* and *Munificentissimus Deus*.

- Still others have taken a moderate approach that is prepared to acknowledge that the conditions for infallibility are "manifestly evident" in the case of more documents than two but not as many as proposed in the *Dictionnaire*.

518. If we revise the *Dictionnaire*'s list to include documents widely regarded as containing infallible definitions (as opposed to teachings taught infallibly by later councils), the result would look something like this:

- Benedict XII, *Benedictus Deus* (1336; DH 1000-1002)
- Innocent X, *Cum Occasione* (1653; DH 2001-2007)
- Alexander VII, *Ad Sanctam Beati Petri Sedem* (1656; DH 2010-2012)
- Innocent XI, *Caelestis Pastor* (1687; DH 2201-2269)
- Pius VI, *Auctorem Fidei* (1794; DH 2600-2700)
- Pius IX, *Ineffibilis Deus* (1854; DH 2800-2804)
- Leo XIII, *Apostolicae Curae* (1896; DH 3315-3319)?
- Pius XII, *Munificentissimus Deus* (1950; DH 3903)

This corresponds well to Cardinal Dulles's assessment that, of papal documents issued before Vatican I (1870), "Most authors would agree on about half a dozen statements."[105] Bear in mind that some of these define more than one truth, so the number of doctrines defined is higher than the number of documents. Also, this doesn't deal with definitions by ecumenical councils or the ordinary Magisterium of the Church, so the total number of infallibly defined doctrines is higher yet.

CHAPTER 17

Theological Opinion

519. Church doctrines call for the faithful to respond with "religious submission of will and intellect" or with an even firmer response in the case of infallible teachings. However, the faithful are not bound in matters of theological opinion, and they may hold those opinions that seem plausible to them.

520. In some scholarly works, a permitted theological opinion is referred to as a *theologoumenon* (pl. *theologoumena*), from the Greek *theos* ("God") and *logein* ("to speak"). However, this term is also used in other senses, and to avoid confusion we will avoid it.

The Nature of Permission

521. The question of how you can know whether an opinion is permitted often arises in times of doctrinal unsettlement and of rapid social and intellectual change, such as our own day. Unfortunately, the answer is not always simple. When people ask, "Is this a permitted opinion?" they are generally looking for a yes or no answer, and sometimes the situation is complex. The reason has to do with the nature of permission. If an opinion is permitted, it has to be permitted by *something*, so we need to ask the follow-up question, "Permitted by *what*?"

Truth

522. The ultimate criterion is truth. If an opinion is true then it is permitted (and mandated), but if it is false then it isn't. However, since we are not God, we don't have unmediated knowledge of the truth and must turn to some source of information.

Revelation

523. In theology, the primary source of information is divine revelation, which can establish a number of things regarding an opinion:

- Revelation may indicate it is true.
- Revelation may indicate it is false.
- Revelation may not indicate anything about it.
- Revelation may offer some evidence but not enough to settle the matter.
- Revelation may be unclear.

If divine revelation indicates that a view is true then it is not only permitted but mandated. Scripture indicates that God exists, therefore this is what we must believe. Similarly, if revelation indicates that a view is false then it is not permitted. Scripture indicates that only one God exists, therefore, there are no other gods.

In the other cases, things are not so clear. God hasn't told us everything. For example, the total number of angels is either even or odd, but revelation doesn't contain evidence about that. In this type of case, it is permissible to speculate, to wonder whether the number is odd or even, but without additional evidence from some source (e.g., reason), it wouldn't seem permissible to adopt a firm view.

If revelation contains some information on a question but not enough to settle it then we may assign the view a probability consistent with the evidence, but we still need to acknowledge the view might be either true or false.

Finally, we must acknowledge revelation can be unclear. As the Ethiopian eunuch said when Philip the Evangelist asked if he understood Isaiah's prophecy, "How can I, unless someone guides me?" (Acts 8:31).

Reason

524. In addition to revelation, God gives us information through the created world, and some of this information is related to religious questions (Rom. 1:20). Historically, philosophy has been used to shed light on religious questions, but it is not the only relevant field. Ultimately all truth is God's truth, so information from all fields must harmonize with revelation, allowing faith and reason to shed light on each other. Consequently, even if an opinion is permitted by what God has told us in revelation, it may still receive confirmation or disconfirmation by what he allows us to discover through reason.

In Galileo's day, discoveries about the motions of celestial bodies prompted a reexamination of how certain biblical passages should be interpreted. More recently, discoveries about cosmology and biological evolution did the same. In both cases, the Magisterium determined the passages didn't require the interpretations that previously were common.

Infallible Church Teaching

525. When the Magisterium exercises its teaching authority in an infallible way, this forever settles the question under discussion. Anything that has been infallibly defined requires definitive assent. (In the case of a dogma, it also requires theological faith.) Consequently, anything that contradicts an infallible teaching is prohibited.

However, care must be exercised in keeping with the hermeneutic of precision. Since "no doctrine is understood as defined infallibly unless this is manifestly evident" (CIC 748 §3), infallible texts must be read precisely, without trying to make them settle questions they don't expressly discuss. History reveals that future doctrinal development can place an infallible teaching in a new and sometimes surprising context.

Thus in the Middle Ages, the dogma "no salvation outside the Church" was understood to preclude the salvation of non-Catholics, since it was presumed they were in bad faith due to culpable schism, heresy, or refusal to accept the Christian faith.

The discovery of the New World revealed there were millions who had never had the opportunity of accepting the Faith, and this dramatically recontextualized the issue (see §§568-569). The Magisterium thus came to adopt the position that the dogma is not directed at those who are innocently separated from the Church and that they can still be related to it in a saving way, though outside its "visible structure" (*Lumen Gentium*, 8, 14-16).

Non-Infallible Church Teaching

526. On many questions, the Magisterium hasn't exercised its teaching authority infallibly. Because these teachings aren't definitive, they could one day be revised (see §§394-399, 565-570), and, in individual cases, it could be legitimate to hold a contrary view (see chapter twenty). According to the CDF:

> The willingness to submit loyally to the teaching of the Magisterium on matters per se not irreformable must be the rule. It can happen, however, that a theologian may, according to the case, raise questions regarding the timeliness, the form, or even the contents of magisterial interventions (*Donum Veritatis*, 24).

However, it also stresses that one doesn't have the right to engage in "public opposition to the Magisterium of the Church, also called 'dissent'" (ibid., 32). This means a contrary view may or may not be permitted, depending on what you mean:

- In exceptional cases, it could be permitted to question "even the contents" of a non-infallible doctrine. Since it hypothetically could one day be revised, a contrary view might still turn out to be true and thus permitted from the ultimate perspective.

- However, this possibility doesn't create permission to publicly oppose (i.e., dissent from) non-infallible teachings. Contrary views are *not* permitted in this sense.

We thus see a distinction between what is permitted in a veridical sense (i.e., with respect to a view's truth) and what is permitted in a more sociological sense within the Church.

Current Church Authorities

527. The ecclesial-sociological sense is also in focus when we consider the views Church leaders are presently allowing to be discussed.

A dramatic illustration occurred when Pope Francis encouraged a discussion among the world's bishops of the conditions under which Communion might be administered to divorced and civilly remarried Catholics. This began when, at Pope Francis's invitation, Cardinal Walter Kasper gave an address to a meeting of cardinals in which he advanced a proposal that would allow some divorced and civilly remarried Catholics to receive absolution and Communion following a period of penance or reorientation.[106] Many argued this was incompatible with previously established, infallible Catholic principles. Others argued at least some of the affected doctrines weren't infallible or they were capable of undergoing doctrinal development in a way that would allow the Kasper proposal.

Ultimately, Pope Francis opted for a solution that envisioned a change in Church practice but didn't change points of doctrine (§328-335). However, he didn't condemn the Kasper proposal or say debate regarding it was closed. He thus created a situation in which it was suddenly permitted to discuss ideas in the Church that had not been open for discussion during the pontificates of Popes John Paul II and Benedict XVI and that many considered contrary to established doctrine.

There thus can be potential collisions between what is permitted by established teaching and what is permitted by present Church leaders. Such situations will be particularly agonizing when the established doctrines are or appear to be infallible. In other cases, they may be a sign the Magisterium is reconsidering a non-infallible teaching. Either way, such situations illustrate the difference between what is *doctrinally* permitted (i.e., by prior doctrine) and what is *ecclesiologically* permitted (i.e., by current Church authorities).

Popular Opinion in Society

528. What views are permitted in society changes over time. Some that formerly were taboo are now permitted (e.g., favoring abortion), and some that were formerly permitted are now taboo (e.g., favoring slavery). There also are differences between societies in different regions. Thus some views are permitted in Europe that would be taboo in Africa (e.g., favoring homosexuality), and there are views that would be legally permitted under American free speech laws that would be criminal offenses in Europe (e.g., Holocaust denial).

To one degree or another Christians, including Church leaders, naturally absorb the views of the society in which they live, and this has an impact on the views sociologically permitted within the Church. New social situations can even raise questions that spur doctrinal development, as the discovery of the New World did on the question of salvation outside the Church (§525). However, there is a danger that Christians, including churchmen, may absorb ideas from society that are incompatible with Christian doctrine. Fortunately, the Holy Spirit is still guiding the Church "into all truth" (John 16:13), and no matter what bumps there are in the road, we may be confident "that if the truth really is at stake, it will ultimately prevail" (*Donum Veritatis*, 31).

Synthesis

529. The question of whether an opinion is permitted thus may involve more than a simple yes or no answer:

1. Since divine revelation doesn't settle every question, a view might be permitted based on revelation but not permitted based on truths discoverable by reason.
2. If reason and revelation don't clearly rule out a view, it may still be prohibited by infallible Church teaching, which clarifies revelation and, in some cases, reason.
3. If a view is permitted by infallible Church teaching, it may be prohibited by non-infallible teaching. In such a situation, in exceptional cases, it might be legitimate to

question the non-infallible teaching in private but not to publicly oppose it.

4. If a truth isn't permitted by Church teaching, it might still be opened for discussion by Church authorities.
5. Regardless of whether a view is permitted by Church teaching, society may have a different attitude, and this may influence how it is perceived in the Church.

Usually when people ask if a view is permitted for Catholics, they have in mind situations (2) and (3)—is it allowed by infallible and other Church teaching? They generally aren't asking whether it is permitted by revelation or reason, whether it is presently open for discussion even though it appears contrary to Church teaching, or whether it is permitted or taboo in Catholic society. Instead, they want to know if it's permitted by present Church teaching (infallible or otherwise). Often it's possible to give a yes or no answer, but sometimes the answer must be more nuanced:

- If someone asks, "Is it permitted to believe that the moon is made of green cheese?" the answer will be that this is not contrary to Church teaching, but it is ruled out by reason.
- If someone asks, "Is the Kasper proposal a permitted opinion?" my answer would be that it appears contrary to Church doctrine but Pope Francis has permitted it for purposes of discussion.

Basic Principles for Investigation

530. How can we identify legitimate theological opinions—understood in the sense of views neither mandated nor prohibited by Church teaching? Two questions need to be asked:

1) Is the view dealt with in infallible Church teaching?
2) Is it dealt with in current, non-infallible teaching?

If an opinion has been the subject of infallible Church teaching then from that moment forward it will either be forever mandated or prohibited, even if some form of sharpening or re-contextualization takes place due to doctrinal development. On how to determine which teachings are infallible, see chapters fifteen and sixteen.

If an opinion has been discussed by the Magisterium in non-infallible teaching, then a determination must be made about whether the teaching is current. This is because doctrinal development can change which views are open to discussion—either taking previously permitted views out of the realm of legitimate discussion or returning them to it. On how to determine if a teaching is current, see chapters eighteen and nineteen.

If an opinion isn't dealt with by infallible teaching or by current, non-infallible teaching, then it belongs to the realm of free opinion. This is because of the general principle, derived from God's gift of free will, that liberty exists in the absence of either a mandate or a prohibition. It's also in keeping with Pope Pius XII's acknowledgment "that popes generally leave theologians free in those matters which are disputed in various ways by men of very high authority in this field" (*Humani Generis,* 19). One thus doesn't need an explicit statement to show that an opinion is permitted. The burden of proof is on one who would maintain that it's either mandated or prohibited.

Practical Principles for Investigation

531. Suppose you want to check whether a view is permitted by Church teaching. How do you do that in practice?

- A natural first step is checking the *Catechism of the Catholic Church,* which can be counted upon to include the main points of Church teaching.

- Another work to check is Denzinger's *Enchiridion Symbolorum* (§§234-236), a key collection of extracts from magisterial documents down through the centuries.

- You also should look at documents devoted to the general subject you're investigating. If you're researching a view regarding the Eucharist, papal encyclicals devoted to the Eucharist—such as Pope Paul VI's *Mysterium Fidei* and Pope John Paul II's *Ecclesia de Eucharistia*—should be consulted.

- It's now possible to electronically search large collections of Church documents, such as by using Google to search for key terms on the Vatican website (after entering your terms, add the tag "site:vatican.va" to the search field before hitting Enter).[107] Some Church documents are found elsewhere on the web, so broader internet searches also can be useful. Apart from the Vatican website, the largest collection of Church documents in English is probably found on the Verbum software platform (see Verbum.com).

- Manuals of theology (e.g., Ott's *Fundamentals of Catholic Dogma*) also can be useful for finding relevant Church documents.

- A final step is checking with an expert to see if there's anything you have missed.

If you find magisterial statements that pertain to the view you're investigating, you then need to evaluate them using the principles discussed in chapters eight through sixteen. If, after searching, you don't find magisterial statements that pertain to the view, you may tentatively conclude that the Magisterium doesn't presently have a teaching on the subject.

Rules of Thumb for Identification

532. Although liberty of opinion is presumed and the burden of proof falls on the one who holds that a particular view is either mandated or prohibited, there are rules of thumb that can serve as shortcuts to showing an opinion is permitted. Bear in mind these are *rules of thumb*, not absolutes. There are exceptions, which we will discuss. Also, it's important to remember that just because a view is *permitted* doesn't mean it is *true*.

Important Search Terms

533. One shortcut is using certain terms when searching Church documents electronically. These include references to non-magisterial groups ("exegetes," "scholars," "theologians"). Searching on such terms in a document devoted to the subject you're investigating may return references to non-magisterial proposals on the topic. The same is true of terms that may indicate a third party's attitude toward your subject ("according to," "consider," "opinion," "proposed/proposal," "tell us," "theology").

Using terms like "theologians" and "opinion" will return passages like Benedict XVI's statement, "Some recent *theologians* are of the *opinion* that the fire [of purgatory] which both burns and saves is Christ himself" (*Spe Salvi,* 47). You then need to examine the context to see whether the document mandates or prohibits such a proposal. If it does neither (as in this case) then the rule of thumb is that it's a matter of free opinion.

However, a view that is permitted at one time may later be mandated or prohibited, and the chance of that happening grows with time. You thus have to be careful with statements in older documents.

Respected Theologians and Theological Schools

534. Another shortcut to showing an opinion is permitted is to see if it's endorsed by respected theologians—including Doctors of the Church—or by established theological schools. Often consulting a manual of theology will reveal this.

If a highly respected theologian from the Patristic age (Jerome), the Middle Ages (Peter Lombard, St. Thomas Aquinas, St. Bonaventure), or later (St. Teresa of Avila, Francisco Suarez, Luis de Molina) endorsed the view, this constitutes prima facie evidence that it's permitted. The same is true of opinions commonly held in established theological schools (Thomists, Scotists, Franciscans).

However, this is only a rule of thumb because doctrinal development can change the situation. Thus Bl. John Duns Scotus's view that Mary was free from all stain of original sin at conception was subsequently infallibly mandated, and the view of some Dominicans of the Thomist school who in some centuries opposed this teaching was infallibly prohibited.

535. You must be careful when looking to theologians of the post-Vatican II period because of the dissent characterizing this time. The presumption of permissibility doesn't apply to the views of dissident theologians, though it does to the views of theologians known for their support of the Magisterium.

536. A special class of respected theologians are those who have been named cardinals (Bl. John Henry Newman, Hans urs von Balthasar,[108] Avery Dulles). Men in this category were so highly valued for their theological contributions that popes appointed them cardinals even though they weren't bishops. Opinions they express may be considered permitted in most circumstances, though there can be exceptions. For example, although von Balthasar's proposal that we may hope all men are saved[109] is carefully phrased to avoid denying Church teaching on the possibility of going to hell, it isn't obvious this is a permitted opinion. Nevertheless, the theological opinions of men in this category generally should be presumed legitimate.

Non-Magisterial Documents Published by Church Authorities

537. Church authorities publish many documents that aren't acts of magisterium. Examples include:

- Documents published by the dicasteries of the Roman Curia that don't carry the papal approval needed to make them part of the pope's magisterium
- Documents published by bishops' conferences that don't meet the criteria of *Apostolos Suos*
- Documents prepared by advisory groups run by the Holy See (e.g., the Synod of Bishops, the Pontifical Biblical Commission, the International Theological Commission)
- The Vatican newspaper *L'Osservatore Romano*
- The magazine *Civiltà Cattolica* (considered semiofficial; it's actually published by the Jesuits but it's reviewed prior to publication by the Holy See's Secretariat of State)

Although these documents don't represent acts of the Magisterium, they are expected to be in line with Church teaching, and opinions expressed in them generally may be presumed to be legitimate. As always, this is a rule of thumb, both because the Magisterium may later weigh in on a question and because mistakes can be made.

538. The rule of thumb applies only to documents that were authorized to be published. Working documents that have been clandestinely leaked (as with the 1960s pontifical commission on birth control; see §222) do *not* count. However, if the pope authorizes the release of a document by the Synod of Bishops or the Pontifical Biblical Commission—as is required for them to be published— then the rule of thumb applies. The same is true of the International Theological Commission, whose documents can be authorized for publication by the pope or the head of the Congregation for the Doctrine of the Faith "on condition that there is not any difficulty on the part of the Apostolic See" (see §§220-221).

Statements by Members of the Magisterium

539. Finally, members of the Magisterium may express theological opinions, and these generally may be presumed legitimate. Bishops in communion with the pope are commissioned to teach the Faith and are guided by the Holy Spirit. One could not seriously maintain that theological opinions expressed by bishops and the pope should be presumed *illegitimate!*

The presumption of legitimacy applies both when members of the Magisterium express a theological opinion in a magisterial document and when they express it in unofficial works, such as:

- Books (e.g., Benedict XVI's *Jesus of Nazareth* series, Cardinal Robert Sarah's *The Power of Silence*, Archbishop Charles Chaput's *Render unto Caesar*)
- Book-length interviews (e.g., John Paul II's *Crossing the Threshold of Hope*, Benedict XVI's *God and the World*, Cardinal Gerhard Muller's *The Hope of the Family*)

- Interviews given to newspapers and other media outlets
- Speeches
- Articles they write

Basically, the views expressed by a bishop should be considered orthodox (legitimate, permitted) until the contrary is shown.

540. Two bishops deserve special attention in this regard—the pope himself and the head of the Congregation for the Doctrine of the Faith. These are the bishops most responsible for protecting the faith of Christians, and their views carry a stronger presumption of orthodoxy. The pope is the vicar of Christ, empowered by the Holy Spirit to confirm his brother bishops in the Faith (cf. Luke 22:32), and the head of the CDF is the chief doctrinal watchdog of the Church. If you can't presume that these men's views are orthodox, who can you?

The presumption also applies to works they produced prior to entering these offices. If a man were known to be fundamentally unorthodox, the college of cardinals wouldn't have elected him pope, and if a man's theological judgment was fundamentally unsound, the pope wouldn't appoint him to head the CDF.

541. Having said that, the presumption of orthodoxy can be defeated. Examples include:

- Bishops whose views are so problematic they are removed from the pastoral care of souls by the pope (e.g., French bishop Jacques Gaillot, who was removed by John Paul II, and Australian bishop William "Bill" Morris, who was removed by Benedict XVI)
- Bishops who have gone into schism or heresy (e.g., Zambian bishop Emmanuel Milingo)

The views expressed by these bishops—before or after their removal from office—can't be considered reliable guides to whether an opinion is permitted.

The views of other bishops also can be problematic on occasion. If a view appears to contradict Church teaching—as opposed to common theological opinion—the presumption that it's a legitimate view doesn't hold. This appears to be the case with Cardinal Walter Kasper's proposal regarding the divorced and civilly remarried (§§527, 529).

The presumption of orthodoxy *for a particular opinion* can even be overcome in the case of popes. Pope John XXII (1316-1334) held that the souls of the blessed don't receive the full beatific vision until the end of the world and the damned don't enter hell until then. This was contrary to the common doctrine of the Church in his day. Just before his death, he retracted this view (DH 990-991), and his successor, Benedict XII, infallibly defined he had been wrong on both matters (DH 1000-1002).

542. A special word should be said about views that bishops and popes express in press interviews. The nature of these situations means they don't have time to carefully formulate a statement, consult with experts, and revise it as needed. They are speaking off the top of their heads. This is one reason why interviews aren't treated as magisterial acts. It's also why—even after stripping away layers of media distortion—we need to be cautious with statements made in interviews. Bishops and popes may have expressed a legitimate view in an unclear way, omitted important qualifiers, or even misspoken. We thus shouldn't treat remarks made in interviews as fully formed expressions of their settled opinion. If such remarks appear contrary to established doctrines (as opposed to common theological opinion), we should give them the benefit of the doubt and wait to see if a clarification is forthcoming.

543. In the case of popes, it's common in every pontificate for the Holy See's press office to issue clarifications, even when the pope is as careful a speaker as Benedict XVI. His reign saw a notable clarification following a speech in Regensburg, Germany, that set off riots in Muslim countries, and later the CDF issued a note clarifying remarks he made in the interview book *Light of the World* (§314). The same thing has happened with even greater frequency with Pope Francis, given his more freewheeling manner of speaking. In particular, he's given a number of interviews with the non-agenarian, atheist journalist Eugenio Scalfari, and following these, the Holy See's press office issued warnings that Scalfari doesn't use a tape recorder or take notes during conversations with the pope, so words attributed to him shouldn't be relied upon.

544. In the case of bishops, clarifications may be issued by the bishop himself or by a spokesman. It isn't common for the Holy See to do so. The Holy See generally feels it would be imprudent to publicly correct bishops over individual remarks. Doing so would undermine his ministry in his own diocese, call more attention to a problematic statement than it otherwise would have received, and potentially alienate people from the Church for appearing "hard-hearted" and "authoritarian" with respect to the bishop. The Holy See thus tends to remain silent on one-off heterodoxies.

This means that, if an individual bishop makes a statement contrary to Church teaching and no public correction follows, it shouldn't be taken as a sign the Holy See considers this a permitted opinion. However, when there is a well-established pattern—if many bishops express the view on many occasions and no correction follows—it *may* be a sign the Holy See is treating the view as permitted, at least in the ecclesial-sociological sense described above.

Examples of Theological Opinions

545. It's only fitting we conclude this chapter with examples of legitimate theological opinions, though these can be no more than random illustrations. Still, some may be quite surprising, which illustrates the need to carefully distinguish between theological opinions—however common—and the authoritative teaching of the Church.

Various Views on Predestination, Grace, and Freedom

546. The Church has teachings on each of these subjects, but they are modest in scope and leave many questions unanswered. Consequently, a number of theological schools of thought have developed among Thomists, Augustinians, Molinists, and others. Discussion among these schools became harsh in the sixteenth and seventeenth centuries during what was known as the "controversy on grace." A practical resolution arrived in 1607 when Pope Paul V issued a decree prohibiting the parties from censuring each other (DH 1997), thus leaving their views a matter of free theological opinion.[110]

The Choirs of Angels

547. Using various biblical texts, theologians have proposed different ways of classifying and ranking angels. However, as John Paul II indicates, these rankings are a matter of theological opinion and none has "an absolute value":

> They [the angels] are divided into orders and grades, corresponding to the measure of their perfection and to the tasks entrusted to them. The ancient authors and the liturgy itself speak also of the angelic choirs (nine, according to Dionysius the Areopagite). Especially in the Patristic and medieval periods, theology has not rejected these representations. It has sought to explain them in doctrinal and mystical terms, but without attributing an absolute value to them (*General Audience*, August 6, 1986).

The Significance of Jesus' Entrustment of Mary

548. In John 19:26-27, Jesus entrusts the care of his mother to the beloved disciple. Later interpreters have seen this act as having a broader significance in which a maternal relationship is established between Mary and all believers. John Paul II embraced this view but noted that it was a matter of "common ecclesial opinion":

> Interpreted at times as no more than an expression of Jesus' filial piety toward his Mother whom he entrusts for

the future to his beloved disciple, these words go far beyond the contingent need to solve a family problem. In
fact, attentive consideration of the text, confirmed by the
interpretation of many Fathers and by common ecclesial
opinion, presents us, in Jesus' twofold entrustment, with
one of the most important events for understanding the
Virgin's role in the economy of salvation (*General Audience*,
April 23, 1997).

The Validity of Baptism "in Jesus' Name"

549. Based on Matthew 28:19, the Church baptizes using the
trinitarian formula "in the name of the Father, and of the Son,
and of the Holy Spirit." However, in the New Testament we
also read of baptism being administered "in the name of Jesus Christ" (Acts 2:38, 10:48), "in the name of the Lord" (Acts
8:16), and "in the name of the Lord Jesus" (Acts 19:5). This raises
the question of whether such formulas were actually used in the
early Church or whether they are a shorthand way of referring
to Christian baptism (as opposed to John's baptism and Jewish
ritual washings)—the full trinitarian formula being too long to
give on each occasion.

If baptism were administered using a formula like "in Jesus'
name," without denying the doctrine of the Trinity, would it be
valid? The Magisterium hasn't dealt with this question in recent
times, and the statements of prior popes are mixed. In 256, Pope
Steven I apparently referred to both formulas without deciding
between them (DH 111). In 404, Pope Innocent I referred to
being baptized "in the name of Christ" without condemning
it or indicating it was to be understood as shorthand (DH 211).
Around 558, Pope Pelagius I stated failure to use the trinitarian formula would invalidate baptism (DH 445). But in 866,
Pope Nicholas I cited the precedent of Acts and the opinion of
St. Ambrose to indicate that baptism "in the name of the Holy
Trinity or only in the name of Christ" would be valid (DH 646).
Ludwig Ott concludes: "The Church has pronounced no final
decision on the question."[111]

It is noteworthy that when the *Catechism* addresses the issue, it doesn't discuss formulas like "in Jesus' name." Neither does it say the essential form of baptism *is* the trinitarian formula. It merely says that the trinitarian formula is used, in slightly different forms, in the Latin and Eastern liturgies (CCC 1240). In light of the prior mixed doctrinal tradition on this question, this illustrates why the hermeneutic of precision is important and why we need to consider what magisterial documents are *not* saying.

Jesus as a "Human Person"

550. Jesus is a Person who has a complete divine nature and a complete human nature. From this, one might infer he could be described *both* as a divine Person and as a human Person. Scripture even expressly says he is both "God" (John 1:1, 5:18, 20:28; Col. 2:6; Titus 2:13) and a "man" (Acts 2:22-23, 17:31; Rom. 5:15; 1 Tim. 2:5).

Nevertheless, various authors deny Jesus can be described as a "human Person." The intent is to protect against heresies such as Nestorianism, which implies Christ is two Persons, and Ebionitism, which held that he is *merely* a human person (not a divine one). In addition, Christ's divine nature is fundamental to his Person, whereas his human nature is not. God the Son can't be anything but a divine Person in virtue of his eternal, immutable, and essential divine nature. However, he could have refrained from acquiring a human nature if he had chosen not to incarnate. Thus if one had to choose between describing Christ as a divine Person or a human Person, the former would be the only choice.

Yet it doesn't seem possible to find a magisterial document saying Christ can't be described as a human Person. It thus appears the rejection of this phrase is a matter of theological opinion rather than doctrine. Further, one sometimes finds respected theologians who acknowledge that "human Person" can be used. Thus the renown nineteenth-century theologian Matthias Scheeben writes:

Christ may be called "human Person," in the sense of Person having humanity (*persona humanitatis*), as he is called divine Person as having divinity. Yet that designation is not commonly used, because misleading.[112]

Opinions of a Prudential Order

551. The Church's social doctrine articulates moral principles of abiding significance, but their application to concrete situations is ultimately the responsibility of the laity. Consequently, John Paul II stressed the wide latitude of opinion the laity have:

[Lay Christians] express in the world the Church's application of her own social doctrine. Nevertheless, they must be aware of their personal freedom and responsibility in matters of opinion, in which their choices, though always inspired by gospel values, should not be presented as the only alternative for Christians. Respect for legitimate opinions and choices different from one's own is also a requirement of love (*General Audience*, April 13, 1994).

CHAPTER 18

Understanding Doctrinal Development

The Reality of Doctrinal Development

552. Doctrinal development is the process by which the Church's teachings develop over time. It occurs despite the fact the Christian faith was "once for all delivered to the saints" (Jude 3).

However, in Catholic circles, it's common to encounter claims that the Church's teachings "cannot change." This mode of speech has been used to counter Protestant claims that the Church has "added" or "invented" many things not found in the Bible. Catholic controversialists similarly accused Protestants of subtracting from or "varying" from historic Christian teaching. Thus, the seventeenth-century French bishop and apologist Jacques Bossuet devoted a book to the *Variations of the Protestant Churches*. Such authors contrasted Protestant novelties with the unchanging teaching of the Catholic Church. Bossuet stated:

> The Church's doctrine is always the same. . . . The gospel is never different from what it was before. Hence, if at any time someone says that the Faith includes something which yesterday was not said to be of the Faith, it is always *heterodoxy*, which is any doctrine different from *orthodoxy*. There is no difficulty about recognizing false doctrine: there is no argument about it: it is recognized at once, whenever it appears, merely because it is new.[113]

There is a fundamental continuity in Catholic teaching, since the Church is "the pillar and bulwark of the truth" (1 Tim. 3:15). If the assertion that the Church's teaching "can't change" is understood to mean its fundamental content doesn't change, it's quite true. In all ages, the Church maintains the same fundamental doctrine—the deposit of faith that it received from Christ. However, if one maintains individual teachings aren't subject to development, it's false.

Doctrinal Development in Scripture

553. In the biblical age, doctrinal development occurred in a way that no longer takes place. At the time, God was still giving public revelation, and modern authors have termed this process "progressive revelation" because God progressively gave mankind more information about himself. This resulted in the disclosure of fundamentally new truths over time:

- The Israelites always believed in an afterlife (Gen. 25:8; Deut. 18:11; 1 Sam. 28:3-20), but originally little was known about it. By the later books of the Old Testament, the resurrection of the dead had been revealed (Dan. 12:2), and it would be further explored in the New Testament (Matt. 22:23-33; John 11:24; 1 Cor. 15:12-56; 1 Thess. 4:16, etc.).

- Old Testament prophecies began to point to a coming Messiah, who the New Testament revealed to be Jesus Christ. It was further revealed, contrary to the expectations of the day, that the Messiah would suffer and die for the sins of mankind and rise "on the third day," rather than the end of the world, when the general resurrection takes place.

- The Old Testament stressed God's oneness as a way of weaning the Israelites from polytheism (Deut. 6:4), but once this was done, the New Testament revealed that the one God is a Trinity of Persons (Matt. 28:19).

Jesus indicated progressive revelation would continue after the Crucifixion, for he had many things to reveal that the disciples couldn't yet bear (John 16:12). Thus he said the Holy Spirit would lead the disciples "into all the truth" (John 16:13), based on what he was given to disclose by Jesus (John 16:14). Progressive revelation thus continued through the Apostolic Age.

Doctrinal Development in Church History

554. After the Apostolic Age, doctrine continued to develop, but in a new way. The *Catechism of the Catholic Church* states:

> No new public revelation is to be expected before the glorious manifestation of our Lord Jesus Christ. Yet even if Revelation is already complete, it has not been made completely explicit; it remains for Christian faith gradually to grasp its full significance over the course of the centuries (CCC 66).

This process has unfolded over the centuries in a variety of ways. One of the clearest examples is how the doctrines of God and of Christ took shape in the early centuries:

- In the early fourth century, the divinity of Christ was attacked by the Arians, who held Jesus is a created, celestial being. In response, Nicaea I (325) infallibly defined the divinity of Christ.

- In the late fourth century, the divinity of the Holy Spirit was denied by the Pneumatomachians (Greek, "those who fight against the Spirit"). In response, Constantinople I (381) infallibly defined the divinity of the Spirit.

- In the early fifth century, Nestorians took a position that implied Jesus is two persons—one divine and one human. In response, the Council of Ephesus (431) ruled against the Nestorians, indicating Christ is a single Person.

- In the mid-fifth century, Monophysites (Greek, "one-nature"-ists) held Jesus had only a single nature, so he couldn't be both fully divine and fully human. In response, the Council of Chalcedon (451) defined that Jesus has two natures, one divine and one human.

- In the seventh century, Monothelites (Greek, "one-will"-ists) held Jesus had only a single will. In response, Constantinople III (681) defined that he has two wills, one divine and one human, and the two are never opposed.

As this sequence indicates, the Church's doctrine developed by moving from larger questions (e.g., is Jesus God?) to more detailed ones (e.g., does he have two wills?). None of this involved new revelation, only a working out the implications of the original deposit of faith.

Recognizing Doctrinal Development

555. Catholics have always known that popes and councils issue new definitions, particularly in response to doctrinal errors. However, they didn't have a robust way of articulating the development of doctrine until Bl. John Henry Newman (1801-1890). As a man raised Protestant, he was well aware that aspects of Catholic faith and practice aren't found explicitly in Scripture. For a time, this was a barrier between him and the Church, even as he found himself moving closer to it.

The turning point came as he was working on a book titled *An Essay on the Development of Christian Doctrine* (1845), in which he wrestled with the question of which developments should be considered legitimate. Though he planned to publish the book before deciding whether to become Catholic, as it was being printed he decided he had resolved his difficulties, and he entered the Church.

Newman's discussion of doctrinal development wasn't welcomed by all Catholics. Many, including American convert Orestes Brownson, were quite critical. Yet he continued to explore it in both public and private works,[114] and since Newman's death, the idea of doctrinal development has been widely embraced. In view of his theological contributions, Newman may one day be named a Doctor of the Church.[115]

Not all ways of understanding doctrinal development are correct, but the fundamental concept is valid and has undeniably played out across history. Its existence is so clear that the concept is accepted by many non-Catholics, including Protestants who accept the early councils' teachings on the Trinity and Christology.

Causes of Doctrinal Development

556. The ultimate cause of doctrinal development is the Holy Spirit, though the ways it takes place are complex. God can even use evils—like heresy—to stimulate doctrinal development (CCC 311). In general, we can group the causes of development in two classes, based on whether they originate outside or inside the Church.

Factors Outside the Church

557. Catholics exist in a broader society, and things happening outside the Church can influence doctrinal development:

- One of the first was the *response of non-Jews* to the Christian message. This began with the conversion of Samaritans (Acts 8:4-8), the Ethiopian eunuch (Acts 8:26-39), and the household of Cornelius (Acts 10:1-11:18), and it led to the first Church council, in Jerusalem c. A.D. 49 (Acts 15), which established that Gentiles did not need to be circumcised to be Christians.

- *Persecution by Roman authorities* led some Christians to lapse from the Faith or to perform compromising acts such as surrendering copies of the scriptures. This raised the question of what should happen when they repented. Could they be readmitted to the Church? When and on what conditions? This drove doctrinal development on topics like mortal sin, penance, absolution, and eventually indulgences.

- *Developments in society* contributed to development of doctrine on the question of slavery. Around 340, when slavery was unquestioned in the Roman world, we find the local Synod of Gangra stating: "If anyone shall teach a slave, under pretext of piety, to despise his master and to run away from his service, and not to serve his own master with good-will and all honor, let him be anathema" (can. 3). However, today the *Catechism of the Catholic Church* states: "The seventh commandment forbids acts or enterprises that for any reason—selfish or ideological, commercial, or totalitarian—lead to the enslavement of human beings, to their being bought, sold and exchanged like merchandise, in disregard for their personal dignity" (CCC 2414).

- *Economic developments* led to development of doctrine concerning the nature of the sin of usury. At one time this was understood as any taking of interest on loans, but around 1230 Gregory IX indicated some taking of interest is legitimate (DH 828).

- *Biomedical developments* such as modern contraceptives, means of abortion, reproductive technologies, embryology, and genetics currently drive additional theological and magisterial attention to these issues. Thus in documents like *Donum Vitae*, the Magisterium applies Catholic principles to newly raised bioethical questions.

Factors Inside the Church

558. Factors within the Church also drive doctrinal development, such as the early *heresies* regarding the Trinity and Christology.

559. Under the influence of the Holy Spirit, the *sensus fidelium* (Latin, "sense of the faithful") develops and can have an impact on Church teaching. This was explored by Newman in *An Essay on the Development of Christian Doctrine* and *On Consulting the Faithful in Matters of Doctrine* (1859). The sense of the faithful has played a notable role in doctrinal development, including the dogmatic definition of the Immaculate Conception. The International Theological Commission notes:

Before he defined it, [Pius IX] asked the bishops of the world to report to him in writing regarding the devotion of their clergy and faithful people to the conception of the Immaculate Virgin. In the apostolic constitution containing the definition, *Ineffabilis Deus* (1854), Pope Pius IX said that although he already knew the mind of the bishops on this matter, he had particularly asked the bishops to inform him of the piety and devotion of their faithful in this regard (*Sensus Fidei in the Life of the Church,* 38).

560. In addition to the faithful, *the work of theologians* is a force driving doctrinal development. Discussion and debate among them sheds light on issues that the bishops eventually use in formulating doctrine. The CDF notes:

> The living Magisterium of the Church and theology, while having different gifts and functions, ultimately have the same goal: preserving the people of God in the truth which sets free and thereby making them "a light to the nations." This service to the ecclesial community brings the theologian and the Magisterium into a reciprocal relationship. The latter authentically teaches the doctrine of the apostles. And, benefiting from the work of theologians, it refutes objections to and distortions of the faith and promotes, with the authority received from Jesus Christ, new and deeper comprehension, clarification, and application of revealed doctrine (*Donum Veritatis,* 21).

561. Finally, *the bishops themselves,* as members of the Magisterium, drive doctrinal development, both in the exercise of their personal magisteria, in their participation in the worldwide ordinary magisterium, and in ecumenical councils. In particular, popes can drive doctrinal development both through their ordinary magisteria and through infallible definitions.

Types of Doctrinal Development

Adding Weight to Concepts

562. Since there is no new revelation, doctrinal development involves clarifying our understanding of the existing revelation.

This happens in two general ways: adding weight to concepts or removing it from them.

Ideas don't occur for the first time in magisterial documents. The pope doesn't write an encyclical, have a thought strike him that's never been discussed before, and say, "What a great idea! I'm going to make it official Church teaching right now!" Inevitably, the views discussed in magisterial texts have been around previously.

Many go back to the time of the apostles, even if the way they're expressed has changed. The belief that Christ is God goes back to the ministry of Jesus himself. However, this isn't true of everything. Some beliefs were only implicit in the deposit of faith, such as the teaching that Christ has two wills, one divine and one human. Although the Church began with the awareness that Jesus is both God and man, the implications of this for his wills took time to work out.

When a concept first begins to be articulated, it takes time to be evaluated by the Magisterium. Although there are variations in the pattern, a concept frequently begins as a free theological opinion before it's made part of Church teaching. It may then grow in authority to the point of being taught infallibly or even made a dogma.

Case Study: The Immaculate Conception

563. The Immaculate Conception illustrates how a concept that's originally implicit in divine revelation can become explicit and then gain doctrinal authority and become a dogma.

Scripture presents the Virgin Mary as a woman of holiness—as "the handmaid of the Lord" (Luke 1:38)—and as a woman who has been uniquely blessed by God (Luke 1:42). First-century writings outside the New Testament suggest she was free from the penalty of what later would be called original sin. Thus the *Ascension of Isaiah*—likely written in A.D. 67[116]—indicates when Jesus was born, she had a miraculous, painless childbirth (11:2-4), despite the fact that the multiplication of pain in childbirth was a consequence of original sin

(Gen. 3:16). This is also mentioned in other early documents, including the second-century *Odes of Solomon* (19:7-9; cf. *Protoevangelium of James,* 19).

Various early Fathers meditate on Mary's holiness and refer to her as immaculate, meaning "without stain" (Latin, *im-,* "without" and *macula,* "stain"). One such Father is St. Ephrem the Syrian (*Nisibene Hymns* 27:8). After the concept of original sin was formulated to express the Bible's teaching on the fall of man and its consequences, theologians could relate Mary's unique holiness to this concept, and the question was asked whether she was subject to original sin the way ordinary people are or if there was an exception in her case. If Mary was unstained by original sin, at what point? Was she conceived that way or was she only liberated from it at a later point?

> At the beginning of the twelfth century, the British monk Eadmer, a pupil of St. Anselm of Canterbury, and Osbert of Clare, advocated the Immaculate (passive) Conception of Mary, that is, her conception free from original sin. Eadmer wrote the first monograph on this subject.[117]

The concept of the Immaculate Conception thus became explicit in the consciousness of the Church. However, at this point it was a matter of free theological opinion, and not all supported it. Some in the Dominican Order objected that the Immaculate Conception conflicted with Christ's role as Savior of all men (1 Tim. 4:10).

The solution was provided by Bl. John Duns Scotus, who argued that by preserving Mary from original sin, God gave her a greater form of salvation. She wasn't merely saved *despite* having contracted original sin, she was saved *from* contracting it. Following this theological development, the Magisterium began to weigh in on the subject:

> In the year 1439, the Council of Basle, in its thirty-sixth session, which, however, had no ecumenical validity, declared

in favor of the Immaculate Conception. Pope Sixtus IV (1471–1484) endowed the celebration of the feast with indulgences, and forbade the mutual censuring of the disputing factions [DH 1400, 1425-1426]. The Council of Trent, in its *Decree on Original Sin,* makes the significant declaration "that it was not its intention to involve Mary, the Blessed and Immaculate Virgin and Mother of God in this Decree" [DH 1516]. In 1567, Pope Pius V condemned the proposition advanced by Baius, that nobody but Christ had been free from original sin, and that Mary's sorrows and her death were a punishment for actual sins or for original sin [DH 1973]. Popes Paul V (1616), Gregory XV (1622) and Alexander VII (1661), advocated the doctrine. Cf. [DH 2015]. On the eighth day of December, 1854, Pope Pius IX, having consulted the entire episcopate, and speaking *ex cathedra,* declared the doctrine of the Immaculate Conception to be a dogma of the Faith [DH 2803-2804].[118]

Removing Weight from Concepts

564. Doctrinal development also occurs when weight is removed from concepts. One way this happens is when the Magisterium condemns an idea, giving it a negative weight (see §§339, 354-355). When this happens, the Magisterium uses one or another degree of authority, from tentatively warning against an idea to infallibly heretical.

565. However, the Magisterium may also remove weight from an idea without condemning it. This does not happen with infallible teachings, since they cannot lose doctrinal weight (they can only be understood in a deeper way, expressed in other terms, or situated in a new context, as with "no salvation outside the Church"; §§568-569). But it can happen with non-infallible teachings. The CDF notes:

To serve the people of God as well as possible, in particular, by warning them of dangerous opinions which could lead to error, the Magisterium can intervene in questions under discussion which involve, in addition to solid principles, certain contingent and conjectural elements. It often only becomes possible with the passage of time to distinguish between what is necessary and what is contingent. . . .

In fact, the theologian, who cannot pursue his discipline well without a certain competence in history, is aware of the filtering which occurs with the passage of time. This is not to be understood in the sense of a relativization of the tenets of the faith. The theologian knows that some judgments of the Magisterium could be justified at the time in which they were made, because while the pronouncements contained true assertions and others which were not sure, both types were inextricably connected. Only time has permitted discernment and, after deeper study, the attainment of true doctrinal progress (*Donum Veritatis,* 24).

566. Cardinal Joseph Ratzinger referred to this process of separating solid principles from other elements as "essentializing." When asked how the Church might change in the future, given shifting global demographics and the fact many future Catholics will be from non-European cultures, he replied:

For this reason, *essentializing*—one of [Romano] Guardini's words—is in my opinion what is fundamental. This is not so much a matter of making imaginative constructions of something in advance, which will then turn out to be quite different and not something we could have constructed artificially, as of turning our lives toward what is essential, which can then be embodied and represented anew. In this sense, a kind of simplification is important, so that what is truly lasting and fundamental in our teaching, in our faith, can emerge. So that the basic constant factors, the questions about God, about salvation, about hope, about life, about what is fundamental in ethics, can be made visible in their basic elements and be available for the construction of new systems.[119]

He went on to say:

> We can only humbly seek to essentialize our faith, that is,
> to recognize what are the really essential elements in it—
> the things we have not made but have received from the
> Lord—and in this attitude of turning to the Lord and to
> the center, to open ourselves in this essentializing so that
> he may lead us onward, he alone.[120]

567. This process is seen when the Church revises non-infallible
teachings. Because they are based on divine revelation and formulated with the assistance of the Holy Spirit, they invariably
contain elements of truth—solid principles—so that even when
a teaching is revised, these elements are preserved.

Case Study: Limbo and the Salvation of the Unbaptized

568. The importance of baptism for salvation has been understood in every age. In some ages it was thought there were only a
few exceptions, such as martyrs, who have a "baptism of blood,"
and catechumens, who consciously intended to be baptized and
thus have a "baptism of desire."

Infants can't have such an intention, and it was thought those
who died without baptism wouldn't be able to receive the beatific
vision of God in the afterlife—even if they also wouldn't suffer
since they lack personal sin. This led to the idea of limbo as a place
where they wouldn't suffer and wouldn't have the supernatural happiness of heaven, though they might have great natural happiness.

The requirement of baptism for infants to be saved was
stressed in magisterial documents into the twentieth century, as
in these questions from the *Catechism of St. Pius X*:

> Q. *When should infants be brought to the Church to be baptized?*
> A. Infants should be brought to the Church to be baptized as
>   soon as possible.
>
> Q. *Why such anxiety to have infants receive baptism?*

A. There should be the greatest anxiety to have infants baptized because, on account of their tender age, they are exposed to many dangers of death, and cannot be saved without baptism.

569. By this time, theologians were beginning to realize that salvation could be possible for more unbaptized people than previously thought. In the Middle Ages, it was easy to assume that those who hadn't embraced the gospel (e.g., non-Christian Jews, Muslims) had heard it and culpably rejected it. But when the New World was discovered, theologians realized there were millions of people (Native Americans) who'd never heard the gospel and couldn't be at fault. This led to a greater recognition of the possibility of salvation for the unbaptized and other non-Catholics. Pope Pius IX taught:

Those who suffer from invincible ignorance with regard to our most holy religion, by carefully keeping the natural law and its precepts, which have been written by God on the hearts of all, by being disposed to obey God and to lead a virtuous and correct life, can, by the power of divine light and grace, attain eternal life (*Quanto Conficiamur Moerore*, August 10, 1863; DH 2866).

Similarly, in 1949 the Holy Office (later the Congregation for the Doctrine of the Faith) stated:

In order that one may obtain eternal salvation, it is not always required that he be incorporated into the Church actually as a member, but it is necessary that at least he be united to her by desire and longing.

However, this desire need not always be explicit, as it is in catechumens; but when a person suffers from invincible ignorance, God accepts also an implicit desire, so called because it is included in that good disposition of soul whereby a person wishes his will to be conformed to the will of God (*Letter to the Archbishop of Boston;* DH 3870).

Vatican II then held that God offers the possibility of salvation to all, stating:

> Since Christ died for all men, and since the ultimate vocation of man is in fact one, and divine, we ought to believe that the Holy Spirit in a manner known only to God offers to every man the possibility of being associated with this paschal mystery (*Gaudium et Spes*, 22).

570. There had always been an instinctive resistance to saying infants dying without baptism were simply damned, which was what led to the idea of limbo in the first place. As awareness of the number of potential exceptions to the requirement of baptism grew, it prompted a reevaluation of whether there might be ways for unbaptized infants to be saved. When the *Catechism* was issued, it stated:

> As regards children who have died without baptism, the Church can only entrust them to the mercy of God, as she does in her funeral rites for them. Indeed, the great mercy of God who desires that all men should be saved, and Jesus' tenderness toward children which caused him to say: "Let the children come to me, do not hinder them," allow us to hope that there is a way of salvation for children who have died without baptism (CCC 1261).

Finally, in 2007 the International Theological Commission issued a study requested by the Congregation for the Doctrine of the Faith, which stated:

> In the Church's Tradition, the affirmation that children who died unbaptized are deprived of the beatific vision has for a long time been "common doctrine" [Italian, *dottrina comune*]. This common doctrine followed upon a certain way of reconciling the received principles of revelation, but it did not possess the certitude of a statement of faith, or the same

certitude as other affirmations whose rejection would entail the denial of a divinely revealed dogma or of a teaching proclaimed by a definitive act of the Magisterium (*The Hope of Salvation for Infants Who Die Without Being Baptized*, 34).

It also noted:

[Papal interventions] did not endorse the theory of limbo as a doctrine of faith. Limbo, however, was the common Catholic teaching [Italian, *dottrina cattolica comune*] until the mid-twentieth century (26).

Despite the fact both the exclusion of unbaptized infants from the beatific vision and limbo had been "common doctrine" (i.e., non-infallible Church teachings), the doctrinal developments noted above have led to the view that there are, in the ITC's words, "strong grounds for hope that God will save infants when we have not been able to do for them what we would have wished to do, namely, to baptize them into the faith and life of the Church" (103).

The ITC study was then approved for publication by Pope Benedict XVI, indicating that there is "not any difficulty on the part of the Apostolic See" with the document (*Tredecim Anni*, 12). We thus see how the strict requirement of water baptism for salvation lost doctrinal weight as additional exceptions to the rule were discerned, though based on divine revelation the Church acknowledges baptism as the only ordinary means of salvation (CCC 1257-1261).

A Word of Caution

571. However popular it may be in some circles to say that Catholic doctrine "cannot change," this doesn't seem to be the way the Magisterium articulates the continuity in its doctrine. Searches of the Vatican website (vatican.va) for such statements don't turn up results. Instead, the Magisterium has become increasingly frank about the possibility of error in non-infallible teachings (§§395-399).

Because there is continuity in the principles underlying Catholic teaching, the Magisterium appears to prefer the language of development to the language of change (cf. §577), but it avoids making absolute statements like "doctrines *can't* change."

In apologetic discussions, statements like "doctrines can't change, but they do develop" will be unconvincing to skeptical listeners. They will rightly point out that development is a kind of change, and if they are knowledgeable, they may point to doctrines that have undergone significant change, such as slavery, usury, the salvation of non-Catholics, or limbo. Rather than be sidetracked by semantic quibbles about whether something is a "change" or a "development," it is prudent to be frank and to neither minimize nor exaggerate the possibility of change in Church teaching:

- Infallible teachings can never be reversed, though they can be understood more precisely, articulated in other ways, or set in new contexts.

- Non-infallible teachings—such as the absolute exclusion of unbaptized infants from the beatific vision or the doctrine of limbo—can gradually be weakened by new doctrinal development and even lose their status as authoritative teachings. In this process, the Holy Spirit preserves the solid principles contained in Church teaching as they are separated from nonessential elements.

Indicators of Doctrinal Development

572. Doctrinal development is easy to discern in hindsight, when the changes occurred in prior centuries, but how can we tell when it's happening in our own day? Here we will look at several recent examples from Vatican II.

Previously Unaddressed Questions

573. A clear indicator of doctrinal development is when the Magisterium addresses a question it hasn't pronounced upon before. For example, the Council of Trent taught that ordination to the priesthood involves the bestowal of a sacramental character, just as baptism and confirmation do (*Decree on the Sacrament of Orders,* 4; DH 1767), but it didn't discuss what happens when a man is consecrated a bishop. Vatican II did address this question, stating:

> The sacred council teaches that by episcopal consecration the fullness of the sacrament of orders is conferred, that fullness of power, namely, which both in the Church's liturgical practice and in the language of the Fathers of the Church is called the high priesthood, the supreme power of the sacred ministry (*Lumen Gentium,* 21).

New Language

574. Another clear indicator of doctrinal development is when the Magisterium uses significantly different language to articulate a teaching. In his encyclical *Mystici Corporis* (1943), Pope Bl. Pius XII gave this account of what it means to be a member of the Catholic Church:

> Actually only those are to be included as members of the Church who have been baptized and profess the true faith, and who have not been so unfortunate as to separate themselves from the unity of the body, or been excluded by legitimate authority for grave faults committed (n. 22).

He thus names four conditions which are needed for a person to be a member of the Church:

1. The person has been baptized.
2. The person professes the truth faith.
3. The person has not separated from the Church.
4. The person has not been excluded by legitimate authority for grave faults.

However, when Vatican II met, it used markedly different language when describing how people are united to the Church:

They are fully incorporated in the society of the Church who, possessing the Spirit of Christ accept her entire system and all the means of salvation given to her, and are united with her as part of her visible bodily structure and through her with Christ, who rules her through the supreme pontiff and the bishops. The bonds which bind men to the Church in a visible way are profession of faith, the sacraments, and ecclesiastical government and communion. He is not saved, however, who, though part of the body of the Church, does not persevere in charity. He remains indeed in the bosom of the Church, but, as it were, only in a "bodily" manner and not "in his heart" (*Lumen Gentium,* 14).

The council went on to make several additional and relevant remarks:

Catechumens who, moved by the Holy Spirit, seek with explicit intention to be incorporated into the Church are by that very intention joined with her. With love and so-licitude Mother Church already embraces them as her own (ibid.).

The Church recognizes that in many ways she is linked with those who, being baptized, are honored with the name of Christian, though they do not profess the faith in its entirety or do not preserve unity of communion with the successor of Peter (n. 15).

Finally, those who have not yet received the gospel are related in various ways to the people of God (n. 16).

Lumen Gentium is covering the same general territory as *Mystici Corporis.* The things it names as binding men to the Church "in a visible way"—i.e., "profession of faith, the sacraments, and eccle-siastical government and communion"—correspond substantially to the conditions for membership listed by Pius XII. However, *Lumen Gentium* places the subject in a larger context. Instead of speaking simply of "members," it discusses those who are "fully incorporated"—including conditions not listed in *Mystici Corporis*—and it comments on those who are "joined" (catechumens), "linked" (non-Catholic Christians), or "related" (non-Christians) to the Church.

Since it doesn't use the term "members," *Lumen Gentium* doesn't alter the definition of that term. However, the shift in language indicates that the council is conceptualizing people's relationship with the Church in a more complex way than the binary "member"/"non-member" model. It thus represents doctrinal a development that addresses questions not raised in *Mystici Corporis* (i.e., how different kinds of non-members are related to the Church).

Altered Substance

575. A final clear indicator of doctrinal development is when the Magisterium alters the substance of a teaching. In 1943, Pius XII wrote:

> If we would define[121] and describe this true Church of Jesus Christ—which is [Latin, *est*] the one, holy, Catholic, apostolic and Roman Church—we shall find nothing more noble, more sublime, or more divine than the expression "the Mystical Body of Christ"—an expression which springs from and is, as it were, the fair flowering of the repeated teaching of the sacred scriptures and the Holy Fathers (*Mystici Corporis,* 13).

Here Pius XII identifies the Church of Christ with the Catholic Church in a simple and direct way, using the Latin verb *est* ("is"). In 1950, Pius XII returned to this point, stating, disapprovingly:

> Some say they are not bound by the doctrine, explained in our encyclical letter of a few years ago, and based on the sources of revelation, which teaches that the Mystical Body of Christ and the Roman Catholic Church are one and the

same thing (*Humani Generis,* 27).

576. When Vatican II met, a doctrinal development occurred that indicated a more complex relationship between the two. The council fathers described "the Church of Christ," stating:

> This Church, constituted and organized in the world as a society, subsists in [Latin, *subsistit in*] the Catholic Church, which is governed by the successor of Peter and by the bishops in communion with him, although many elements of sanctification and of truth are found outside of its visible structure. These elements, as gifts belonging to the Church of Christ, are forces impelling toward catholic unity (*Lumen Gentium,* 8).

577. The use of "subsists in" rather than "is" produced a great deal of discussion after the council, and in 2007 the CDF issued a document containing several *dubia* on the subject. Responding to the initial question, "Did the Second Vatican Council change [Latin, *mutare*] the Catholic doctrine on the Church?" the congregation replied:

> The Second Vatican Council neither changed nor intended to change this doctrine, rather it developed, deepened, and more fully explained it (*Responses to Some Questions Regarding Certain Aspects of the Doctrine on the Church,* 1).

Here the congregation indicates the council didn't make a wholesale change to the doctrine, though—if we speak frankly—by developing, deepening, and more fully explaining it, a change of some kind occurred.

Responding to the question "What is the meaning of the affirmation that the Church of Christ subsists in the Catholic Church?" the congregation replied:

> "Subsistence" means this perduring, historical continuity

and the permanence of all the elements instituted by Christ in the Catholic Church, in which the Church of Christ is concretely found on this earth.

It is possible, according to Catholic doctrine, to affirm correctly that the Church of Christ is present and operative in the churches and ecclesial communities not yet fully in communion with the Catholic Church, on account of the elements of sanctification and truth that are present in them. Nevertheless, the word "subsists" can only be attributed to the Catholic Church alone precisely because it refers to the mark of unity that we profess in the symbols of the faith (I believe . . . in the "one" Church); and this "one" Church subsists in the Catholic Church (ibid., 2).

Finally for our purposes, when responding to the question "Why was the expression 'subsists in' adopted instead of the simple word 'is'?" the congregation stated:

It comes from and brings out more clearly the fact that there are "numerous elements of sanctification and of truth" which are found outside her structure, but which "as gifts properly belonging to the Church of Christ, impel toward catholic unity" (ibid., 3).

Thus, by using "subsists in," the council wished to express a more complex relationship between the Church of Christ and the Catholic Church than "is" would convey, meaning a doctrinal development took place.

Unlike the previous development—in which the council employed the language of "full incorporation" rather than membership, thus allowing "member" to be used in its established sense—the council here makes a change that affects the substance of an existing teaching. It would no longer be possible (except in colloquial speech where "subsists" wouldn't be understood) to make as simple an identification of the Church of Christ with the Catholic Church. The core of prior teaching has been retained: Christ instituted only one Church on earth, the Catholic Church is the organic continuation of that Church, and only it has all of the aspects of that Church. However, "it is possible, according to Catholic doctrine, to affirm correctly that the Church of Christ is present and operative in the churches and ecclesial communities not yet fully in communion with the Catholic Church."

Notable Indicators

578. In addition to clear indicators that doctrinal development has occurred, there are also signs one may be under way or may soon occur. These reflect the factors used to assess the weight of non-infallible teachings:

> The authoritativeness of [magisterial] interventions . . . becomes clear from the nature of the documents, the insistence with which a teaching is repeated, and the very way in which it is expressed (*Donum Veritatis*, 24).

The three criteria of authoritativeness are:

1. The nature of the documents that contain a teaching
2. The frequency with which it is repeated
3. The language used to express it

Using these criteria, one can plot trajectories with respect to the weight a teaching has:

- If a non-infallible teaching is being mentioned in more authoritative documents, more frequently, or with more emphatic language, these are signs it's being given a higher level of authority.
- If it's being mentioned in less authoritative documents, less frequently, and with less emphatic language, these are signs that it is being given a lower level of authority.

Since doctrinal development involves adding or removing weight from a concept (§§562-570), either of these trends suggests doctrinal development is under way.

579. Another sign doctrinal development may be under way is when the Magisterium allows bishops or theologians to explore alternatives to how a teaching is presently formulated or understood. In these cases, the way the Magisterium responds is key:

- If it responds by reiterating its current teaching, this is a sign discussion to the contrary is *not* legitimate. Thus when bishops and theologians began to question or reject the teaching of *Humanae Vitae* on contraception, or to advocate the ordination of women to the priesthood, the Magisterium responded by forcefully repeating both of these teachings, showing the position of these individuals was illegitimate and doctrinal development was *not* under way on these questions.

- However, if the discussion goes on for a significant period and the Magisterium doesn't reiterate current teaching, it *may* be a sign doctrinal development is happening. Thus when bishops and theologians began to explore alternatives to limbo, the Magisterium remained silent and allowed the discussion to progress, and eventually limbo ceased to be part of the common doctrine of the Church (§§568-570).

Magisterial Silence

580. For magisterial silence to indicate doctrinal development, it must go on for some time. The Holy See tends not to respond to individual variations from its teachings and, especially in the case of bishops, treats them as one-off heterodox expressions (§544). However, if there is an ongoing pattern of alternatives being proposed and the Holy See remains silent, it's significant. Rome may be allowing the subject to be explored by theologians and by bishops in their particular magisteria. At a later time, it may or may not reengage the issue.

581. Because periods of silence may indicate doctrinal development, one must be careful appealing to older documents to support non-infallible teachings that haven't been mentioned in a long time.

582. In fact, prolonged magisterial silence may be a sign that a teaching has already ceased to be part of Church doctrine. This is essentially the same as the legal concept of desuetude, according to which a law can lose its force due to long disuse. The same thing can happen with Church teachings. Rather than bringing on the disruption that would occur by issuing a formal retraction, the Church can allow a teaching to quietly lapse.

For example, the *Roman Catechism* (aka the *Catechism of the Council of Trent*) said this about the origin of tonsure (a way men cut their hair to signal clerical status):

> In tonsure the hair of the head is cut in form of a crown, and should always be worn in that form, so as to enlarge the crown according as any one advances in orders. This form of the tonsure the Church teaches [Latin, *docet*] to be derived from apostolic Tradition, as it is mentioned by St. Dionysius the Areopagite, Augustine, Jerome, fathers of the greatest antiquity and authority. Tonsure is said to have been first introduced by the prince of the apostles, in honor of the crown of thorns which was pressed upon the head of our Savior (2:7:14).

Note that the *Roman Catechism* stated that tonsure "is said" to have been introduced by St. Peter. That would qualify as a non-doctrinal statement since the *Catechism* doesn't insist on it. However, it also says that the Church "teaches" clerical tonsure "to be derived from apostolic Tradition." This would qualify as doctrine at the time the *Roman Catechism* was issued.

Yet nobody holds that to be Church teaching today, and it appears the Magisterium simply allowed this teaching to fall into desuetude. By 1912, the *Catholic Encyclopedia*, which carries an imprimatur, could state based on subsequent research:

Historically the tonsure was not in use in the primitive Church during the age of persecution. Even later, St. Jerome (in *Ezech.* 44) disapproves of clerics shaving their heads. Indeed, among the Greeks and Romans such a custom was a badge of slavery. On this very account, the shaving of the head was adopted by the monks. Toward the end of the fifth, or beginning of the sixth, century, the custom passed over to the secular clergy (s.v. "Tonsure").

It's therefore risky to cite older Church documents as proofs for teachings that haven't been repeated in centuries, though this doesn't apply to infallible doctrines, for those never lose their status.

CHAPTER 19

Difficulties with Doctrinal Development

583. Any process involving fallen man creates difficulties, and therefore doctrinal development can. Here we will look at three types:

- Seeming invention of doctrine
- Seeming contradiction of doctrine
- Seeming non-reception of doctrine

Seeming Invention of Doctrine

584. This was the charge Bl. John Henry Newman set out to address in *An Essay on the Development of Christian Doctrine*. It had been a staple of anti-Catholic polemics since the Reformation that Catholics invented doctrines that had no foundation in divine revelation (conceived, per *sola scriptura*, as just the Bible). In response, Newman proposed seven criteria indicating the legitimacy of doctrinal developments. Failure to conform to these criteria would, for Newman, indicate doctrinal corruption. In the end, he concluded Catholic doctrinal developments met the criteria and were legitimate. We don't have space to explore the criteria in detail, however, they were summarized by the International Theological Commission:

1. The conservation of the type, which is to say the basic form, and of the proportions and relationships existing between

the whole and the parts. When the structure as a totality remains, its type holds fast, even if some particular concepts change. But this total structure may become corrupt, even in the case where the concepts remain unchanged, if the latter are made part of a context or a system of coordinates which is altogether different.

2. The continuity of principle: The different doctrines represent principles existing at a deeper level, even when these are often not recognized until a later stage. The same doctrine, if detached from its founding principle, may be interpreted in more ways than one, and lead to contradictory conclusions. Continuity of principle then is a criterion which can distinguish proper and legitimate development from the erroneous.

3. Capacity for being assimilated: A living idea shows its edge by its ability to get at reality, attract other ideas to itself, stimulate reflection and develop itself further without loss of its internal unity. This capacity for being integrated is a criterion of legitimate development.

4. Logical coherence: The development of dogmas is a vital process which is too complex to be regarded simply a logical explanation and deduction from given premises. Nevertheless, there must be logical coherence between the conclusions and the initial data. Conversely, one can judge what a development is from its consequences or recognize it as legitimate or otherwise by its fruits.

5. Anticipation of the future: Trends which come to realization and succeed only later may make themselves noticeable early on, even if as isolated phenomena where the outline is still dim. Such advance trends are signs of the agreement of subsequent development with the original idea.

6. The conservation of past values: Development becomes corruption when it contradicts the original doctrine or earlier development. True development conserves and safeguards the development and formulations that went before.

7. Durability: Corruption leads to disintegration. Whatever corrupts itself cannot last for long. Whatever is vital and durable on the contrary is a sign of authentic development (*The Interpretation of Dogma,* III:5).

Seeming Contradiction of Doctrine

585. Difficulties also arise when a doctrinal development appears to contradict previous doctrine. This can be a wrenching experience, and it occurred for many in the traditionalist movement following Vatican II.

Members of the Society of St. Pius X, in particular, have argued that the council's teaching on religious liberty (see *Dignitas Humanae*) contradicts prior teaching. We don't have space to go into this subject in detail, but I would recommend Fr. Brian Harrison's work on the question. In his piece "Pius IX, Vatican II, and Religious Liberty,"[122] he argues that the council doesn't change or contradict prior teaching but considers issues that formerly were not addressed. This is similar to how *Lumen Gentium* did not alter Pope Pius XII's definition for who count as members of the Catholic Church but offered a fuller consideration of the ways in which people can be related to the Catholic Church (§574).

586. Rather than looking at particular cases, we will consider general principles for examining instances of seeming contradiction. This process is similar to resolving apparent contradictions in Scripture, though the two aren't strictly the same since Scripture is divinely inspired, whereas Church documents are written with a lesser form of heavenly assistance.

In general, when relating the magisterial documents of one era to those of another, you need to employ the principles discussed in chapters ten and eleven, in particular, the hermeneutics of precision, continuity, reform, and charity.

Applying the Hermeneutic of Precision (cf. §§299-307)

587. It is especially important, when looking at seeming contradictions in Church teaching, to apply the hermeneutic of precision. This is no time to get sloppy in how you read or think about magisterial statements! You must not be led astray by emotion or hasty inferences. You must make a calm, objective, and precise assessment of what the documents say. In doing that, you should ask:

- Are the statements that appear to be in conflict doctrinal at all? Magisterial documents contain many non-doctrinal statements (see chapter thirteen), including pastoral ones. Any pastor knows there is a time to be harsh and a time to be gentle. This is often responsible for the different approaches documents take. If one or both of the seemingly contrary statements is non-doctrinal in nature then, by definition, you don't have a doctrinal contradiction.

- What *exactly* do the documents say? Take into account everything you know about them, the historical situation that led to their creation, and how language was used when they were written. Resist the temptation to draw inferences and focus strictly on the meaning required by the words they use. This is an essential step in determining whether there is an actual contradiction.

Applying the Hermeneutic of Continuity (cf. §§288-291)

588. Although Church documents are not written under divine inspiration, the Holy Spirit guides and unites the Magisterium across all ages in Church history. Consequently, a fundamental continuity in its teaching should be presumed. This has practical applications when examining seeming contradictions, and you should ask several questions:

- What do the documents have in common—i.e., what do they agree on? This will narrow the focus of discussion to just the apparent differences.

- Could apparent differences be due to differences in language or emphasis? If so, there is no contradiction.

- Could they be applying similar principles to different situations, such as those brought on by changes in society? In this case also there would be no contradiction.

Applying the Hermeneutic of Reform (cf. §§292-295)

589. The Magisterium doesn't just conserve teachings from the past. If it did, doctrinal development wouldn't occur. Thus you mustn't apply the hermeneutic of continuity so rigidly that it would prevent doctrinal development. After using the hermeneutic of continuity to identify the common ground between documents, you should ask questions about remaining differences:

- Does the later document address things the earlier document didn't? If so, these may represent additions to but not contradictions of previous teaching.

- Does the later document omit things that the earlier document covered? If so, it may mean: (1) the later document isn't denying what the previous one said; its authors simply chose not to go into those subjects; (2) parts of what the earlier document said are currently being reevaluated (§580-581); (3) parts of what the earlier document said have fallen into desuetude and are no longer authoritative (§582).

Applying the Hermeneutic of Charity (cf. §§296-298)

590. If you're examining a seeming contradiction in Church teaching, you're likely to have feelings about which version you prefer. Fallen human nature can produce hostile feelings toward members of the Magisterium who write things we don't like. Our doctrinal preferences can even become tokens of our identity and membership in particular groups:

- Some progressives quote older documents and denigrate them as a way of showing how benighted the Magisterium was back in the olden days. They then argue the Church needs to shed its prior teachings and embrace the future.

- Some traditionalists quote newer documents and deni-grate them as a way of showing how benighted the Mag-isterium has become in recent days. They then argue the Church needs to shed its current teachings and embrace its prior ones.

The derision shown by both kinds of authors is a form of virtue signaling, and it displays a lack of charity that is in-consistent with a proper attitude toward the shepherds Christ has appointed to oversee his flock. Yes, members of the Mag-isterium have flaws, just as all people do. However, to adopt a fundamentally hostile attitude toward them is inconsistent with the ethic of love Jesus taught, with the respect due their office, and the recognition due to the work of the Holy Spirit in their ministry.

We must not *allow* ourselves to fall into this trap. We must "keep Satan from gaining the advantage over us; for we are not ignorant of his designs" (2 Cor. 2:11). This means taking a fun-damental attitude of charity toward the authors of magisterial documents in all ages, recognizing the good they were seeking to do, and doing "nothing from selfishness or conceit, but in humility count others better than yourselves" (Phil. 2:3).

Arriving at an Overall Assessment

591. Applying the above principles may lead to a quick resolution of seeming contradictions in Church teaching, but it may not. In such cases, you should do additional research. Have there been any books or papers written on the subject you are considering by respected authors who are faithful to the Magisterium? Are there orthodox experts you could consult to get more information?

592. Ultimately, seeming contradictions between Church teach-ing have one of two resolutions:

- There is no contradiction—the documents merely use dif-ferent language or explore different questions.

- There is a contradiction—a material difference in what the documents say about a doctrine, such that both cannot be true.

In the latter case, only one of the contrary statements can be true, but which? If one is infallible then the choice is simple: the infallible one is true and the other is mistaken in some way. However, one must not quickly conclude that a teaching is infallible. One needs to apply the tests discussed in chapter sixteen and remember that "no doctrine is understood as defined infallibly unless this is manifestly evident" (CIC 749 §3).

593. If both statements are non-infallible, the situation is harder to sort out. However, the fact that doctrinal development is progressive provides a point of reference. There can be ups and downs in history, but the fundamental trajectory is of the Holy Spirit leading the Magisterium into a greater understanding of the deposit of faith. This parallels the process of progressive revelation in Scripture, and later texts—such as the teachings of Jesus in the Gospels—are to be given priority when seeking to understand earlier teachings—such as those of Moses. Consequently, if there is a genuine conflict between earlier and later expressions of doctrine, the more recent ones are presumed to offer a deeper understanding. This isn't an infallible rule because later churchmen, when not speaking infallibly, can make mistakes. However, the ongoing leading of the Holy Spirit creates a presumption favoring more recent magisterial statements.

594. Finally, a few words should be said about our present day and objections to some teachings of Vatican II. Representatives of the Society of St. Pius X are correct that the documents of Vatican II shouldn't be treated as infallible (*Lumen Gentium*, appendix). The council chose not to issue any new infallible definitions. This means there can be imperfections in how it articulated matters and that these could be improved. Indeed, one would always expect future doctrinal developments to improve on current magisterial statements. Also, the Church acknowledges there can be situations in which theologians may have legitimate difficulties with Church documents (§§612-623).

However, it would be wrong to adopt a hostile attitude toward Vatican II. Its non-infallible teachings, like all such teachings, call for "religious submission of will and intellect" (*Lumen Gentium,* 25; cf. *Humani Generis,* 20). Even if there is room for critique and improvement, the fundamental legitimacy of the council is guaranteed by the Holy Spirit and expressed, in human terms, both by the approval given its documents by the fathers of the council and by Pope Paul VI. It's also guaranteed by the subsequent reception of the council by the later popes and by the worldwide episcopate.

It isn't credible to hold that, if the council were fundamentally illegitimate, it would have received the approval of the more than 2,400 bishops of the worldwide episcopate who participated or the thousands of bishops who have succeeded them. A handful of dissenting voices does not overcome the overwhelming approval that the council received. And, as Msgr. Fernando Ocáriz Braña remarks:

> Lastly, in this regard, it does not seem superfluous to call to mind that almost half a century has passed since the conclusion of the Second Vatican Council and that in these decades four Roman pontiffs have succeeded one another on the Chair of Peter. An assessment of the teaching of these popes and the corresponding assent of the episcopate to that teaching should transform a possible situation of difficulty into a serene and joyful acceptance of the Magisterium, the authentic interpreter of the doctrine of the faith. This must be possible and is to be hoped for, even if aspects that are not entirely understood remain.[123]

Seeming Non-Reception of Doctrine

595. Although Vatican II received an overwhelming approval or "reception"—by faithful, bishops, and popes—there are cases when it isn't obvious a Church teaching has been received by the faithful. That's not surprising since the Church, like Christ, has always been "a sign that is spoken against" (Luke 2:34).

Today opinion polls reveal widespread rejection by Catholics of its teaching on contraception, and some consequently argue this teaching has not been received by the faithful and therefore isn't authoritative. This argument has been advanced by Fr. Charles E. Curran.[124] Fr. James Martin, S.J., has proposed a similar argument concerning homosexual behavior.[125] What are they talking about?

Reception and the Sense of the Faithful

596. Discussing how the Holy Spirit assists the Church when it infallibly defines a teaching, Vatican II stated:

> To these definitions the assent of the Church can never be wanting, on account of the activity of that same Holy Spirit, by which the whole flock of Christ is preserved and progresses in unity of faith (*Lumen Gentium*, 25).

When the Magisterium infallibly defines a teaching, the Holy Spirit guides the faithful to accept—or "receive"—that teaching. This reception reflects what theologians call the "sense of the faithful" (*sensus fidelium*), who possess a supernatural "sense of the Faith" (*sensus fidei*). According to Vatican II:

> The whole body of the faithful . . . cannot err in matters of belief. This characteristic is shown in the supernatural appreciation of faith (*sensus fidei*) on the part of the whole people, when, from the bishops to the last of the faithful, they manifest a universal consent in matters of faith and morals (*Lumen Gentium*, 12; CCC 92).

The Holy Spirit therefore gives the Church—including the ordinary faithful—a supernatural awareness of what constitutes the true faith, and when the Magisterium infallibly defines a teaching, he guides the faithful members to receive this teaching. Following *Humanae Vitae*, authors like Curran argued that so many Catholics reject its teaching that the process of reception had not occurred. But if the Holy Spirit guarantees such reception, it would follow that the teaching is not infallible, and Curran would argue it is also mistaken.

597. Setting aside the specific issue of contraception,[126] it should be pointed out that the process of reception is just that: a process. You can't look at the immediate reaction to a teaching as a definitive guide. The Holy Spirit takes time to do his work in guiding the faithful, and this is complicated by free will. Once people have arrived at a conclusion, they don't easily change it. As physicist Max Planck remarked:

> A new scientific truth does not triumph by convincing its opponents and making them see the light, but rather because its opponents eventually die, and a new generation grows up that is familiar with it.[127]

This insight is sometimes paraphrased as, "Science progresses one funeral at a time," and—though it's grim to say so—something similar happens with doctrinal development, especially after major teaching moments. Thus after ecumenical councils there is frequently a period of doctrinal conflict, with some thinking the council went too far and others thinking it didn't go far enough. It often takes a couple of generations for this to settle down and for the council's teaching to be fully received. Cardinal Dulles points out:

> The Creed of Nicaea was fully received only after fifty-six years of violent contentions. The Council of Constantinople of 381 marked the end of these quarrels.[128]

It may be possible to look back at a magisterial act at a distance of hundreds of years and assess that it wasn't received by the faithful, but this can't be done in the first generation or two after the announcement of a controversial teaching.

598. In recent years a number of documents have appeared that discuss reception and the sense of the faithful. One of the most significant is the International Theological Commission's *Sensus Fidei in the Life of the Church* (2014). The Commission notes that, despite the generally smooth reception of magisterial teachings:

> There are occasions, however, when the reception of mag-isterial teaching by the faithful meets with difficulty and resistance, and appropriate action on both sides is required in such situations. The faithful must reflect on the teach-ing that has been given, making every effort to understand and accept it. Resistance, as a matter of principle, to the teaching of the Magisterium is incompatible with the au-thentic *sensus fidei.* The Magisterium must likewise reflect on the teaching that has been given and consider whether it needs clarification or reformulation in order to commu-nicate more effectively the essential message (n. 80).

Who Are the Faithful?

599. The ITC points out that just because a person is a Catholic, this doesn't mean he's authentically displaying a true sense of the Faith. When Catholics disagree, they can't all be right, and it's obvious some are more faithful than others. God offers all the baptized guidance (James 1:5), but we have free will and must cooperate with his guidance to bear fruit (James 1:6-8). The Commission thus identified criteria an individual needs to meet to authentically display the sense of the faithful (nn. 88-105):

a) participation in the life of the Church
b) listening to the word of God
c) openness to reason
d) adherence to the Magisterium
e) holiness—humility, freedom, and joy

f) seeking the edification of the Church

All of these are common sense.

- If a person was baptized Catholic but never darkens a church door, he's so disconnected from his faith that he can't be said to display a supernatural sense of the Faith.
- The Faith is contained in the word of God, so willingness to listen to Scripture and Tradition is essential.
- A person who won't listen to reason, who's determined to hold his opinions regardless of the arguments brought forward, isn't displaying the discernment needed to distinguish truth from falsehood.
- Christ gave us the Magisterium, and a person who fundamentally refuses to listen to it isn't authentically faithful.
- Holiness is a key goal of God's work in our lives, and a person who doesn't seek and display holiness isn't cooperating with God.
- Finally, God leads individuals to build up or edify their fellow Christians, and someone fundamentally oriented toward creating division and disedification isn't cooperating with him.

Public Opinion and the Sense of the Faithful

600. In many parts of the world, including America, most Catholics don't even go to Mass on a regular basis. They thus don't have the level of involvement in their faith needed to meet even the first criterion for displaying the sense of the faithful. When you consider how many Catholics don't display the qualities listed above, it's clear public opinion polls can't be relied upon as a guide to the sense of the authentically faithful. The Commission comments:

> i) First of all, the *sensus fidei* is obviously related to faith, and faith is a gift not necessarily possessed by all people, so the *sensus fidei* can certainly not be likened to public opinion in society

at large. Then also, while Christian faith is, of course, the primary factor uniting members of the Church, many different influences combine to shape the views of Christians living in the modern world. As the above discussion of dispositions implicitly shows, the *sensus fidei* cannot simply be identified, therefore, with public or majority opinion in the Church, either. Faith, not opinion, is the necessary focus of attention. Opinion is often just an expression, frequently changeable and transient, of the mood or desires of a certain group or culture, whereas faith is the echo of the one gospel which is valid for all places and times.

ii) In the history of the people of God, it has often been not the majority but rather a minority which has truly lived and witnessed to the faith. The Old Testament knew the "holy remnant" of believers, sometimes very few in number, over against the kings and priests and most of the Israelites. . . . In many countries today, Christians are under strong pressure from other religions or secular ideologies to neglect the truth of faith and weaken the boundaries of ecclesial community. It is therefore particularly important to discern and listen to the voices of the "little ones who believe" (Mark 9:42) (n. 118).

Obviously, some who dissent from Church teaching are regular churchgoers, and they may meet multiple criteria identified by the Commission. However, the point remains that a true sense of the Faith is displayed by those who are authentically faithful, not simply those who are baptized. Cardinal Dulles notes:

Sometimes it happens that a given teaching or set of teachings encounters resistance. In the case of non-infallible teaching, it could be a sign that the Magisterium has erred. Alternately, it could mean that the teaching, as currently formulated, is ill-timed, one-sided, or poorly presented. But a third possibility must always be considered: that the faithful are not sufficiently attuned to the Holy Spirit.[129]

CHAPTER 20

Difficulties with Church Teaching

The Reality of Difficulties

601. One year as Passover approached, Jesus declared we must eat his flesh and drink his blood. This prompted a dispute:

> Many of his disciples, when they heard it, said, "This is a hard saying; who can listen to it?" . . . After this many of his disciples drew back and no longer went about with him.
>
> Jesus said to the Twelve, "Will you also go away?"
>
> Simon Peter answered him, "Lord, to whom shall we go? You have the words of eternal life; and we have believed, and have come to know, that you are the Holy One of God." (John 6:60, 66-69)

As this incident reveals, Jesus' teachings contain "hard sayings"—things that can be difficult to accept. Some can be so challenging even followers of Jesus may turn away and leave the Faith. Others have a different response: St. Peter didn't deny the difficulty of Jesus' teaching, but he recognized that Jesus had "the words of eternal life." Therefore, no matter how difficult it was to accept Jesus' teaching, it *must* be true.

Both the unfaithful response to difficult teachings and the faithful one have been repeated down through the ages. In this chapter, we will look at both.

Offenses Against the Faith and the Church

Heresy, Apostasy, and Schism

602. Finding a Church teaching difficult to accept is understandable, for God has given the Church "hard sayings" to proclaim, but there are destructive ways of responding. The *Catechism of the Catholic Church* lists four:

> Incredulity is the neglect of revealed truth or the willful refusal to assent to it. "Heresy is the obstinate post-baptismal denial of some truth which must be believed with divine and catholic faith, or it is likewise an obstinate doubt concerning the same; apostasy is the total repudiation of the Christian faith; schism is the refusal of submission to the Roman pontiff or of communion with the members of the Church subject to him" (CCC 2089, quoting CIC 751).

603. We've discussed the conditions that need to be fulfilled for heresy, apostasy, and schism in §§263-266, and we don't need to repeat the details here. However, it's worth noting a remark made by the U.S. bishops' Committee on Doctrine about making *charges* of heresy:

> The Church has been deliberately careful in its description of something so serious, so harmful to its identity. Unfortunately, in the context of intra-Church polemics, *heresy* is often used rather loosely to designate any form of non-acceptance of Church teaching or any proposal of novel theological opinions or pastoral practices. To use the technical term *heresy* in such a broad way would be erroneous and unjust (*The Teaching Ministry of the Diocesan Bishop,* 17).

This principle also applies to the similarly grave charges of apostasy and schism. These are all serious ecclesiastical crimes, and they carry correspondingly serious penalties (CIC 1364 §1; cf. 1321-1325, 1330). Such charges are not to be made casually.

Just as you shouldn't accuse another person of spousal abuse or murder without rigorous evidence, neither should you accuse another person of heresy, apostasy, or schism without it. The *Code of Canon Law* provides:

> No one is permitted to harm illegitimately the good reputation which a person possesses (can. 220).

604. The *Catechism* contains a serious discussion of offenses against another's good name:

> Respect for the reputation of persons forbids every attitude and word likely to cause them unjust injury. He becomes guilty:
>
> - of rash judgment who, even tacitly, assumes as true, without sufficient foundation, the moral fault of a neighbor;
> - of detraction who, without objectively valid reason, discloses another's faults and failings to persons who did not know them;
> - of calumny who, by remarks contrary to the truth, harms the reputation of others and gives occasion for false judgments concerning them.
>
> To avoid rash judgment, everyone should be careful to interpret insofar as possible his neighbor's thoughts, words, and deeds in a favorable way:

> Every good Christian ought to be more ready to give a favorable interpretation to another's statement than to condemn it. But if he cannot do so, let him ask how the other understands it. And if the latter understands it badly, let the former correct him with love. If that does not suffice, let the Christian try all suitable ways to bring the other to a correct interpretation so that he may be saved (Ignatius of Loyola, *Spiritual Exercises*, 22).

Detraction and calumny destroy the reputation and honor of one's neighbor. Honor is the social witness given to human dignity, and everyone enjoys a natural right to the honor of his name and reputation and to respect. Thus, detraction and calumny offend against the virtues of justice and charity (CCC 2477-2479).

When one has committed such offenses, there is a duty of making reparation:

Every offense committed against justice and truth entails the duty of reparation, even if its author has been forgiven. When it is impossible publicly to make reparation for a wrong, it must be made secretly. If someone who has suffered harm cannot be directly compensated, he must be given moral satisfaction in the name of charity. This duty of reparation also concerns offenses against another's reputation. This reparation, moral and sometimes material, must be evaluated in terms of the extent of the damage inflicted. It obliges in conscience (CCC 2487).

Incredulity

605. The *Catechism* also lists incredulity as an offense against the Faith. As "the neglect of revealed truth or the willful refusal to assent to it," it constitutes a grave one. Incredulity is a form of nonbelief (Latin, *in-,* "not," and *credo,* "I believe"). It may involve a refusal to study the truths of the Faith or to take them seriously, since doing so would interfere with a valued belief or behavior. It also can involve a willful act of defiance, even though one knows the truths of the Faith.

Incredulity doesn't presuppose baptism. In the sense the *Catechism* uses the term, incredulity involves only revealed truth and would not result if one rejected non-revealed infallible teachings (§§345-347), though rejecting the latter would still be a grave sin. Whether it would be a mortal or venial sin would depend—for both Christians and non-Christians—on the degree of knowledge and deliberation a person had (CCC 1857-1860).

Dissent

606. In recent decades, dissent has done a great deal of damage both inside and outside the Church. *Donum Veritatis* notes:

> The Magisterium has drawn attention several times to the serious harm done to the community of the Church by attitudes of general opposition to Church teaching which even come to expression in organized groups. In his apostolic exhortation *Paterna cum Benevolentia*, Paul VI offered a diagnosis of this problem which is still apropos. In particular, he addresses here that public opposition to the Magisterium of the Church also called "dissent," which must be distinguished from the situation of personal difficulties treated above (n. 32).

Dissent broke out on a large scale following Pope Paul VI's encyclical *Humanae Vitae* (1968). Within days of its release, the American moral theologian Fr. Charles E. Curran began a campaign against its teaching on contraception, and it grew to international proportions. This forced the Magisterium to deal with large-scale opposition to its teaching—in Catholic circles—for the first time in a long time.

607. It is important to note that dissent involves *public* opposition. The U.S. bishops' Committee on Doctrine observes:

> [*Donum Veritatis*] restricts the meaning of the word *dissent* to "public opposition to the Magisterium of the Church, which must be distinguished from the situation of personal difficulties" (DV 32). This should be noted because in American usage the term *dissent* is used more broadly to include even the private expression of rejection of reformable magisterial teaching (*The Teaching Ministry of the Diocesan Bishop*, 18).

This means personal difficulties one may have accepting magisterial teaching don't constitute dissent as long as they don't take the form of public opposition. The Committee on Doctrine states:

> Obviously, "public opposition" does not encompass the private denial of teaching on the part of an individual.
>
> More important, however, it does not seem appropriate to apply the term *public* to the professional discussions that occur among theologians within the confines of scholarly meetings and dialogues or to the scholarly publication of views.

608. However, there is a point at which disagreement becomes dissent:

> When, however, a judgment rejecting magisterial teaching is widely disseminated in the public forum (*dissent* in the proper sense as formulated by [*Donum Veritatis*]), such as may occur through popular religious journals or through books intended for mass distribution or through the press and electronic media, then a situation of public dissent is at hand.

Most of the faithful don't write such articles or books, but everyone has access to social media and publishing on the internet. This means, if you have a disagreement with Church teaching, you shouldn't start trash talking the Magisterium online.

609. Even if it doesn't result in apostasy, heresy, or schism, dissent can result in a number of penalties. In the case of theologians, this can cause the loss of their teaching positions, and the same applies to anyone who teaches in a Church setting, including catechists and parish study group leaders.

Dealing with Difficulties

Doubts and Difficulties

610. Not all ways of responding to difficult teachings are as destructive as these. Some are constructive. Peter didn't deny the difficulty of accepting Jesus' teaching on the Eucharist, but he accepted it anyway since Jesus has the words of eternal life (John 6:68). This illustrates a distinction discussed by Bl. John Henry Newman:

> Many persons are very sensitive of the difficulties of religion; I am as sensitive as any one; but I have never been able to see a connection between apprehending those difficulties, however keenly, and multiplying them to any extent, and doubting the doctrines to which they are attached. Ten thousand difficulties do not make one doubt, as I understand the subject; difficulty and doubt are incommensurate. . . . A man may be annoyed that he cannot work out a mathematical problem, of which the answer is or is not given to him, without doubting that it admits of an answer, or that a particular answer is the true one (*Apologia Pro Vita Sua*, Part VII).

In ordinary English, we often use the word *doubt* to refer to an emotional sensation—specifically, a lack of feeling confident. However, Newman uses the word not to describe an emotional state but for a state of the will. In his sense, doubt is a refusal to agree with a claim. If a person says, "I *don't know* whether I agree," or, "I *don't* agree," he doubts in Newman's sense. But if he says, "I agree," he doesn't doubt, no matter how much he may lack a feeling of confidence or how uncertain he is that he can prove something or answer objections to it. The latter factors are what Newman calls *difficulties*. They can be emotional (not feeling confidence) or intellectual (not knowing how to provide proof or answer objections).

Understanding the terms this way, Newman is right: doubts and difficulties are two different things. Peter and the Twelve may have had difficulties with Jesus' hard saying, but they accepted it and so didn't doubt it in Newman's sense.

611. Since God is the source of all truth, whatever he reveals is certainly true. Yet we may encounter emotional or intellectual difficulties. Our feelings fluctuate, and at times we feel more or less confident. Similarly, we may not know how to prove a teaching of the Faith or how to deal with objections to it. But we can still accept its truth because God reveals it. According to the *Catechism* (which quotes Newman):

> Faith is certain. It is more certain than all human knowledge because it is founded on the very word of God who cannot lie. To be sure, revealed truths can seem obscure to human reason and experience, but the certainty that the divine light gives is greater than that which the light of natural reason gives. "Ten thousand difficulties do not make one doubt" (CCC 157).

612. Because God has given the Church hard sayings to proclaim, people at times will encounter difficulties. This is an expected situation, and the Church has offered guidance on how to deal with it, especially in the CDF's instruction *Donum Veritatis* (1990). It focuses on the role of theologians, but its principles apply to ordinary members of the faithful. So what should we do when we find it difficult to accept a Church teaching?

Assessing Meaning

613. First you must make sure you accurately understand what the Magisterium has said. This is not a step to be glossed over lightly. The Magisterium often uses specialized language designed for professionals, like bishops and theologians, to communicate with each other in a very precise way. As we discussed in §§263-273, it uses unfamiliar terms and it uses familiar words in unfamiliar ways. People who don't carefully attend to how a statement is worded can easily misunderstand.

A different problem can happen when members of the Magisterium give interviews. By trying to express complex theological ideas in a simple, impromptu way, they may use imprecise language, omit important qualifiers, or even misstate things. Further, the press may offer only partial quotations, coupled with inadequate, inaccurate, and sensationalistic summaries of what was said.

These factors make it important, when you encounter a statement that's hard to accept, to give it a careful reading. You should *always* look up the original text and read it in full. Don't just accept that someone's summary of what a pope or bishop said is accurate. Read it for yourself (see chapter twenty-one).

You may need to consult experts to figure out a text's meaning, and as we discussed in §§299-307, it's important to pay attention both to what *is* being said and to what is *not* being said. The latter is necessary because the Magisterium doesn't want to close off options on questions it isn't specifically addressing. If we don't pay attention, we can mistakenly infer something the Magisterium wasn't teaching. We also need to recognize that sometimes statements are ambiguous, and there may be no way to determine what is intended. On occasion, magisterial documents use ambiguity deliberately to avoid closing off possible views (§§253-255, 277-279).

But suppose you've done all these things and you still find a teaching hard to accept. What then?

Assessing Level of Authority

614. The next step is to determine the level of authority the statement (called an "intervention") possesses. According to *Donum Veritatis*:

> The theologian will need, first of all, to assess accurately the authoritativeness of the interventions, which becomes clear from the nature of the documents, the insistence with which a teaching is repeated, and the very way in which it is expressed (24).

Determining a statement's level of authority may require the assistance of experts. In general, statements in magisterial documents fall into three broad categories (see chapter twelve):

1. Some aren't doctrinal statements at all (see chapter thirteen).
2. Some have been taught authoritatively but not infallibly (see chapter fourteen).
3. Some have been taught infallibly (see chapters fifteen and sixteen).

It's important to assess which category a magisterial statement belongs to as objectively as possible, because it's easy to allow our feelings to influence our judgment. If we view a statement favorably, we want to put it in a more authoritative category, and if we view it negatively, we want to put it in a less authoritative one.

Non-Doctrinal Matters

615. If a difficult statement belongs to this category, we are not obliged to accept it. As Msgr. Fernando Ocáriz Braña points out, "Such matters are received with respect and gratitude, but do not require an intellectual assent in the strictest sense."[130] In other words, we should give such statements serious and favorable consideration, knowing that God is guiding the pastors of the Church, but the nature of these statements ultimately doesn't require us to agree.

Infallible Matters

616. By contrast, when the Church has infallibly taught something, we are required to agree:

- If the Church has infallibly taught that something is divinely revealed, the correct response is theological faith, because God has revealed the matter, and God cannot lie.
- If the Church has infallibly taught something without specifying that it's divinely revealed, the correct response is to hold it definitively because by his gift of infallibility, God has protected the Church from teaching error on this point.

Therefore, if you determine the Church has infallibly taught something you find difficult, the thing to do is remind yourself of these principles: God guarantees that it's true—either by directly revealing it or by protecting the Church from teaching error.

Non-Infallible Matters

617. This category is the trickiest. What do we do when we find it hard to accept something the Church teaches authoritatively but not infallibly? *Donum Veritatis* notes that, in any given age, non-infallible Church teachings can contain both elements that are certain and elements that are less sure. With time, doctrinal development allows the Magisterium to discern which elements must be preserved from those that need not be, but what should our attitude be while that process plays out?

> The willingness to submit loyally to the teaching of the Magisterium on matters per se not irreformable must be the rule. It can happen, however, that a theologian may, according to the case, raise questions regarding the timeliness, the form, or even the contents of magisterial interventions (*Donum Veritatis,* 24).

In other words: it's possible for a theologian to question whether a magisterial statement is being given at an appropriate time, whether it's phrased in an appropriate way, or even—in the case of non-infallible teachings—whether it's correct. *Donum Veritatis* says this particularly applies with prudential matters, as in the Church's social teaching:

> When it comes to the question of interventions in the prudential order, it could happen that some magisterial documents might not be free from all deficiencies. Bishops and their advisors have not always taken into immediate consideration every aspect or the entire complexity of a question (ibid.).

However, this doesn't mean the Church's prudential judgments can be ignored:

> It would be contrary to the truth, if, proceeding from some particular cases, one were to conclude that the Church's Magisterium can be habitually mistaken in its prudential judgments, or that it does not enjoy divine assistance in the integral [i.e., complete, overall] exercise of its mission. In fact, the theologian, who cannot pursue his discipline well without a certain competence in history, is aware of the filtering which occurs with the passage of time. This is not to be understood in the sense of a relativization of the tenets of the faith. The theologian knows that some judgments of the Magisterium could be justified at the time in which they were made, because while the pronouncements contained true assertions and others which were not sure, both types were inextricably connected. Only time has permitted discernment and, after deeper study, the attainment of true doctrinal progress (ibid.).

You thus shouldn't view the Church's prudential judgments as "habitually mistaken." God is still guiding the Church, even if the Magisterium sometimes makes problematic prudential judgments that are later corrected as doctrinal development progresses.

Before You Disagree

618. Orthodox theologians acknowledge there are exceptional situations in which it's possible, without sin, to disagree with non-infallible Church teaching. Germain Grisez observes that such teaching ordinarily requires religious assent and that "this obligation admits of exception only if there is some superior theological source for a contrary judgment."[131] He also notes that a review of various pre-conciliar theological manuals shows that "all admit the possibility that one might not be obliged to assent to certain teachings—those neither defined nor proposed infallibly by the ordinary magisterium. But none asserts that theologians may publicly dissent from teachings proposed by the Magisterium."[132]

In *Donum Veritatis*, the CDF acknowledges there are situations in which, even after study and dialogue, the "difficulty remains because the arguments to the contrary seem more persuasive" and thus the theologian "feels he cannot give his intellectual assent" (31; cf. §623).

Under what conditions would this be morally permissible? In 1968, the U.S. bishops stated that such disagreement "is in order only if the reasons are serious and well-founded, if the manner of the dissent does not question or impugn the teaching authority of the Church and is such as not to give scandal" (*Human Life in Our Day*, 51).[133]

Cardinal Avery Dulles remarked that these conditions "proved difficult to apply. Who was to say whether the reasons were well-founded? How could one establish that the authority of the Magisterium was not being impugned when its teaching was being denied? How could scandal be avoided when theologians were openly saying that the pope's teaching was wrong?"[134]

A more authoritative attempt to address this question was made by the Congregation for the Doctrine of the Faith (CDF). According to *Donum Veritatis*:

Such a disagreement could not be justified if it were based solely upon the fact that the validity of the given teaching is not evident or upon the opinion that the opposite position would be the more probable. Nor, furthermore, would the judgment of the subjective conscience of the theologian justify it because conscience does not constitute an autonomous and exclusive authority for deciding the truth of a doctrine (28).

This identifies three grounds that are insufficient for disagreeing with a magisterial teaching:

1. It isn't enough if the basis of a teaching isn't *obvious* to you. The Magisterium has been given teaching authority by

God (1 Tim. 3:15), who guides it. We thus need to be receptive to its teaching. The burden of proof is on you if you want to disagree.

2. It isn't enough that another view merely strikes you as more probable. In view of the divine guidance the Magisterium receives, there need to be *serious reasons* favoring another view before you'd be warranted in disagreeing on a point of doctrine.

3. Appeals to one's subjective conscience aren't sufficient. There need to be serious, *objective* reasons.

The last ground is particularly noteworthy since appeals to one's conscience were frequently made to justify dissent from *Humanae Vitae*. This focused magisterial attention on the proper role and formation of conscience, and it is one of the reasons why the *Catechism of the Catholic Church* has twenty-seven paragraphs on conscience (CCC 1776-1802), compared to just four on purgatory (CCC 1030-1032, 1054).

If the above conditions are insufficient for theologians, they also are insufficient for ordinary members of the faithful. Indeed, an ordinary person should be even more cautious in disagreeing with the Magisterium since he's not a specialist. *Donum Veritatis* adds:

> In any case there should never be a diminishment of that fundamental openness loyally to accept the teaching of the Magisterium as is fitting for every believer by reason of the obedience of faith (29).

Study

619. If there seem to be serious reasons to doubt a non-infallible teaching, the next step is to study it and see if the difficulty can be resolved:

> The theologian will strive then to understand this teaching in its contents, arguments, and purposes. This will mean

an intense and patient reflection on his part and a readi-
ness, if need be, to revise his own opinions and examine
the objections which his colleagues might offer him (ibid.).

Just as a theologian should consult his colleagues, an ordinary
member of the faithful should consult others, including catechists, priests, and theological experts he may be able to contact.

Dialogue

620. If his own study and discussions with colleagues do not
resolve a theologian's difficulties, he may need to engage in dialogue with the Magisterium itself:

> If, despite a loyal effort on the theologian's part, the diffi-
> culties persist, the theologian has the duty to make known
> to the magisterial authorities the problems raised by the
> teaching in itself, in the arguments proposed to justify it,
> or even in the manner in which it is presented. He should
> do this in an evangelical spirit and with a profound desire
> to resolve the difficulties (30).

Donum Veritatis notes that the fact that there are tensions to be
resolved is not necessarily a bad thing:

> If tensions do not spring from hostile and contrary feel-
> ings, they can become a dynamic factor, a stimulus to both
> the Magisterium and theologians to fulfill their respective
> roles while practicing dialogue (25).
>
> His objections could then contribute to real progress
> and provide a stimulus to the Magisterium to propose the
> teaching of the Church in greater depth and with a clearer
> presentation of the arguments (30).

621. In the dialogue, the theologian needs to be cautious about
how much confidence he places in his own views:

Even if the doctrine of the faith is not in question, the theologian will not present his own opinions or divergent hypotheses as though they were non-arguable conclusions. Respect for the truth as well as for the people of God requires this discretion (cf. Rom. 14:1-15; 1 Cor. 8, 10:23-33). For the same reasons, the theologian will refrain from giving untimely public expression to them (27).

Because of the disruption dissent causes in the life of the Church—and the scandal that could be given to outsiders—the dialogue needs to take place discreetly:

In cases like these, the theologian should avoid turning to the "mass media," but have recourse to the responsible authority, for it is not by seeking to exert the pressure of public opinion that one contributes to the clarification of doctrinal issues and renders service to the truth (30).

622. Theologians may engage in dialogue with their bishop, their episcopal conference's committee on doctrine, or the CDF itself. However, the only member of the Magisterium an ordinary member of the faithful could potentially engage in dialogue would be his bishop. Broader bodies like the national conference's committee on doctrine or the CDF would be overwhelmed if they tried to engage in dialogue every time an ordinary churchgoer had difficulties with something the Magisterium said.

Nevertheless, the same principles apply when ordinary members of the faithful discuss their difficulties with a pastor or bishop. They should be cautious in advancing their views, make a sincere effort to resolve the difficulties, and discuss them discreetly rather than going on Facebook or Twitter to trash talk the Magisterium.

Living with Unresolved Difficulties

623. *Donum Veritatis* notes that it isn't always possible to clear up a theologian's difficulties:

It can also happen that at the conclusion of a serious study, undertaken with the desire to heed the Magisterium's teaching without hesitation, the theologian's difficulty remains because the arguments to the contrary seem more persuasive to him. Faced with a proposition to which he feels he cannot give his intellectual assent, the theologian nevertheless has the duty to remain open to a deeper examination of the question.

For a loyal spirit, animated by love for the Church, such a situation can certainly prove a difficult trial. It can be a call to suffer for the truth, in silence and prayer, but with the certainty, that if the truth really is at stake, it will ultimately prevail (31).

Ordinary members of the faithful, too, may find themselves having to live with an unresolved disagreement with non-infallible Church teaching, and that is a painful experience. The pain should be offered up for the sake of the Church and for one's own sanctification. As the document indicates, they also should remain prayerful and open to reexamining the question. A powerful consolation is that, if the Magisterium has been wrong on something, the situation will not last, for the Holy Spirit guides the Church "into all truth" (John 16:13).

CHAPTER 21

The Papal Rumor Net

624. There are many people who make sketchy claims about what popes have said. Sometimes it's the current pope; sometimes it's a pope from long ago. Sometimes it concerns a doctrinal matter; sometimes it concerns a practice. Whatever the case, the phenomenon is widespread. I call it the papal rumor net.

When you encounter it, there is a series of questions you can use to get past the rumors. These synthesize principles we've discussed in this book, and they serve as a model for dealing with sketchy claims about Church teaching.

Question 1: What's your source?

625. Just because somebody tells you something, you aren't obliged to believe it. The burden of proof is on the person who tells it to you. This is especially true in an area known to be infested by rumors, half-truths, and outright falsehoods, such as the papal rumor net is. Therefore, the first thing to do is ask what a person's source is. The answer may be remarkably unsatisfying: "I don't know." "Everybody knows this." "I've always heard this." "Somebody told me." "I read an article somewhere." This leads to our next question.

Question 2: Why don't you get back to me when you have a source?

626. If you don't bear the burden of proof, you also don't bear the burden of research. When someone wants you to believe something, it's *his* job to come up with evidence. Don't think you need to drop everything and do his research for him. You're perfectly entitled to say, "Tell you what: Why don't you find a source—preferably a primary source. If you do, we can examine it together."

Question 3: Is the source authentic?

627. If the person comes back with a source, the next step is to determine if it's authentic, because in the last two thousand years there have been countless papal misattributions, hoaxes, and forgeries.

For a long time, an ancient Christian document known as *2 Clement* was thought to be written by Pope St. Clement I, who reigned in the late first century. However, today scholars generally think it was by an unknown author and was, at some point, accidentally attributed to Clement.

There have also been deliberate hoaxes. In recent years "news parody" websites have run stories claiming the pope said outrageous things. They ostensibly do this for humor, but some sites take such pains to make their stories look authentic it seems the only "humor" involved is the amusement the authors get by hoodwinking people. News parody sites are recent, but similar hoaxes are found in older anti-Catholic literature. In the days before people could quickly look stuff up on the internet, it was easy to simply make up a papal quote, and authors hostile to the Church did so for polemical purposes.

Sometimes entire documents would be forged in the name of a pope, even by people who favored the Church. A ninth-century author who went by the name Isidore Mercator released a collection of forged papal letters (some of which contained authentic material) to bolster papal authority. They are now known as the pseudo-Isidorian Decretals or the False Decretals.

628. If you encounter a quote you think may not be authentic, how do you check it out? If it's attributed to a recent pope, the first step is to check the Vatican website (vatican.va). It has most of the documents from recent popes, though they aren't always in English. If it's attributed to an older pope, your best bet is to check Denzinger (see §§234-236).

If you're trying to authenticate something a pope allegedly said to the press, checking the website where the account appeared is important. News parody sites may explain their nature on an "About" page, or it may be obvious if the rest of the site contains implausible stories.

If a site tries to do serious journalism—say, it's the *New York Times* or the *Wall Street Journal*—you're on safer ground, but it's important to get the context of what the pope said. Secular newspapers generally only give snippets of what someone said, and the surrounding text can be highly misleading. One way to find the original text is to search on a string of words attributed to the pope, with additional terms like "speech," "interview," "full transcript," or "full text."

Question 4: Is this a primary or secondary source?

629. If a source is authentic, it's important to know whether it's primary or secondary. For our purposes, a primary source is one that gives the words of the pope in their full, original context (e.g., encyclicals, audiences, speeches). These include recordings that haven't been edited to remove the context of what the pope said. Anything else will be a secondary source.

630. A special kind of secondary source consists of things a pope supposedly said in private. Claims made by such sources can be interesting, but they shouldn't be given much weight. All private statements are non-official and not binding. At most they convey a pope's private opinion on a matter. If a pope really wanted to lend his name to an idea, he would address it publicly.

Further, reports of private papal statements are notoriously unreliable. For example, a priest named Ingo Dollinger once claimed then–Cardinal Joseph Ratzinger told him that the entire secret of Fatima hadn't been released. However, the Vatican Press Office issued a statement from former Pope Benedict XVI in which he "declares 'never to have spoken with Professor Dollinger about Fatima,' clearly affirming that the remarks attributed to Professor Dollinger on the matter 'are pure inventions, absolutely untrue,' and he confirms decisively that 'the publication of the Third Secret of Fatima is complete.'"[135]

Question 5: How reliable is the source?

631. Sources differ widely in reliability. Primary sources are what you want, because they present the exact words of the pope, in context, though you have to watch out for possible translation problems.

Secondary sources can be very unreliable. Sometimes people make claims on Facebook or other online forums and offer no way to investigate further. They just splash the claim out there. In such situations, the best response may be, "Sorry, but I need a better source than that." On the other hand, secondary sources written by scholars carry much more weight, though even here you need to be cautious. Scholars aren't always correct, particularly when they're writing outside their field of expertise. Key questions to ask when evaluating secondary sources are:

1. How much of the pope's original words and their context is being given?
2. How much bias does the source display?
3. What reputation for reliability does the source have?

In general, your goal should be to get back behind a secondary source and find a primary one. Without that, you can't be sure what the pope said.

Question 6: Does this involve a doctrine or something else?

632. Once you have the text of what a pope said, you need to determine whether he's talking about a matter of doctrine. This is important because often people assume everything a pope says is Church teaching. However, a pope may be doing any number of things besides teaching. He may be:

- establishing a rule for Catholics to follow as a matter of Church law
- discussing history

- expressing appreciation for something
- providing advice or counsel
- giving a personal opinion

In none of these matters is a pope *teaching* (see chapter thirteen).

Question 7: What level of authority does the statement have?

633. You also need to establish the level of authority of what the pope says. Not everything is infallible (see chapters fifteen and sixteen). There is a spectrum of levels of authority a papal statement can have (see chapter twelve). And popes are free to express matters of personal opinion without making them matters of Church teaching, as in press interviews.

Question 8: Does the statement still apply?

634. If a papal statement was authoritative when it was made, it may not apply today. This is true for statements of both doctrine and statements of law. Because of doctrinal development, non-infallible statements of doctrine can be superseded by later ones (see chapter eighteen). Similarly, using the power of the keys given to govern the Church (Matt. 16:19), popes modify Church law to better suit new conditions. Doctrinal and legal changes can occur in more than one way:

- Popes may directly revoke previous statements. This happens most commonly with legal ones.
- Popes may make a new statement that supersedes a previous one without deprecating it. This is more common in matters of doctrine.
- Popes may allow a statement of doctrine or law to lose its force by not repeating it for a long period of time, allowing it to fall into disuse or what scholars refer to as "desuetude" (§§580–582).

Whatever mechanism popes choose to accomplish these changes, the fact they occur means that you can't take a random papal statement from centuries ago and assume it applies today. You must look at more recent Church teaching and law if you want to know what applies now.

Case Study: Gregory III and Horsemeat

635. I was once contacted by a person who was disturbed by claims on the internet that Pope Gregory III (731-741) prohibited eating horsemeat. Wikipedia's page on horsemeat even cited a scholarly source: Calvin W. Schwabe's book *Unmentionable Cuisine* (University of Virginia Press, 1979). According to Schwabe, "In pre-Christian times, horsemeat eating in northern Europe figured prominently in Teutonic religious ceremonies, particularly those associated with the worship of the god Odin. So much so, in fact, that in A.D. 732 Pope Gregory III began a concerted effort to stop this pagan practice" (p. 157).

Schwabe, who died in 2006, was a scholar. He had a doctorate in parasitology and public health from Harvard, and he's commonly known as the father of veterinary epidemiology. But he wasn't a scholar of the history of the papacy, so he probably didn't consult primary source papal documents for his claim about horsemeat. He probably got it from a book or paper in his own field of veterinary science. Whoever wrote that work also probably wasn't an expert in the history of the papacy and also probably didn't check primary sources. This means we likely have the transmission of a rumor by non-experts writing in a separate field, with no clear source for the claim. Schwabe doesn't cite one, not even a veterinary text. And a check of the current edition of Denzinger doesn't reveal Gregory III having said anything on this subject.

But suppose that he did. How would we evaluate the matter? Without a precise quotation to examine, we can only discuss some possibilities. It is clear from the New Testament that eating horsemeat isn't a sin, for Jesus "declared all foods clean" (Mark 7:19). Medieval popes knew this, so a prohibition on horsemeat should be understood as a matter of discipline rather than doctrine. This is suggested by the report that Gregory's efforts were directed against the worship of deities like Odin in German-speaking territories.

Presumably, any such ban would have taken the form of a law that Germanic Christians would be expected to follow to protect them from falling back into paganism or trying to blend it with Christianity. However, Church law has been completely reorganized since the eighth century, and it doesn't presently have a prohibition on eating horsemeat. Consequently, even if Gregory III or other popes prohibited the practice, today it isn't Church teaching or law.

About the Author

Jimmy Akin is an internationally known author and speaker. As the senior apologist at Catholic Answers, he has more than twenty years of experience defending and explaining the Faith.

Jimmy is a convert to the Faith and has an extensive background in the Bible, theology, the Church Fathers, philosophy, canon law, and liturgy. Jimmy is a weekly guest on the national radio program Catholic Answers Live, a regular contributor to *Catholic Answers Magazine*, and a popular blogger and podcaster. His books include *The Fathers Know Best* and *A Daily Defense*. His personal website is JimmyAkin.com.

Endnotes

1   C.S. Lewis, *Mere Christianity* (New York: HarperCollins, 1980), 62.

2   James T. O'Connor and Vincent Gasser, *The Gift of Infallibility: The Official Relatio on Infallibility of Bishop Vincent Gasser at Vatican Council I* (Boston: St. Paul Editions, 1986), 21–22.

3   See Francis J. Sullivan, S.J., "The Teaching Authority of Episcopal Conferences," *Theological Studies* 63(2002):472–493, available online at TheologicalStudies.net. See also Thomas J. Reese, S.J., ed., *Episcopal Conferences: Historical, Canonical, and Theological Studies* (Washington, D.C.: Georgetown University Press, 1989).

4   For example, see "Certitude" in the 1908 edition of *The Catholic Encyclopedia,* and Sylvester J. Hunter, S.J., *Outlines of Dogmatic Theology,* 3rd ed. (New York: Benzinger Brothers, 1896), I:102.

5   James A. H. Murray, ed., *A New English Dictionary* (Oxford: Clarendon Press, 1897), s.v. "Discipline," 6b.

6   Joseph T. Martin de Agar, *A Handbook on Canon Law* (Montreal: Wilson & Lafleur, 1999), 19–20.

7   Avery Dulles, *Magisterium* (Naples, Fla.: Sapientia Press, 2007), 77.

8   Dulles, *Magisterium,* 77.

9   Pierre Adnes, "Revelations, Private" in Rene Latourelle and Rino Fisichella, *Dictionary of Fundamental Theology* (New York: Crossroad, 1995).

10 The modern Nicene Creed is more formally known as the Niceno–Constantinopolitan Creed. It consists of the original Creed of Nicaea, which defined the divinity of Christ, as supplemented by the First Council of Constantinople (381) to also define the divinity of the Holy Spirit.

11 Francis Morrisey, *Papal and Curial Pronouncements: Their Canonical Significance in Light of the Code of Canon Law,* 2nd ed. (Ottawa: Faculty of Canon Law, Saint Paul University, 1995), 21.

12 Morrisey, *Papal and Curial Pronouncements,* 15.

13 *Apud* J. Michael Miller, *The Encyclicals of John Paul II* (Huntington, Ind.: Our Sunday Visitor, 2001), 11.

14 J. Michael Miller, *The Encyclicals of John Paul II,* 12–14.

15 Miller, *The Encyclicals of John Paul II,* 15.

16 Miller, *The Encyclicals of John Paul II,* 20–21.

17 Morrisey, *Papal and Curial Pronouncements,* 17–18.

18 Morrisey, *Papal and Curial Pronouncements,* 13.

19 E.g., see Edward Peters, "A Non-Magisterial Magisterial Statement?," December 15, 2015, at *In the Light of the Law,* canonlawblog.wordpress.com. See also "Why the Holy See Issues Non-Magisterial Statements" at jimmyakin.com.

20 *Apud* O'Connor, *The Gift of Infallibility,* 73.

21 Morrisey, *Papal and Curial Pronouncements,* 25.

22 Morrisey, *Papal and Curial Pronouncements,* 29.

23 Morrisey, *Papal and Curial Pronouncements,* 29.

24 Morrisey, *Papal and Curial Pronouncements,* 34–35.

25 Joseph Ratzinger, "Theology Is Not Private Idea of Theologian," *L'Osservatore Romano,* English Weekly Edition, July 2, 1990, 5.

26 Joseph Ratzinger, *Relationship Between Magisterium and Exegetes,* May 5, 2003.

27 William Levada, Address at the Pontifical Athenaeum of St. Anselm, "Dei Verbum—Forty Years Later," October 10, 2005.

28 Joseph Ratzinger, Foreword, in Michael Sharkey, ed., *International Theological Commission, vol. 1: Texts and Documents, 1969–1985.*

29 For a discussion of this change and its doctrinal significance, see "Understanding the Catechism's Death Penalty Revision" at jimmyakin.com.

30 Joseph Ratzinger and Christoph Schonborn, *Introduction to the Catechism of the Catholic Church* (San Francisco: Ignatius Press, 1994), 25–27.

31 Heinrich Denzinger et al., eds., *Enchiridion Symbolorum, Definitionum, et Declarationum de Rebus Fidei et Morum* (San Francisco: Ignatius Press, 2012), 10.

32 Nicole Winfield, Associated Press, September 11, 2017, 9:55 A.M. EDT, online at www.apnews.com.

33 Catholic News Agency, "Full Text of Pope Francis' In-Flight Press Conference from Colombia," September 11, 2017, 10:10 A.M., online at catholicnewsagency.com.

34 Zenit, May 25, 2015, 9:34 A.M., online at zenit.org. Note that the story has since been corrected.

35 Origen, *Origen: Prayer, Exhortation to Martyrdom*, ed. Johannes Quasten and Joseph C. Plumpe, trans. John J. O'Meara, vol. 19, *Ancient Christian Writers* (New York, N.Y. and Mahwah, N.J.: Newman Press, 1954), 96.

36 Austin Flannery, O.P., ed., *Vatican Council II: The Conciliar and Post Conciliar Documents*, new rev. ed., vol. 1, (Northport, N.Y.: Costello Publishing, 1992), 757.

37 Walter M. Abbott, S.J., ed., *The Documents of Vatican II* (New York: Herder & Herder and Association Press, 1966), 119.

38 "Does the Catholic Church Teach We Are Gods?," online at timstaples.com.

39 Basil Studer, "Dogma, History Of," ed., Angelo Di Berardino and James Hoover, trans. Joseph T. Papa, Erik A. Koenke, and Eric E. Hewett, *Encyclopedia of Ancient Christianity* (Downers Grove, Ill.: IVP Academic; InterVarsity Press, 2014), 731.

40 Karl Rahner, ed., *Encyclopedia of Theology: The Concise Sacramentum Mundi* (New York: Seabury Press, 1975), s.v. "Dogma"; bibliographic citations omitted.

41 John P. Beal, James A. Coriden, and Thomas J. Green, eds., *New Commentary on the Code of Canon Law* (New York: Paulist Press, 2000), 914.

42 Gerhard Muller, *Catholic Dogmatics for the Study and Practice of Theology*, vol. 1 (New York: Crossroad, 2017), xii–xiii.

43 R.S. Wallace and G.W. Bromiley, "Sacraments," *The International Standard Bible Encyclopedia, Revised*, ed. Geoffrey W. Bromiley (Grand Rapids, Mich.: Wm. B. Eerdmans, 1979–1988), 256.

44 William E. Addis and Thomas Arnold, *A Catholic Dictionary* (New York: Catholic Publication Society Co., 1887), 735.

45 Daniel Kennedy in *The Catholic Encyclopedia* (New York: Robert Appleton Company, 1912), s.v. "Sacraments."

46 Rocco Palmo, "'There Is No Turning Back Now'—In Historic Abuse Summit, Vatican Says Chilean Bench to Face 'Consequences,'" May 12, 2018, online at whispersintheloggia.blogspot.com.

47 Hubert Jedin, *A History of the Council of Trent, vol. II: The First Sessions at Trent, 1545–1547* (New York: Thomas Nelson and Sons, 1961), 309.

48 Claudia Carlen, ed., *The Papal Encyclicals: 1958–1981* (Ypsilanti, Mich.: Pierian Press, 1990), 227.

49 P.G.W. Glare, ed., *Oxford Latin Dictionary* (Oxford: Oxford University Press, 2012). Citations of classical Latin literature omitted.

50 Leo F. Stelten, *Dictionary of Ecclesiastical Latin* (Peabody, Mass.: Hendrickson Publishers, 1995).

51 See also "The Meaning of 'Marital Intercourse'" at jimmyakin.com.

52 John L. Allen, Jr., "Pope Takes the Classic Vatican Approach to Birth Control and Zika," February 20, 2016, online at cruxnow.com.

53 Benedict XVI and Peter Seewald, *Light of the World* (San Francisco: Ignatius Press, 2010), 119.

54 John L. Allen, Jr., "Pope Signals Nuance on Condoms," November 20, 2010, online at ncronline.org.

55 Not even *Ethical and Religious Directives for Catholic Health Care Services* appears to be an official act of magisterium, since it does not carry a notice indicating it was approved in a way that would qualify under the conditions laid out in *Apostolos Suos*.

56 "Communion to the Remarried, Muller, 'There Can Be Mitigating Factors in Guilt,'" online at lastampa.it; translated from Cardinal Muller's introduction to the book *Risposte (Amichevoli) ai Critici di Amoris Laetitia* by Rocco Buttiglione (Milan: Edizione Ares, 2017).

57 Fr. Regis Scanlon, "What History May Tell Us About *Amoris Laetitia*," January 26, 2017, online at crisismagazine.com.

58 Edward Peters, "Do Footnotes Count?" January 27, 2017, online at canonlawblog.wordpress.com.

59 Avery Dulles, *The Craft of Theology: From Symbol to System*, 2nd ed. (New York: Crossroad, 1996), 43.

60 Ludwig Ott, *Fundamentals of Catholic Dogma* (St. Louis: B. Herder Book Company, 1957), 9–10.

61 Ott, *Fundamentals of Catholic Dogma*, 10.

62 Johann Finsterholzl, in K. Rahner, et al., *Sacramentum Mundi: An Encyclopedia of Theology*, vol. 6 (New York: Herder and Herder, 1970), s.v. "Theological Notes."

63 Dulles, *The Craft of Theology*, 121–122.

64 *"Notificationes" Given by the Secretary General of the Council*, November 16, 1964; cf. Harold E. Ernst, "The Theological Notes and the Interpretation of Doctrine, *Theological Studies* 63(2002):813–825.

65 Ott, *Fundamentals of Catholic Dogma*, 5.

66 Beal et al., eds., *New Commentary on the Code of Canon Law*; on CIC 750.

67 Dulles, *Magisterium*, 89.

68 Msgr. Fernando Ocáriz Braña, "On Adhesion to the Second Vatican Council," *L'Osservatore Romano*, December 2, 2011.

69 He does not mention that, in his earlier books, then–Fr. Ratzinger was an advocate of this view. See Joseph Ratzinger, *Eschatology: Death and Eternal Life*, 2nd ed., (Washington, D.C.: The Catholic University of America Press, 1988), 228–233.

70 Ocáriz, "On Adhesion to the Second Vatican Council."

71 On August 1, 2018, the head of the Congregation for the Doctrine of the Faith, Cardinal Luis Ladaria, issued a letter to the bishops of the world announcing that Pope Francis had approved a change to the section of the *Catechism of the Catholic Church* dealing with the death penalty. For a discussion of this change and its doctrinal significance, see "Understanding the Catechism's Death Penalty Revision" at jimmyakin.com.

72 This has to be understood with some nuance; although heresy was defined in the 1500s, following St. Thomas Aquinas, as the corruption of the Church's dogmas, the modern understanding of a dogma was not yet in use and the term was used more loosely, meaning that the concept of heresy was correspondingly looser. See §§270–271.

73 See International Theological Commission, *Memory and Reconciliation: The Church and the Faults of the Past* (1999); see also Luigi Accattoli, *When a Pope Asks Forgiveness: The Mea Culpa's of John Paul II* (Boston: Pauline Books & Media, 1998).

74 Ocáriz, "On Adhesion to the Second Vatican Council."

75 Joseph Ratzinger, *The Nature and Mission of Theology: Essays to Orient Theology in Today's Debates*, trans. Adrian Walker (San Francisco: Ignatius Press, 1995), 106.

76 Stelten, *Dictionary of Ecclesiastical Latin*, s.v. "Mos."

77 Glare, ed., *Oxford Latin Dictionary*, s.v. "Mōs."

78 Francis J. Sullivan, S.J., *Magisterium: Teaching Authority in the Catholic Church* (Eugene, Oregon: Wipf and Stock Publishers, 2002), 128.

79 *Acta Synodalia* III/8 (Vatican City: Libreria Editrice Vaticana, 1970), 89; *apud* Dulles, *Magisterium*, 73–74.

80 Hunter, S.J., *Outlines of Dogmatic Theology*, §211.

81 Ott, *Fundamentals of Catholic Dogma*, introduction, §6.

82 Dulles, *Magisterium*, 78.

83 Dulles, *Magisterium*, 77.

84 Avery Dulles notes: "The [Latin] term *mores*—here translated 'morals'—takes on different nuances in different documents. It often means something like 'patterns of behavior commended by the gospel'" (*Magisterium*, 63). This includes more than just moral truths. However, because it does include moral truths, the Magisterium would still be able to infallibly define these.

85 Congregation for the Doctrine of the Faith, ed., *Proclaiming the Truth of Jesus Christ; Papers from the Vallombrosa Meeting* (Washington: USCCB, 2000), 66.

86 CDF, *Proclaiming the Truth of Jesus Christ*, 66.

87 "Press Conference on Encyclical '*Humanae Vitae*,'" *L'Osservatore Romano*, weekly edition in English, August 8, 1968, 7.

88 One could quibble even with this question. Cardinal Avery Dulles notes: "Strictly speaking, infallibility is a property of the Magisterium in its activity of teaching, not a property of magisterial statements. The statement protected by infallibility are said to be 'irreformable'" (*Magisterium*, 66).

89 *Dictionnaire de Théologie Catholique*, s.v. "Infaillibilité du Pape," vol. 7, pt. 2, columns 1703–1704.

90 See, e.g., Ludovico Billot, S.J., *Tractatus De Ecclesia Christi* (Rome: Typographia Polyglotta of the S. C. de Propaganda Fide, 1903), 657–659.

91 Dulles, *Magisterium*, 71. Dulles recommends consulting Francis Sullivan, *Creative Fidelity: Weighing and Interpreting Documents of the Magisterium* (New York: Paulist Press, 1996), 80–92, for further discussion of proposed papal definitions.

92 O'Connor, *The Gift of Infallibility*, 47.

93 Sullivan, *Creative Fidelity*, 50.

94 Sullivan, *Creative Fidelity*, 50.

95 Cf. Sullivan, *Creative Fidelity*, 53–54.

96 Stelten, *Dictionary of Ecclesiastical Latin*.

97 Avery Dulles, *The Survival of Dogma* (New York: Crossroad, 1985), 153.

98 Sullivan, *Creative Fidelity*, 52.

99 Hunter, *Outlines of Dogmatic Theology*, §221.

100 Sullivan, *Creative Fidelity*, 51–52.

101 Sullivan, *Creative Fidelity*, 41–79. Despite the problematic title of this book, Sullivan seeks to be faithful to the Magisterium. A former professor at the Pontifical Gregorian University in Rome, he is one of the major scholars in this area, and Cardinal Dulles's recommendation of this work (*Magisterium*, 71, fn. 14) illustrates its utility, even if one doesn't agree with everything he argues.

102 The current edition of *Denzinger* has bracketed numbers suggesting which censures apply to which propositions. Because they are not part of the original document, it thus remains unclear which documents should be given which censures according to Innocent XI.

103 As with *Caelestis Pastor*, the current edition of *Denzinger* has bracketed numbers suggesting which censures apply to which propositions. Because they aren't part of the original document, it remains unclear which documents should be given which censures according to Innocent XII.

104 Sullivan, *Creative Fidelity*, 81.

105 Dulles, *Magisterium*, 71.

106 For the text of the address, see Walter Kasper, *The Gospel of the Family* (New York: Paulist Press, 2014).

107 You could also use the native search feature on the Vatican website, but Google will generate better search results for you than that one will.

108 Von Balthasar died before he could be installed as cardinal, but the fact John Paul II appointed him to the office indicates the value of his theological contributions.

109 See his book *Dare We Hope "That All Men Be Saved"?*, 2nd ed. (San Francisco: Ignatius Press, 2014).

110 For a discussion of the issues, see Ott, *Fundamentals of Catholic Dogma*, 242–249.

111 Ott, *Fundamentals of Catholic Dogma*, 353–354.

112 Joseph Wilhelm and Thomas B. Scannell, trans., *A Manual of Catholic Theology: Based on Scheeben's "Dogmatik,"* vol. II, 3rd ed., rev. (London: Kegan Paul, Trench, Trübner & Co. Ltd., 1908), 88.

113 Quoted by Owen Chadwick, *From Bossuet to Newman: The Idea of Doctrinal Development*, 2nd ed. (Cambridge: Cambridge University Press, 1987), 17.

114 See James Gaffney, trans., ed., *Roman Catholic Writings on Doctrinal Development by John Henry Newman* (Kansas City, Mo.: Sheed & Ward, 1997), and James Gaffney, ed., *Conscience, Consensus, and the Development of Doctrine: Revolutionary Texts by John Henry Cardinal Newman* (New York: Image, 1992).

115 This is a view I have long held, and in recent times I have seen it proposed by others, including Newman experts. Cf. "Cardinal Newman: Doctor of the Church? Father Ian Ker on the Priest's Cause, Teachings," Zenit, October 22, 2008.

116 Jimmy Akin, "Dating the Ascension of Isaiah" (unpublished).

117 Ott, *Fundamentals of Catholic Dogma*, 201.

118 Ott, *Fundamentals of Catholic Dogma*, 202.

119 Joseph Ratzinger and Peter Seewald, *God and the World: Believing and Living in Our Time: A Conversation with Peter Seewald*, trans. Henry Taylor (San Francisco: Ignatius Press, 2002), 446.

120 Ratzinger and Seewald, *God and the World*, 453.

121 Note that this use of the term *define* does not create an *ex cathedra* statement. If Pius XII intended to make one, he would have used the kind of language Pius IX used in *Ineffibilis Deus* and that he himself used in *Munificentissimus Deus*. No scholars regard this as an *ex cathedra* statement. Here the term is being used in its ordinary sense of an explanation, as when a dictionary defines a word. This is confirmed by the parallel verb "describe."

122 Online at catholicculture.org.

123 Ocáriz Braña, "On Adhesion to the Second Vatican Council."

124 Charles E. Curran, "*Humanae Vitae*' and the *Sensus Fidelium*," *National Catholic Reporter*, June 25, 2018, online at ncronline.org.

125 James Martin, S.J., "Father James Martin Answers 5 Common Questions about 'Building a Bridge,'" *America*, July 14, 2017, online at americamagazine.org.

126 See also Dulles, *Magisterium*, 107–108.

127 *Apud* Thomas Kuhn, *The Structure of Scientific Revolutions*, 4th ed. (Chicago: University of Chicago Press, 2012), 150.

128 Dulles, *Magisterium*, 104.

129 Dulles, *Magisterium*, 106.

130 Ocáriz Braña, "On Adhesion to the Second Vatican Council."

131 Germain Grisez, *The Way of the Lord Jesus, Volume One: Christian Moral Principles* (Quincy, Ill.: Franciscan Press, 1997), 871.

132 Grisez, *The Way of the Lord Jesus*, 873.

133 In this document, the U.S. bishops refer to "licit dissent," using *dissent* in the American sense of disagreement. This differs from the way the Holy See uses *dissent* to refer to public opposition to the Magisterium (§§268, 606–609). The U.S. bishops thus mean legitimate disagreement.

134 Dulles, *The Craft of Theology*, 113.

135 Holy See Press Office, "Communiqué: On Various Articles Regarding the 'Third Secret of Fatima,'" May 21, 2016, online at press.vatican.va.

Glossary

Anathema: (Greek, "an offering, something cursed, a curse"): In magisterial documents, a form of major excommunication. This penalty no longer exists but the phrase "let him be anathema" may indicate the presence of an infallible definition (§§480-488).

Apostasy: (Greek, *apostasia,* "standing apart"): The total repudiation of the Christian faith (§§263, 265).

Authentic: In ecclesiastical documents, this frequently means "authoritative" rather than "genuine." "Authentic" teaching is authoritative teaching (§§14, 267).

Authorial intent: What an author intends to communicate in a work (§242).

Canon: (Greek, *kanon,* "rule"): (1) The canon of Scripture (i.e., the books that belong in the Bible), (2) a provision in canon law, as found in the *Code of Canon Law,* (3) a rule issued by an ecumenical council, sometimes using the formula "let him be anathema" (§318).

Censure: (1) A kind of punishment in canon law, (2) a negative theological note indicating the problematic nature of an opinion (§§339-340).

Church document: As used in this book, a document that is issued by a Church official or agency, whether or not it deals with doctrine or carries the approval needed to give it magisterial authority. Cf. "Magisterial document."

De fide: (Latin, "of the Faith"): Theological note applied to dogmas (§§337-338).

Define: (Latin, *de-,* "completely" and *finis,* "end"): To teach in a definitive way so that legitimate dispute is completely ended. In contemporary theology, to define a teaching means to settle it infallibly (§§475, 489-495).

Definition: (1) The act of teaching definitively or (2) a statement that is definitively taught (§475).

Definitive assent: The response called for by infallible teachings that have not been proclaimed dogmas (§346).

Definitive: The quality of being defined so that there can be no further legitimate dispute (§413).

Denzinger: The author of an influential collection of excerpts from Church documents. Alternately, the collection itself (§§234-236).

Deposit of faith: The body of revelation that God gave to the Church through Christ and the apostles. It includes the revelation given in the Old Testament era, which Jesus and the apostles endorsed (§117).

Dicastery: (Greek, *dikastērion,* "court of law"): Any of the departments in the Roman Curia (§44).

Discipline: (Latin, *disciplina,* "instruction"): A custom that carries an obligation (§92).

Dissent: In American usage, disagreement. In Vatican documents, public opposition to the Magisterium of the Church (§§268, 606–608).

Divine and catholic faith: Also called theological faith. The response called for by dogmas (§344).

Doctrinal development: The process by which Church doctrine develops over time—e.g., as the contents of the deposit of faith come to be more clearly understood and expressed, under the impulse of the Holy Spirit (§§552, 554–555).

Doctrine: (Latin, *doctrina,* "teaching"): Any authentic (authoritative) teaching of the Church, including but not limited to dogmas (§85).

Dogma: (Greek, "opinion, belief"): A doctrine that is (1) divinely revealed and (2) infallibly taught by the Magisterium *as divinely revealed* (§§85, 343–344). For the historical use of this term, see §271.

Dogmatic fact: A non-revealed truth capable of being defined due to its relationship with divine revelation—e.g., that a particular council was ecumenical, that a particular man was a valid pope (§437).

Doubt: The refusal, as an act of the will, to assent to a teaching, either by suspending judgment on it or by denying it outright. Not to be confused with feelings, e.g., a lack of confidence (§610).

Ecumenical council: Ideally, a council involving the worldwide episcopate; to be authoritative, its decrees must be approved or at least accepted by the pope (§§40–41, 464).

***Editio typica*:** (Latin, "typical edition"): The official, authoritative version of a document (§246).

Eisegesis: (Greek, *eis,* "into," and "exegesis"): Reading into a work instead of interpreting it properly (§244).

***Ex cathedra*:** (Latin, "from the chair"): Term used for statements in which the pope infallibly defines a dogma (§§427, 470–471).

Exegesis: (Greek, *ek,* "out," and *hegeisthai,* "guide"): The process of explanation or interpretation. Alternately, an individual explanation or interpretation. The goal of exegesis is to determine authorial intent (§243).

Extraordinary magisterium: The way the Church's teaching authority is exercised (1) when the pope issues an infallible definition or (2) when the bishops issue an infallible definition in an ecumenical council (or when they teach when they are simply gathered in an ecumenical council) (§13).

Faith and morals: Matters the Church is capable of infallibly defining (§428). Note that "morals" indicates a broader set of things than the English term suggests (§429).

Heresy: (Greek, *hairesis,* "opinion, choice"): The obstinate, post-baptismal doubt or denial of a teaching that must be believed with divine and catholic faith (i.e., a dogma) (§§263-264). For the historical use of this term, see §270.

Hermeneutic: (Greek, *hermēneutēs* = "interpreter"): The process of interpretation or an individual principle of interpretation (§245).

Inerrant: The quality of not containing error (§141).

Infallible: The quality of not being able to make an error (in the case of humans, this means being protected by God from making an error) (§142).

Inspired: The quality of being "breathed by God" so that God is the ultimate author of a statement, though he may use a human agent. This term is applied to the books of Scripture but not to other documents (§143).

Irreformable: Not capable of being changed. An older term for infallibly defined propositions. It is uncommon today (§413).

Magisterial document: As used in this book, a document that carries magisterial authority. Cf. "Church document."

Magisterium: (Latin, *magister,* "teacher"): (1) The authority to teach, (2) those who have the authority to teach (i.e., the bishops in union with the pope), (3) a body of authoritative teachings (§11).

Object of infallibility: Truths that the Church is capable of infallibly defining (§428). Cf. "Primary object of infallibility," "Secondary object of infallibility."

Ordinary and universal magisterium: The teaching authority of the bishops in union with the Roman pontiff when they (1) are not gathered in an ecumenical council but (2) are teaching for the whole of the faithful. The ordinary and universal magisterium can teach infallibly (§457).

Ordinary magisterium: The way the Church's teaching authority is normally exercised (e.g., by the bishops dispersed throughout the world or by the pope when not making an infallible definition) (§13).

Particular magisterium: A synonym for "personal magisterium" (§12).

Personal magisterium: (1) The teaching authority possessed by an individual bishop or pope; (2) the body of things taught by that bishop or pope (§12).

Primary object of infallibility: The primary truths God has given the Church the ability to infallibly define (i.e., divine revelation, the truths in the deposit of faith) (§431).

Private revelation: Revelation given by God to particular people or groups. It is ongoing and does not require divine faith, even when approved by the Church (§§118-123).

Public revelation: Revelation given by God and directed to the whole of humanity living after the coming of Christ. It is finished and requires divine faith. *Synonym:* "the deposit of faith" (§116-117).

Reason: The divine gift that allows us to discover information without divine revelation (§110).

Reception: The process by which the Holy Spirit guides the faithful to accept the teachings of the Church. Alternately, the response that this process produces (§596).

Religious submission of will and intellect: The response ordinarily called for by non-definitive magisterial teachings (§349).

Revelation: Truths directly revealed by God through his words and actions (§§112-113).

Roman Curia: The group of dicasteries in Rome that assist the pope in governing the Church (§§43-45).

Schism: (Greek, *skhisma,* "division"): The refusal of submission to the supreme pontiff or of communion with the members of the Church subject to him (§§263, 266).

Scripture: (Latin, *scriptura,* "writing"): The divinely inspired writings of the Bible (§135).

Secondary object of infallibility: Truths the Church has the ability to infallibly define because they are necessary to properly guard or expound divine revelation (§§434-435).

Sensus fidei: (Latin, "sense of the Faith"): (1) The supernaturally guided understanding that the Church or the individual believer has of the contents of the Faith, (2) the capacity to properly discern the Faith (§596).

Sensus fidelium: (Latin, "the sense of the faithful"): The supernaturally guided understanding that the faithful have of the contents of the Faith (§596).

Subject of infallibility: One who exercises the gift of infallibility (§§418-427). Cf. "Object of infallibility."

Theologian: A specialist in theology who has a canonical mission to teach (§80).

Theological note: Also called a doctrinal note. A rank indicating the doctrinal weight of a view. Not commonly used today. Typically, theological notes were unofficial and assigned by theologians rather than the Magisterium (§§337-341).

Theological opinion: A view on theological subjects that is not mandated as a matter of Church doctrine (§530).

Theology: (Greek, *theos*, "God," and *logia*, "discussion"): The study of God, based on divine revelation (§73). Theology is not the same as doctrine (§84).

Tradition: (Latin, *trans-*, "across," and *dare*, "to give"): Something that is handed down in a community (e.g., "This is one of our traditions") or the entire body of things that are handed down (e.g., "This is part of our tradition") (§§126-127). When capitalized, "Tradition" signifies authoritative, divinely revealed traditions (§§130-131).

Universal magisterium: (1) The worldwide body of bishops teaching in union with the pope; (2) teaching directed to and binding on the worldwide Church (§12).

Bibliography

Walter M. Abbott, S.J., ed., *The Documents of Vatican II* (New York: Herder & Herder and Association Press, 1966).

Luigi Accattoli, *When a Pope Asks Forgiveness: The Mea Culpa's of John Paul II* (Boston: Pauline Books & Media, 1998).

William E. Addis and Thomas Arnold, *A Catholic Dictionary* (New York: Catholic Publication Society Co., 1887).

Pierre Adnes, "Revelations, Private" in Rene Latourelle and Rino Fisichella, *Dictionary of Fundamental Theology* (New York: Crossroad, 1995).

Jimmy Akin, "The Meaning of 'Marital Intercourse'" online at jimmyakin.com.

——, "Understanding the Catechism's Death Penalty Revision" online at jimmyakin.com.

John L. Allen, Jr., "Pope Signals Nuance on Condoms," November 20, 2010, online at ncronline.org.

——, "Pope Takes the Classic Vatican Approach to Birth Control and Zika," February 20, 2016, online at cruxnow.com.

John P. Beal, James A. Coriden, and Thomas J. Green, eds., *New Commentary on the Code of Canon Law* (New York: Paulist Press, 2000).

Benedict XVI and Peter Seewald, *Light of the World* (San Francisco: Ignatius Press, 2010).

Ludovico Billot, S.J., *Tractatus De Ecclesia* Christi (Rome: Typographia Polyglotta of the S. C. de Propaganda Fide, 1903).

Claudia Carlen, ed., *The Papal Encyclicals: 1958–1981* (Ypsilanti, Mich.: Pierian Press, 1990).

Catholic News Agency, "Full Text of Pope Francis' In-Flight Press Conference from Colombia," September 11, 2017, 10:10 A.M., online at catholicnewsagency.com.

Owen Chadwick, *From Bossuet to Newman: The Idea of Doctrinal Development*, 2nd ed. (Cambridge: Cambridge University Press, 1987),

Charles E. Curran, "'*Humanae Vitae*' and the *Sensus Fidelium*," *National Catholic Reporter*, June 25, 2018, online at ncronline.org.

Joseph T. Martin de Agar, *A Handbook on Canon Law* (Montreal: Wilson & Lafleur, 1999).

Heinrich Denzinger et al., eds., *Enchiridion Symbolorum, Definitionum, et*

Declarationum de Rebus Fidei et Morum (San Francisco: Ignatius Press, 2012).

Avery Dulles, *The Craft of Theology: From Symbol to System*, 2nd ed. (New York: Crossroad, 1996).

—, *Magisterium* (Naples, Fla.: Sapientia Press, 2007).

—, *The Survival of Dogma* (New York: Crossroad, 1985).

Harold E. Ernst, "The Theological Notes and the Interpretation of Doctrine," *Theological Studies* 63(2002):813-825.

Johann Finsterholzl, in K. Rahner, et al., *Sacramentum Mundi: An Encyclopedia of Theology*, vol. 6 (New York: Herder and Herder, 1970), s.v. "Theological Notes."

Austin Flannery, O.P., ed., *Vatican Council II: The Conciliar and Post Conciliar Documents*, new rev. ed., vol. 1, (Northport, N.Y.: Costello Publishing, 1992).

James Gaffney, ed., *Conscience, Consensus, and the Development of Doctrine: Revolutionary Texts by John Henry Cardinal Newman* (New York: Image, 1992).

—, trans., ed., *Roman Catholic Writings on Doctrinal Development by John Henry Newman* (Kansas City, Mo.: Sheed & Ward, 1997).

P.G.W. Glare, ed., *Oxford Latin Dictionary* (Oxford: Oxford University Press, 2012).

Germain Grisez, *The Way of the Lord Jesus, Volume One: Christian Moral Principles* (Quincy, Ill.: Franciscan Press, 1997).

Fr. Brian Harrison, "Pius IX, Vatican II, and Religious Liberty," online at catholicculture.org.

Holy See Press Office, "Communiqué: On Various Articles Regarding the 'Third Secret of Fatima,'" May 21, 2016, online at press.vatican.va.

Sylvester J. Hunter, S.J., *Outlines of Dogmatic Theology*, 3rd ed. (New York: Benzinger Brothers, 1896).

Hubert Jedin, *A History of the Council of Trent, vol. II: The First Sessions at Trent, 1545-1547* (New York: Thomas Nelson and Sons, 1961).

Daniel Kennedy in *The Catholic Encyclopedia* (New York: Robert Appleton Company, 1912), s.v. "Sacraments."

William Levada, Address at the Pontifical Athenaeum of St. Anselm, "Dei Verbum—Forty Years Later," October 10, 2005.

C.S. Lewis, *Mere Christianity* (New York: HarperCollins, 1980).

International Theological Commission, *Memory and Reconciliation: The Church and the Faults of the Past* (1999).

Walter Kasper, *The Gospel of the Family* (New York: Paulist Press, 2014).

Thomas Kuhn, *The Structure of Scientific Revolutions*, 4th ed. (Chicago: University of Chicago Press, 2012).

James Martin, S.J., "Father James Martin Answers 5 Common Questions about 'Building a Bridge,'" *America*, July 14, 2017, online at americamagazine.org.

J. Michael Miller, *The Encyclicals of John Paul II* (Huntington, Ind.: Our Sunday Visitor, 2001).

Francis Morrisey, *Papal and Curial Pronouncements: Their Canonical Significance in Light of the Code of Canon Law*, 2nd ed. (Ottawa: Faculty of Canon Law, Saint Paul University, 1995).

Gerhard Muller, *Catholic Dogmatics for the Study and Practice of Theology*, vol. 1 (New York: Crossroad, 2017).

—, "Communion to the Remarried, Muller, 'There Can Be Mitigating Factors in Guilt,'" online at lastampa.it; translated from Cardinal Muller's introduction to the book *Risposte (Amichevoli) ai Critici di Amoris Laetitia* by Rocco Buttiglione (Milan: Edizione Ares, 2017).

James A. H. Murray, ed., *A New English Dictionary* (Oxford: Clarendon Press, 1897), s.v. "Discipline," 6b.

Msgr. Fernando Ocáriz Braña, "On Adhesion to the Second Vatican Council," *L'Osservatore Romano*, December 2, 2011.

James T. O'Connor and Vincent Gasser, *The Gift of Infallibility: The Official Relatio on Infallibility of Bishop Vincent Gasser at Vatican Council I* (Boston: St. Paul Editions, 1986).

Origen, *Origen: Prayer, Exhortation to Martyrdom*, ed. Johannes Quasten and Joseph C. Plumpe, trans. John J. O'Meara, vol. 19, *Ancient Christian Writers* (New York, N.Y. and Mahwah, N.J.: Newman Press, 1954).

Ludwig Ott, *Fundamentals of Catholic Dogma* (St. Louis: B. Herder Book Company, 1957).

Rocco Palmo, "'There Is No Turning Back Now'—In Historic Abuse Summit, Vatican Says Chilean Bench to Face 'Consequences,'" May 12, 2018, online at whispersintheloggia.blogspot.com.

Edward Peters, "A Non-Magisterial Magisterial Statement?," December 15, 2015, online at canonlawblog.wordpress.com.

—, "Do Footnotes Count?" January 27, 2017, online at canonlawblog. wordpress.com.

—, trans., *The 1917 or Pio-Benedictine Code of Canon Law* (San Francisco: Ignatius Press, 2001).

Karl Rahner, ed., *Encyclopedia of Theology: The Concise Sacramentum Mundi* (New York: Seabury Press, 1975), s.v. "Dogma."

Joseph Ratzinger, *Eschatology: Death and Eternal Life*, 2nd ed., (Washington, D.C.: The Catholic University of America Press, 1988).

—, Foreword, in Michael Sharkey, ed., *International Theological Commission, vol. 1: Texts and Documents, 1969-1985*.

—, *The Nature and Mission of Theology: Essays to Orient Theology in Today's Debates*, trans. Adrian Walker (San Francisco: Ignatius Press, 1995).

—, *Relationship Between Magisterium and Exegetes*, May 5, 2003.

—, "Theology Is Not Private Idea of Theologian," *L'Osservatore Romano*, English Weekly Edition, July 2, 1990.

Joseph Ratzinger and Christoph Schonborn, *Introduction to the Catechism of the Catholic Church* (San Francisco: Ignatius Press, 1994).

Joseph Ratzinger and Peter Seewald, *God and the World: Believing and Living in Our Time: A Conversation with Peter Seewald*, trans. Henry Taylor (San Francisco: Ignatius Press, 2002).

Thomas J. Reese, S.J., ed., *Episcopal Conferences: Historical, Canonical, and Theological Studies* (Washington, D.C.: Georgetown University Press, 1989).

Fr. Regis Scanlon, "What History May Tell Us About *Amoris Laetitia*," January 26, 2017, online at crisismagazine.com.

Tim Staples, "Does the Catholic Church Teach We Are Gods?," online at timstaples.com.

Leo F. Stelten, *Dictionary of Ecclesiastical Latin* (Peabody, Mass.: Hendrickson Publishers, 1995).

Basil Studer, "Dogma, History Of," ed., Angelo Di Berardino and James Hoover, trans. Joseph T. Papa, Erik A. Koenke, and Eric E. Hewett, *Encyclopedia of Ancient Christianity* (Downers Grove, Ill.: IVP Academic; InterVarsity Press, 2014).

Francis J. Sullivan, S.J., *Creative Fidelity: Weighing and Interpreting Documents of the Magisterium* (New York: Paulist Press, 1996).

—, *Matisterium: Teaching Authority in the Catholic Church* (Eugene, Oregon:

Wipf and Stock Publishers, 2002).

—, "The Teaching Authority of Episcopal Conferences," *Theological Studies* 63(2002):472–493, online at TheologicalStudies.net.

R.S. Wallace and G.W. Bromiley, "Sacraments," *The International Standard Bible Encyclopedia, Revised,* ed. Geoffrey W. Bromiley (Grand Rapids, Mich.: Wm. B. Eerdmans, 1979–1988).

Joseph Wilhelm and Thomas B. Scannell, trans., *A Manual of Catholic Theology: Based on Scheeben's "Dogmatik,"* vol. II, 3rd ed., rev. (London: Kegan Paul, Trench, Trübner & Co. Ltd., 1908).

Nicole Winfield, Associated Press, September 11, 2017, 9:55 A.M. EDT, online at www.apnews.com.

Zenit, "Cardinal Newman: Doctor of the Church? Father Ian Ker on the Priest's Cause, Teachings," October 22, 2008, online at zenit.org.

—, "Pope to U.S. Christian Unity Event: Jesus Knows All Christians Are One, Doesn't Care What Type," May 25, 2015, 9:34 A.M., online at zenit.org.

Index

This index lists notable sections in which topics are discussed. The numbers given are for the sections (e.g., §195) rather than page numbers.